Children, Home and School

Regulation, autonomy
or connection?

Edited by Rosalind Edwards

London and New York

First published 2002 by RoutledgeFalmer
11 New Fetter Lane, London EC4P 4EE

Simultaneously published in the USA and Canada
by RoutledgeFalmer
29 West 35th Street, New York, NY 10001

RoutledgeFalmer is an imprint of the Taylor & Francis Group

© 2002 Rosalind Edwards

Typeset in Bembo by
HWA Text and Data Management, Tunbridge Wells
Printed and bound in Great Britain by
The Cromwell Press, Trowbridge, Wiltshire

British Library Cataloguing in Publication Data
A catalogue record for this book is available from the British Library

Library of Congress Cataloging in Publication Data
Children, home, and school : regulation, autonomy or connection? /
edited by Rosalind Edwards.
  p. cm. – (Future of childhood series)
  Includes bibliographical references and index.
  1. Home and school–Cross-cultural studies. I. Edwards, Rosalind.
  II. Series.

LC225 .C42 2001
371.19–dc21   2001052002

ISBN 0-415-25043-9 (hbk)
ISBN 0-415-25044-7 (pbk)

Contents

Tables and figures

Tables

Figures

Contributors

Priscilla Alderson is Professor in Childhood Studies at the Social Science Research Unit, Institute of Education, University of London. She researches children's consent, competence and participation. Her books include: *Children's Consent to Surgery* (Open University Press, 1993); *Listening to Children: Ethics and Social Research* (Barnardos, 1995); *Health Care Choices: Making Decisions With Children* (with J. Montgomery, IPPR, 1996); *Enabling Education: Experiences in Special and Ordinary Schools* (with C. Goodey, Tufnell Press, 1998); *Learning and Inclusion* (David Fulton, 1999); and *Young Children's Rights* (Jessica Kingsley, 2000).

Pam Alldred is currently researching young people's views on Sex and Relationship Education in the Department of Education, Keele University. She is a contributor to *Feminist Dilemmas in Qualitative Research* (edited by J. Ribbens and R. Edwards, Sage, 1998), and was a member of the *Challenging Women: Psychology's Exclusions, Feminist Possibilities* and *Psychology, Discourse, Practice: From Regulation to Resistance* collectives with E. Burman et al. 1996. Her interests include debates about 'family values', researching childhood and new movements for social justice.

Elisabeth Backe-Hansen is a senior researcher at NOVA (Norwegian Social Research). She has published extensively within the areas of child protection, foster care, ethics in child research and social competence among children and young people. Her most recent publications include: *10-åringer i Norden: Kompetanse, risiko og oppvekstmiljø* (co-edited with T. Ogden, Nordisk Ministerråd, 1998); *Sakkyndighetsarbeid: Fag og beslutninger om barn* (co-authored with H. Øvreeide, Ad Notam Gyldenal, 1999); and *Oppvekst i barnets århundre: Historier om tventydighet* (co-edited with A. Jensen, H. Bache-Wiig and K. Heggen, Ad Notam Gyldenal, 1999).

John Barker is a Research Officer in the Department of Geography at Brunel University. His research interests include the provision of out-of-school child care, and the changing patterns of children's mobility (in particular, children's growing reliance on car travel) and access to spaces. John has published, with Fiona Smith, in journals such as *Childhood, Youth and Policy* and *Area and Built Environment*.

Lise Bird is Senior Lecturer in the School of Education at Victoria University of Wellington in Aotearoa New Zealand. She is interested in cross-disciplinary, critical approaches to child development and is co-author of *Human Development in Aotearoa* (with W. Drewery, McGraw-Hill, 2000). She also researches and teaches on issues of difference and normalisation in education.

Mano Candappa is a Research Officer at the Thomas Coram Research Unit, Institute of Education, University of London. Her main research interests are in children and childhood, socially marginalized groups, and research methodology. Recent publications include: *Why Do They Have to Fight? Refugee Children's Stories From Bosnia, Kurdistan, Somalia and Sri Lanka* (with J. Rutter, 1998); 'Building a new life: the role of the school in supporting refugee children', *Multicultural Teaching* (2000, 19:1); and 'Human rights and refugee children in the UK' (in B. Franklin, ed. *The Handbook of Children's Rights*, 2nd edn, 2001).

Mairian Corker is an independent disability studies scholar who currently holds a visiting Senior Research Fellowship at King's College London. Her main research interest is the development of a discourse analytical approach to the study of disability as a form of social oppression. She has authored and edited numerous publications, including *Deaf Transitions*; *Deaf and Disabled or Deafness Disabled*; *Disability Discourses* (with Sally French); and the forthcoming *Disability/Postmodernity: Embodying Disability Theory* (with Tom Shakespeare), and *Disabling Language: Analyzing Disability Discourse*. She is Executive Editor of the leading disability studies journal *Disability & Society*.

William A. Corsaro is Robert H. Shaffer Class of 1967 Endowed Professor of Sociology at Indiana University, Bloomington. He is the author of *Friendship and Peer Culture in the Early Years* (Ablex, 1995) and *The Sociology of Childhood* (Pine Forge Press, 1997). His research interests are in the areas of sociology of childhood, children's peer cultures, and early childhood education.

Miriam David has held the post of Professor of Policy Studies and Director of the Ed.D in the Department of Education at Keele University since September 1999. She is also a Visiting Professor at the London Institute of Education and at Kings College London. She has an international reputation for her research on family, education and social policy. Her publications include: *Closing the Gender Gap: Post War Education and Social Change* (with M. Arnot and G. Weiner, Polity Press, 1999); *Negotiating the Glass Ceiling: Senior Women in the Academic World* (edited with D. Woodward, Falmer Press, 1998); *Parental Choice, Involvement and Expectations of Achievement in Education* (with A. West, P. Noden, A. Edge and J. Davies, London School of Economics, 1997); and *Mother's Intuition? Choosing Secondary Schools* (with A. West and J. Ribbens, Falmer Press, 1994).

John Davis is now Evaluation Consultant: Children and Social Exclusion, Sport Included Ltd, and was previously a Research Fellow at the Research Unit in Health and Behavioural Change, University of Edinburgh. He has carried out ethnographic research projects in the areas of curriculum innovation, disability, education, health and sport.

Rosalind Edwards is Professor in Social Policy at South Bank University, and Director of the ESRC-funded Families and Social Capital Research Group. She has carried out research on a variety of family issues, including: mothers and education; lone and partnered mothers, employment and childcare; step-families; and children's understandings of parental involvement in education. Recent publications include: *Feminist Dilemmas in Qualitative Research: Public Knowledge and Private Lives* (edited with J. Ribbens, Sage, 1998); *Lone Mothers, Paid Work and Gendered Moral Rationalities* (with S. Duncan, Macmillan, 1999); and *Risk and Citizenship: Key Issues in Welfare* (edited with J. Glover, RoutledgeFalmer, 2001). She co-edits (with J. Brannen) *The International Journal of Social Research Methodology: Theory and Practice*.

Itohan Egharevba is a former Research Officer at the Thomas Coram Research Unit, Institute of Education, University of London. Her main research interests are in equal opportunities and socially marginalized groups. She is currently completing her doctoral thesis on access to initial teacher education for minority ethnic groups, based at Edge Hill University College, Lancashire.

Kjersti Ericsson is professor in criminology in the Department of Criminology at the University of Oslo. She has published a number of books on total institutions, juvenile delinquency, education, gender relations and child welfare. Her most recent published books are: *Barnevern som samfunnsspeil (Child welfare as a mirror of society)* (1996); *Drift og dyd (Vice and virtue)* (1997); and *Skolebarn og skoleforeldre (School children and school parents)* (with G. Larsen, 2000). She also writes fiction, and has published eight volumes of poetry and two novels.

Guri Larsen is a research fellow in the Department of Criminology at the University of Oslo. Her most prominent research interests have been immigration, the situation of refugees, majority/minority relations, and child welfare. She is the author of *Brødre (Brothers)* (1992), and co-author of *Skolebarn og skoleforeldre (School children and school parents)* (with K. Ericsson, 2000).

Cleopatra Montandon is Professor of Sociology of Education at the University of Geneva, Switzerland. She has conducted research on socialisation, on the division of labour between families and schools, and more recently on children's perspectives as regards their education. Among her publications are: *Les strategies éducatives des familles* (with J. Kellerhals, Delachaux et Niestlé, 1991), and *L'éducation du point de vue des enfants* (L'Harmattan, 1997).

Katherine Brown Rosier is Assistant Professor of Sociology at Louisiana State University, Baton Rouge. She is the author of *Mothering Inner City Children: The Early School Years* (Rutgers University Press, 2000). Her research interests are in the areas of family, childhood, race and ethnic relations, and poverty.

Fiona Smith is Lecturer in Human Geography at Brunel University. Her research interests include the geography of out-of-school child care, the changing life of children and children's use of space. She participated in the Economic and Social Research Council's Children 5–16 Research Programme, and has published widely in journals such as *Childhood, Youth and Policy*, and *Area and Built Environment*.

Preface

Despite its title *The Future of Childhood* Series is not an exercise in outmoded futurology. It does not aim to make simple-minded predictions of the future. Rather, it takes important aspects of contemporary children's lives and through research about current practices and emergent trends poses questions about possible, and alternative, future directions. This inevitably intersects with social and political controversies about values: why should we care about children; what constitutes a good childhood; who should be involved in shaping it and how? The series is, therefore, intended to provoke serious discussion about what childhood is, what it could and what it should be. Existing volumes have accomplished this in relation to inter-generational relationships, work and technology. An important collection on children and the city will be available in 2002 and further volumes on children and the family, social policy and identity are planned thereafter.

The aim of the Series is well exemplified by this particular volume on home-school relationships. The growth of official interest in links between home and school is an international phenomenon. It is fuelled by responses to intensified global economic competition that identify children as a potentially controllable part of the 'supply side'. This brackets children as a very important source of 'human capital' that can be shaped according to the skills anticipated as crucial to future economic competitiveness. This is, of course, a very instrumental and rather impoverished vision of education. Nevertheless, children's performance at school, which in this view is closely tied in with these economic goals, is thought to be influenced by parental involvement in their child's education. This is, therefore, increasingly targeted for intervention and regulation.

Children's voices and experiences are largely missing from this discourse – indeed, are thought unnecessary to it – because children's main importance is seen in their future adult economic roles rather than their active contemporary social participation. This volume, like the rest of the Series, begins to correct this by focusing on children as social actors. Its contributors document children's own experiences of the relationships between home and school (and cognate organisations). In doing so they also show how social forces that are at least partially contradictory shape childhood as an institution. So, for example, it is clear that the 'human capital' version of childhood is not the only possibility. Children are also growing up amidst more generalised tendencies towards individualisation, which constructs not a fatalistic willingness to be shaped but a consciousness of (relative) independence, autonomy and choice.

The contributors to this volume explore home–school relationships within several different national contexts (including Britain, New Zealand, Norway and the United States) and from angles (such as the experience of disabled children and refugee children) that are often missing or muted. In doing so they raise many challenges to taken-for-granted assumptions and underline the need for public discussion that is more informed and aware of children's perspective than is presently the case. These are the very qualities that make *The Future of Childhood* not an exercise in crystal ball gazing but an active engagement with current directions.

Alan Prout
Series Editor

Acknowledgements

Thanks to Alan Prout (University of Stirling) and Simon Duncan (University of Bradford) for comments on my introduction, and to Alan generally for support in editing this collection.

Thanks also to Olivia, my granddaughter, for giving me insights into another generation of home–school relations.

Introduction

Conceptualising relationships between home and school in children's lives

Rosalind Edwards

Home and school[1] are two of the main settings and experiences in contemporary children's lives in developed and post-industrial societies. Indeed, they can be said to play a major role in constructing and shaping the current parameters of childhood. Children in the home and at school are thus subject to much political and popular attention. Changes in family forms and lifestyles, an increased focus on assessment of educational performance, and the relationship between the two, are causing concern about the implications for children. While there have long been worries about children's home lives and educational attainment, their form changes according to contemporary issues. In particular, home–school links have emerged as a pressing issue and an explicit target for policy intervention and debate.

The rise in attention to home–school relations can be linked to the large and rapid economic, political and cultural changes that are taking place globally in the way people live. These are said to have resulted in a widespread and pervasive sense of anxiety and insecurity, so that we live in what is often termed a 'risk society' (Beck 1992, 1999). Manifestations of a general social climate increasingly dominated by uncertainty include a greater cultural confusion about the appropriate form that childhood should take, attempts to shape the future by intervening to make particular kinds of adults out of children, and a focus on the roles of home and school in this process.

This collection examines a particular aspect of these manifestations. It explores the settings of home and school, as well as other educationally linked organised spaces in children's lives, and the relationship between them. The predominant concern of most texts on the topic is with parents' and/or teachers' views and activities. In contrast, the key focus of the contributions to this book is on children's positioning and social practices within and between the two locations. The authors present in-depth discussions of their research in a range of national contexts: Britain (Chapters 1, 3, 4, 7 and 9), New Zealand (Chapter 2), Norway (Chapters 5 and 10), Switzerland (Chapter 6) and the USA (Chapter 8), and for children from a variety of backgrounds and circumstances. They consider various aspects of these children's, and sometimes the adults' in their lives, own understandings and activities in home and school, pre-school and out of school club settings, and their movements between them. The collection addresses key tensions in how children may be positioned and see themselves as dependent and regulated by and between their home and school lives, as autonomous and individualised social actors within and between these settings, or as connected in interdependent relationships.

Identification of the issues of regulation, autonomy and connection as relevant to children's experiences is underpinned by different ways of conceptualising the relationship between home and school for children, and which this introduction attempts to lay out. It provides an overview of the relevant trends in childhood in developed and post-industrialised countries, and reviews the ways in which they may be understood. It forms a 'macro' contextual backdrop to the more 'micro' studies of the chapter contributions addressing the specifics of everyday lived childhoods.

This introduction begins with a brief assessment of the policy trend towards encouraging closer relations between home and school that is occurring in many countries. Initiatives in this area are underpinned by socialisation and developmental perspectives on children, which pose them as adults in the making. Home and school, and attempts to promote home–school links, are implicated in the deepening emphasis on children's familial dependency and their increasing location in separate organised settings. These broad processes of familialisation and institutionalisation are elaborated, and home–school relations identified as marking their interaction in various ways. This perspective on children's lives reveals home and school as shaping and regulating children's lives in developing and post-industrialised countries.

Such overarching trends, however, are occurring in specific national contexts, where there are diverse conceptions and histories of the relationship between families, markets and the state, and of the nature of childhood, and of home and school, within this. In an edited collection that encompasses contributions from several countries, it is important to acknowledge and explore this issue. A variety of concepts are available to help in this, from social policy and childhood studies disciplines. Such analyses operate at the level of broad social structures and identify the ways in which children's lives are implicated in these structures, and how children are positioned specifically in relation to home and school.

Another overarching process that has been identified as shaping children's lives is a trend towards acknowledging children's rights, autonomy and self-regulation. Facets of this individualisation are discussed, as is how it draws conceptual attention 'down' from wider structures towards the ways in which children are social actors involved in the construction and negotiation of the social orders of home and school. In turn, this also draws attention to the predominant concepts of autonomy and dependency in understanding home and school in children's lives.

As is pointed out, however, while this perspective reveals much, as a binary opposition it also tends to leave aside the relationships of connection and inter-dependency in which children are involved. Feminist concepts of care have been turned to in some recent work in order to illuminate the complexity of children's negotiations and practices at home and in school.

Finally, this introduction ends by reviewing the main concerns and arguments of each of the chapter contributions in this book, showing how the key issues of regulation, autonomy and connection are woven throughout them.

CHILDREN, HOME AND SCHOOL: THE POLICY TREND

Over the past four decades or so, an orthodoxy has developed that it is in children's best educational interests if home (parents) and school (teachers) work together in partnership. A lack of dissonance between home and school, and parental involvement in children's education in both settings, is promoted both professionally and politically (David 1993). Such a broad consensus can be seen most notably in western post-industrialised countries (see CERI 1997), including the five represented in contributions to this book: Britain, New Zealand, Norway, Switzerland and the United States. For example, at the policy level, in Britain the 1998 School Standards and Framework Act seeks to provide a firm base for home–school links through mandating home–school agreements to be issued by schools, detailing parents' responsibilities for their children's schooling and noting the school's role, which parents are expected to sign. The United States federal Goals 2000: Educate America Act similarly seeks 'to strengthen the partnerships between parents and professionals in meeting the educational needs of children … and the working relationship between home and school' (US Department of Education, online). Further, pre-school education intervention initiatives, such as Head Start in the USA and Sure Start in Britain, are often posed in terms of early contact between practitioners and parents building good home–'school' relationships that will continue into the compulsory schooling period (for example, Hallgarten 2000). Belief about the necessity for close home–school relations is also taking hold in developing countries and those other than the West. Mavis Sanders and Joyce Epstein's (1998) journal collection, for example, contains contributions addressing good home–school links practice in countries such as Japan and Chile, commenting that: 'Home, school and community connections around the world are becoming more formal and purposeful, to ensure that all students receive the support necessary for academic and personal success' (p. 340).

Such strategies are underpinned by academic studies showing that parental attitudes towards and involvement in their children's learning activities at home and in school have an influence on children's level and quality of learning development and attainment at all ages (see David 1993; Epstein 1992). Sociologists of education have also developed typologies covering the forms and extent of parents' participation and involvement in their children's education. For example, Joyce Epstein's (1995) influential classification covers parents' obligations; schools' obligations; parental involvement at school, at home and in governance; and community collaboration. Both political and academic formulations in the area of home–school relations, however, contain a curious silence about the children who are the object of these endeavours (Edwards and David 1997). The dominant socialisation and developmental perspectives informing many initiatives and much research pose children as immature 'becomings' – as future adults. They presuppose a one-way set of relationships between parents, teachers and children. It is adults' attitudes and actions that are regarded as crucial while children are positioned as passive and inert recipients, and as educational outcomes or products. The forces of socialisation (family/home and education/school) receive greater attention than the children themselves. In contrast, contributions to this collection, while still addressing these forces, turn the spotlight on children as social actors moving between and negotiating home and school.

As Carol Vincent and Sally Tomlinson (1997) have pointed out, home–school agreements and the wider promotion of home–school links are part of a broader construction of what constitutes 'good parenting'. Parents, and in particular mothers, are co-opted and positioned as responsible for the social behaviour and educational attainment of their children (see also Smith 1998). The 'soft' language of partnership is becoming a more hard-edged attempt to direct and regulate family and home life for both parents and children. Their analysis can be extended to encompass the ways that home–school relations initiatives are also an integral part of the broader construction and shaping of the nature of contemporary childhood.

THE FAMILIALISED AND INSTITUTIONALISED CHILDHOOD

Childhood is increasingly familialised and institutionalised – two processes that have been identified as broadly constituting contemporary childhood and affecting children's lives (Brannen and O'Brien 1995; Qvortrup *et al.* 1994). (A third process – individualisation – is discussed later.) Home and school are firmly implicated within these processes. They are bounded settings where children not only empirically tend to spend increasing amounts of time, but also prescriptively where they should be located. Children's independent unsupervised location outside of home or school has come to be regarded as both posing risks to vulnerable children's safety and well-being, and as a danger to others and a threat to the social order from unruly children (Scott, Jackson and Backett-Milburn 1998). Home and school as the primary sites of childhood are particularly and predominantly the case in developed and post-industrial societies, but this location is also becoming the 'proper' standard against which childhoods in developing countries are judged. For example, Jo Boyden (1991) has argued that Western normative assumptions about childhood experiences and locations have been encoded in the United Nations Convention on the Rights of the Child.

Familialisation

The concept of the familialisation of childhood captures the emphasis on children being the responsibility of their parents and on their upbringing and home lives as shaping their behaviour and attitudes. Their identities and activities are being incorporated into their family, with home as a physical and conceptual space in which they are increasingly located.

The historically specific construction of the modern nuclear family over the past two centuries has defined a bounded 'private sphere' of home and family, to which children 'naturally' belong (Alanen 1998; James, Jenks and Prout 1998). Indeed, the historical meaning of the familialisation of childhood has been interlinked with notions about women's place in relation to the domestic sphere of the home

(Cockburn 1998; Oakley 1994). The familialisation of childhood occurred alongside the 'domestication' of motherhood in the nineteenth century. More recently, as mothers are increasing their labour market participation, so too have changes occurred in ideas about home care by mothers as the appropriate (sole) place for young children, with a growing emphasis on educating pre-school children (see below). Nevertheless, children's everyday lives outside of formal institutionalised settings such as school are the organisational and managerial responsibility of their parents – an expectation that falls largely on mothers.

Western childhoods have also been argued to have become 'feminised' as, with the growth in lone motherhood (single, separated, divorced), women tend to live with children more than do men (Jensen 1994, 2001). Thus feminisation may be regarded as an aspect of children's familialisation. Western children are said to be increasingly 'economically useless' but 'emotionally priceless', with high levels of economic and emotional investment and obligation required from their parents (Beck 1992; Zelitzer 1985). An-Magritt Jensen (2001) has argued that this shift is strongly linked to the feminisation of childhood: as children have declined as economic assets for parents, so they have become more a female interest and responsibility. Others have linked children's increased emotional pricelessness to the individualisation process described later (Beck and Beck-Gernsheim 1995). Either way, a view of children's economic redundancy is subject to challenge if schooling is conceptualised as self and societal capitalisation, also discussed later.

Children are conceptualised in terms of their familial dependency whatever the family form, but again the feminisation aspect of familialisation has an impact. Such dependency is material as well as cultural, with children largely reliant on their parents for their standard of living and the basic conditions of their lives. Children living in lone mother families are often subject to relatively deprived socio-economic conditions.

Institutionalisation

The trend towards familialisation has been accompanied, and reinforced, by the concept of the institutionalisation of childhood. It has been historically promoted by the introduction of compulsory schooling in the industrialised world, and children's accompanying exclusion from substantial paid work activity. This process addresses children's increasing compartmentalisation in specifically designated, separate and protected organised settings, hierarchically supervised by professionals and hierarchically structured according to age and ability (Nasman 1994). Like familialisation, it also entails feminisation in that increases in mothers' employment have meant women being employed in 'child work' occupations in the labour market, including in jobs that men historically held such as teaching (Jensen 2001).

Children's institutionalisation encompasses an emphasis on children's status and location as pupils in schools, accompanied by a focus on their educational attainment that can steadily increase as an institutional structure for their lives as they work towards educational qualifications (Brannen, Heptinstall and Bhopal 2000). Schooling has come to represent an ordered passage from child to adult status, and has gradually been extended 'upwards' as an institutionalised period (i.e. raising of the leaving age for compulsory schooling) in order to meet the need for a numerate and literate educated workforce. There is also the growing emphasis on pre-school education and nursery provision noted above to extend the institutionalisation of childhood 'downwards' (Moss, Dillon and Statham 2000). Thus the process of institutionalisation bounds and structures the arenas for, nature and range of social competence accorded to children (Hutchby and Moran-Ellis 1998).

The process of the institutionalisation of childhood can also be conceptualised as including the growing extent of children's subjection to and definition by specific bodies of institutional knowledge and practice, including those that lay out 'normal' educational and social development stages and trajectories (Woodhead 1997). Such professional models and theories turn children into 'programmes' requiring careful measurement and monitoring, such as in the school through development, intelligence and attainment tests, as well as within the home. Indeed, this surveillance and regulation through expert practices is another area where there are links between mothers and children, as 'parenting' becomes an institutionalised 'skill' to be taught and assessed: 'science's conquest of the child is also a conquest of the mother' (Beck and Beck-Gernsheim 1995, p. 130).

The focus on home–school relations discussed earlier can be seen as marking an interaction between the familialisation and institutionalisation of childhood in various ways. Policy-makers and professionals increasingly regard home and school, parents and teachers, as having similar functions in relation to children, which require them to work in 'partnership'. Both home–school links initiatives and research unthinkingly familialise and institutionalise children by occluding their role as social actors in the school and at home, and in relations between the two (Edwards and Alldred 2000). Furthermore, while champions of home–school links can pose this as a desire to promote 'family-like schools' (for example, Hallgarten 2000), there are concerns that such initiatives represent the state (institutional educational) colonisation and regulation of family life, parents (mothers) and children (Crozier 1998; Edwards and Alldred 2000; Edwards and Warin 1999; and see Vincent and Tomlinson discussed above). As David Morgan has generally remarked about the development of schooling, it entails 'schooling the family' (Morgan 1996, p. 147; see also Bernstein 1977).

CHILDHOOD AND THE STATE – COMPARATIVE ANALYSES

The broad trends towards the familialisation and institutionalisation of contemporary childhood in developed and post-industrialised societies are, of course, just that – broad trends. They, and thus home–school relations, are occurring in different contexts however (Edwards and Alldred 1999). These contexts include countries with different welfare state regimes that have quite distinct conceptions and histories of the relationship between families, markets and the state, and thus of the nature of childhood. The roots and development of state policies towards family and dependency relations (in particular the extent to which children should be collectively and socially, or individually and privately, provided for) are evident in the current range of provisions for children and the normative visions of family life embedded within them. Interestingly, these varying contexts are rarely acknowledged in the typologies describing and classifying parental involvement and home–school relations, which are posed as conceptually universal.

Comparative analysts have produced various classifications of welfare state regimes based on distinctions about what the welfare state does (see Duncan and Edwards 1999, for broad discussion). However, most of these imply, rather than explicitly address, the constitution of childhood because they focus on relations between the state, labour market and family. Children almost drop out of the picture in a situation where younger children are prohibited from, and older children only allowed minimal, labour market engagement in developed regimes.

Gøsta Esping-Andersen's (1990) influential classification of the emergence and divergence of post-industrial welfare state regimes is based on levels of decommodification – how far people are independent from selling their labour through state income transfers for sickness, unemployment and old age. In this formulation the contributors to this edited collection discuss children, home and school in the context of the range of developed welfare regimes identified by Esping-Andersen: liberal, conservative and social democratic.

In broadly liberal regimes, including Britain, New Zealand and the United States, the relationship between families and the state has historically been one where the state does not intervene to offer support, other than in a limited and imposed way to stigmatised and/or 'dysfunctional' groups. Indeed, a privatised realm of the traditional family is crucial to socialisation into notions of personal regulation that are compatible with liberal capitalism (Rose 1990). Mothers can 'choose' to be positioned as decommodified in the home caring for children, through dependency on their male partner (or minimally through the state in their absence), or commodified through paid labour. The welfare regime largely does not promote either course and largely does not provide institutionalised care for children outside of compulsory schooling. The emphasis is more on children's familialisation, with the extent of their institutionalisation posed as a private parental choice. Thus home–school relations policies are promoted in a context where parents, and in particular mothers (ideally in two-parent families), are placed as materially and culturally responsible, and held accountable for, their children. The state traditionally takes a background role other than regulatory. State regulation and parental accountability are being exacerbated as state welfare services in liberal regimes, such as the UK, become increasingly subject to market relations as competing 'producers', and parents placed as 'consumers' (see Ball 1994; David 1993 on education). Children's citizenship in terms of consultation, for example about changes in education policy and practice, receives little attention within such liberal familialisation (Pringle 1998; Wyness 1999).

In broadly conservative regimes, including Switzerland, the state acts to support traditional male breadwinner and female home-maker families. Institutionalised care for children, including the school system in the length of the school day, assumes that mothers are decommodified. 'Day' care similarly often offers short hours, assuming that if mothers are employed it will be part time. As in liberal regimes, historically the emphasis is more on the familialisation of childhood and far less on state promoted institutionalisation outside of compulsory schooling. Arguably, however, there is less emphasis on the marketisation of welfare services such as education. Similarly, though, home–school relations are promoted in the context of parents (normatively in nuclear – mother, father, child/ren – families) holding the primary material and cultural responsibilities for their children.

In social democratic welfare regimes, where Norway is positioned in Esping-Anderson's model, the state takes a far more active role in supporting and shaping the nature of family life. Mothers – with or without male partners – are both commodified as paid workers, with the state providing pervasive day and after school care, and yet decommodified independent of, and alongside, any male partner through extensive state benefits providing for parental leave when children are young. The state promotes the institutionalisation of childhood in this and other ways. For example, children have stronger citizenship rights in terms of having their interests represented (for example, the Norwegian Ombudsman for Children – see Norwegian Ministry for Children and the Family 1996)[2]. In this context, home–school relations are conducted in a situation in which material and cultural responsibility for children is shared between parents (of no preferred family form) and the state.

The above brief depiction of family–state relations and the extent of the familialisation and/or institutionalisation of childhood in these welfare regimes draws on Esping-Andersen's classification. It goes considerably beyond his formulation, however (a pragmatic but critical strategy also adopted by Keith Pringle 1998, in focusing on children and social welfare in European regimes). Esping-Anderson's categorical analysis does not address the decommodification of children or consider the implications for the familialisation and institutionalisation of childhood. Feminist writers have heavily criticised his work for being gender-blind. They have produced various alternatives that place gender relations in a more central role, and which position countries in different configurations to, and/or highlight differences between countries grouped together in, Esping-Anderson's categorisation system (for example, Leira 1994; Lewis 1992; McLaughlin and Glendinning 1994; and see review in Duncan 1995). Nevertheless, while children are obviously central to such analyses in terms of who should care for them and in what location, they are subsumed within the main emphasis on relations between men and women. Eithne McLaughlin and Caroline Glendinning's (1994) focus on familialisation/defamilialisation – the extent to which people engage in and can move away from the (patriarchal) family in living independently – for example, takes children's familialisation unremarked and for granted (as does Esping-Anderson's 1999, response to his critics, now identifying 'familialist' and 'non-familialist' welfare state groups).

Birgit Pfau-Effinger's work (1998) provides some exception to this. Her concept of the dominant 'gender culture' begins to place an emphasis on the notions of 'good' childhood inherent in welfare regime forms. She points to their roots in the historical development of dominant models of: the ideal regarding the social spheres through which women and men are integrated into society; societal valuation of these spheres; the structure of dependencies between women and men within families; and cultural constructions of the relationship between generations, including the main social sphere for children's upbringing. This approach highlights the way that children and childhood are regarded as belonging to the private sphere, with motherhood as a specific unpaid gender role (i.e. the familialisation of childhood), or the extent to which childhood is constructed as a long phase of life with its own worth and caring for children is seen as a task for the welfare state (i.e. the institutionalisation of childhood). Ultimately, it can be argued, Pfau-Effinger's analysis remains adult-centred in that it still retains gender roles, rather than childhood, as its pivot. For example, building on her gender arrangement stage categorisation, the welfare regimes of the countries represented in this book become placed as 'The Male Breadwinner/Female Part-Time Child-Care Provider Model' (Britain, New Zealand, Switzerland and the USA) and 'The Dual Breadwinner/State Child-Care Provider Model' (Norway). Nevertheless (and given the strong historical links between the positions of women and children), her analysis has potential in pointing the way to a comparative analysis of the relationship between families and the state that engages with and gives prominence to childhood. It also allows for flexible comparative analyses that can move below the level of the nation state, to look at regional and local differences within states. For example, Switzerland's federalist system is divided into 26 cantons and around 3000 municipalities, each of which has different socio-economic structures and school systems, and there are distinct conservative (German speaking) and modernised conservative (French speaking) underpinnings (see Bühler 1998). Pfau-Effinger's approach can thus avoid the criticism often levelled at such work, that it ignores diversity within a national context, including at regional and local levels (see James, Jenks and Prout 1998, for discussion of this issue in relation to researching childhood).

On their part, researchers working within childhood studies tend not to engage with social policy analysts attempting to produce welfare state regime classifications (for an exception see Pringle 1998). This is not to say that there has been no comparative work undertaken at the level of states that places children centre stage. In addition to Keith Pringle's (1998) review of child welfare policies across Europe (which curiously does not address education and schooling), most notably there has been the 'Childhood as a Social Phenomenon' programme (Qvortrup *et al.* 1994). This five year international programme of research measured and assessed the comparative living conditions of children in developed and post-industrialised societies in 12 European countries. It covered topics such as birth, morbidity and mortality trends, the distribution of wealth, and educational achievement and disadvantage, and discussed a variety of legal and social policy matters and their impact on and shaping of childhood. This approach enabled those involved to identify trends in contemporary childhood that the countries under study had in common: the processes of familialisation and institutionalisation already discussed, and the process of individualisation discussed below. The programme did not aim to produce a welfare regime classification that centred on children, though. Rather, it focused on social forces that shape children's everyday lives cross-nationally.

A fruitful concept that could be useful in a comparative welfare regime analysis that centres on children is Leena Alanen and Magritt Bardy's (1991) notion of historically constructed 'generational contracts' as a social and cultural system. This cross-cuts and resonates with the concept of 'gender culture' discussed above (as Alanen has pointed out, 1998), and has its inherent flexibility as well. It brings to the fore material, social and emotional relationships of provision and dependency and the division of labour that governs relations between the generations. Such generational contracts are initiated by adults and based on adults' understandings. There can, however, be differences in what is allowed to and required of children within that framework. Alanen and Bardy's conceptualisation of generational contracts is largely concerned with family relationships (see also Alanen 1998). Its analytical potential may be broader than this, however.

Analyses of the historical development of national social policies as these conceive of children and formulate childhood have been undertaken (for example, for New Zealand see Dalley 1998; and for Britain see Hendricks 1994). These carefully chart the ways that images of childhood are inseparable from social policy developments, with the health, welfare and rearing of children linked in varying ways to the economic and morality orders and future destiny of the nation. Thus, while there maybe different analyses of children–family–state relations in different welfare state regimes, it is probably fair to say that children predominantly are regarded and treated as investments and 'becomings' rather than 'beings' in social policy developments. An aspect of the generational contract regime is that it is largely understood as one of current (adult) political welfare investment cost in dependent children for future benefit rather than regarding children as important in themselves (albeit Nordic societies' emphasis on children's representation). Education provision is an exemplar of this view of children. Compulsory schooling is provided as a present investment in children in order that they will become the productive workforce and rational self-controlled citizens of the nation in the future. Arguably, this policy emphasis on children as a means of shaping and controlling the societal future is intensifying as the general social climate is pervaded by a sense of risk and uncertainty (see Prout 2000, on Britain).

While it may be a dominant force in policy stances however, this dependent 'becomings' view of children and education has been challenged by some childhood writers. Jens Qvortrup (1985, 1995), for example, argues that children have always participated in the social division of labour that characterises the society in which they live (in terms of both time and place). For children living in developed and post-industrialised countries, that labour consists of large amounts of scholarly work. David Oldman (1994) makes a similar point in taking an economic relations perspective, describing children as providing 'child work' employment for adults. He poses schooling as children working for their own self, as well as social, 'capital-isation'. Oldman also emphasises that family, as a bounded social system, produces and is structured by stratification. In other words, these sorts of approaches to understanding children's position can be regarded as unpacking parts of the generational contract.

Both Qvortrup and Oldman are concerned with conceptualising children as an age 'class' in their analyses. This approach, however, subsumes and can gloss over divisions between children, including divisions in more traditional social class terms. While all children, not just upper and middle classes, may have been institutionalised within education systems, Pierre Bourdieu (1986) has drawn attention to the significance of educational processes for the transmission of class position. Thus working class children's 'self capitalisation' is not the same as that of upper and middle class children, and reproduces social stratification. In terms of day care provision, mainly within broadly liberal and conservative welfare regimes, children in poor and lone mother families may be subject to surveillance and regulation through institutionalisation because familialisation in their case is regarded as dysfunctional. The Head Start initiative in the USA is a good example of this, and in a situation where class and ethnicity overlap to mean that such surveillance proportionally impacts more on African-American children (Deacon 2002). Gender is also an issue in divisions of labour of the generational contract within families and the home sphere, and where cross-cutting with gender culture is most obvious. Most notably, girls have been found to carry out more housework and care than do boys (for Britain see Morrow 1994; Reid 1995). Further, in terms of schooling, several authors have noted that boys and girls are allowed/learn to take on radically different subject identities, with girls performing and rewarded for docile and nurturant behaviour, and boys performing and allowed 'masculine' activities and 'naughtiness' (for example, James 1993; Walkerdine 1985).

Analyses of family–state relations and of the broad processes that constitute contemporary childhood in developed and post-industrial societies, point to the different balances of parental responsibility, and state and professional regulation of children. However, the latter type of analysis has also identified trends towards a third process (in addition to familialisation and institutionalisation) shaping children's lives – children's self-regulation, or individualisation.

THE INDIVIDUALISATION OF CHILDHOOD

Individualisation represents an increasing emphasis on children as individual social actors who reflexively shape their own biography and are responsible for their 'project of the self'. This encompasses a focus on children's civil rights under the law and on their being able to determine, or at least participate and have a say in, their own lives (Nasman 1994): 'Children are now seen as individuals, whose autonomy should be safeguarded and fostered and whose being can no longer be simply nested into the family or the institution' (James *et al.* 1998, p.6–7). Again, the extent and form of this trend can vary between and within different welfare state regimes.

At first sight, as has been pointed out (Brannen and O'Brien 1995), the process of individualisation may appear to be in tension with the trends of familialisation and institutionalisation. This is especially the case in formulations associated with the political right, where moves towards children's individualisation are regarded as contributing to the corrosion of the fundamental moral values of 'the family', and discipline in schools and on the streets. From another perspective, however, familial-isation and institutionalisation can be harnessed to produce individualisation (although this may still involve tensions). Following notions of socialisation and a developmental trajectory, parents' and schools' responsibilities towards children are often posed as ensuring that children are guided towards such values and competencies (Edwards and Alldred 2000). This goal of individualisation, however, is double-edged. As raised earlier in discussing liberal welfare regimes, family is regarded as crucial in producing self-control. The same is also true of schooling. Autonomy is thus not completely unregulated; rather the site of control and governance shifts from the familial and institutional to the subject self (Rose 1990). As Alison James, Chris Jenks and Alan Prout evocatively put it, 'Modernity's child, at school, on the street and even at home, becomes its own policeman' (1998, p. 56).

Parents' and schools' responsibilities for ensuring children's (adult) individualisation are evident in several commentaries and studies. Anthony Giddens, for example, in his influential discussion of democratisation and intimacy, contends that parents should treat their children 'as a putative equal of the adult', that is as if they were able to exercise autonomous choice and reflexively deploy arguments (1992, p. 91). Such familial efforts towards children's future inculcated individualisation may be class based, however. For example, as part of the BASUN study of modern childhood in Nordic countries (Andenaes 1996), Gunilla Dahlberg (1996) identified middle-class childrearing as more orientated to the future and engaging with reflexive individualisation, while working-class childrearing was more rooted in a bounded 'here and now'.

The social order in schools is also said to have changed from 'closure' to an 'openness' that requires personalised control and autonomy (James, Jenks and Prout 1998, drawing on Bernstein 1967). For example, in Britain, Julia Brannen, Ellen Heptinstall and Kalwant Bhopal (2000) have pointed to the way that children are expected to take on increasing self-responsibility in school, as demonstrated in their management of mobility between classrooms, interpretation of the differentiated school curriculum and negotiation of peer relationships.

For those in childhood studies, the focus is on children's individualisation as beings rather than becomings – a stance that underlies the majority of the contributions to this edited collection. Children are regarded as social actors who negotiate and participate in the construction of their daily lives, and who can be legitimate and competent informants about those lives in social research (Hutchby and Moran-Ellis 1998; James and Prout 1997). The increasing familialisation and institutional-isation of childhood, as involving children in having to deal with being located in a number of social sites, has resulted in attention to their agency and individualisation.

In-depth studies of children's lives have addressed their competence in moving between home and school, regardless of age. They negotiate different value systems and disparate versions of 'the child' as, in the former, a particular person in a family/household, and for the latter, a batch member of the pupil and peer group. For example, Elisa Klein (1988) addresses the ways that pre-school children in the U.S. construct mothers and teachers (mainly female) as fulfilling different social roles in relation to themselves (see also Andenaes 1996, on Nordic pre-school children's negotiation of familial and institution care contexts). Berry Mayall (1993, 1994a and b) has discussed how British primary school children experience more encourage-ment towards independence in relation to health care in the home, while at school such competence is subject to more bureaucratic restriction. Brannen, Heptinstall and Bhophal (2000) point to older children's negotiation of a continuing attachment to family in the context of becoming competent in the arena of schooling and peer relationships.

Children's competence and social action are argued to both shape and be shaped by the construction of childhood (Hutchby and Moran-Ellis 1998; James, Jenks and Prout 1998). The construction of childhood is also the process through which children's agency arises so that children themselves engage with and participate in its construction at the same time as they are both subject to and reproduce it. So for example, in relation to familialisation, Brannen, Heptinstall and Bhopal's (2000) finding that British children place great value on their parents 'being there' for them could be regarded as some acceptance of and desire for familialisation. In relation to the trend of individualisation, Anna Solberg (1994) has described how Norwegian children manipulate their parents' encouragement of their independence and competence, and the wider social acceptance of this, to carve out and control unsupervised time in the home for short periods.

Studies of children's agency and carving out of their own agendas within the constraints of the structures of childhood stress a particular configuration of the relationship between autonomy and dependency. This impacts on how the relationship between children, home/familialisation and school/institutionalisation is conceptualised and understood.

THE 'AUTONOMY–DEPENDENCY AXIS'

Ian Hutchby and Jo Moran-Ellis refer to the 'autonomy–dependency axis' as 'one around which the vast majority of work in the new social studies of childhood … can be said to revolve' (1998, p. 21). The trends of familialisation and institutionalisation, as discussed earlier, are regarded as key in (re)producing children's structural dependence, regulating and constraining their autonomy. The process of individualisation, however, draws attention to children's agentic autonomy, often focusing attention on their own agendas, resistance to regulation and subversion of control – albeit the process also involves self-regulation, as discussed above.

Allison James, Chris Jenks and Alan Prout's (1998) influential discussion of the ways in which childhood can and may best be theorised, uses the autonomy–dependency lens (as linked to the agency–structure dichotomy) as part of the way they consider home and school as examples of the material and cultural contexts of childhood. This draws attention to the issues of power and control that they pose as a key feature in theorising childhood.

Home and school are 'dedicated to the control and regulation of the child's body and mind through regimes of discipline, learning, development, maturation and skill' (James, Jenks and Prout 1998, p. 38). Home and school parallel and echo each other in being bounded and constraining, and are both social locations in which children are dependent on, and subject to monitoring, control and assessment by, adults: parents and teachers. They both implement timetables that specifically and broadly instil regularity and rhythm into all the activities and tasks of childhood: from eating, sleeping, washing, excreting and playing, to age-progression through a structured sequence of educational, skill and responsibility stages.

Nevertheless, from an autonomy–dependency axis perspective, the structural contexts of both settings do not only constrain children's autonomy but also enable it. Home and school also provide spaces and times that are left empty by the material and cultural timetables of the adult world, for example in the playground at school. In particular, children's peer relationships and friendships are fitted into these inter-stices and are often posed as providing a collective autonomous, if contingent and partial, alternative 'culture'. Furthermore, as indicated in the discussion on individual-isation, home and school represent arenas of action whose structures and rules provide resources that children can subvert, appropriate and manipulate in dealing with parents' and teachers' agendas and in working out their own (see, for example, Holloway and Valentine 2000; Hutchby and Moran-Ellis 1998).

From this conceptual perspective then, there are indeed strong links between home and school, but these are of a quite different type from those promoted in home–school relations policies and practice. The picture painted of these links, however, may be somewhat overdrawn. As noted in discussing the individualisation of childhood, there are different value bases and constructions of 'the child' in each, and which children negotiate in moving between the two, as well as being able, to varying extents, to negotiate within each. These differences can play a key role in separating off children's home existence from their school existence.

The autonomy-dependency axis provides an important viewpoint on children's lives at home and school, in particular drawing attention to issues of power and control. It makes a useful counter to orthodox developmental and socialisation perspectives on the role of home and parents, and of school and teachers, that occlude adult–child power relations and ignore children's agentic role. The axis is rooted, however, in a liberal conception of personhood and may therefore be subject to criticisms that, in turn, it also occludes equally important aspects of people's lives, including those of children.

CONNECTION AND INTERDEPENDENCY

Much of the critique of the liberal political conception of a binary opposition between autonomy and dependence comes from feminist writers (for example, Elshtain 1981; Frazer and Lacey 1993; Pateman 1988; Sevenhuijsen 1998). Within the traditional liberal notion of individualised personhood, autonomy is reified as freedom and equality, and dependency is denigrated as constraint and subjugation. This dichotomy is infused with both age and gender: a self-determining and self-sufficient individual who does not have to rely on others is symbolically and implicitly adult and male. Autonomy is associated with adulthood and dependency with childhood, so that adults who become dependent (such as in old age) are infantilised (Hockey and James 1993). It is associated with maleness because it is based on distinctions between public and private spheres, with the public sphere of employment and politics providing the resources and arena for individualised autonomy.

Feminist political thought has gone further than questioning such oppositional logic by means of arguing, for example, that children can and do exhibit autonomy (such as within and between their familialised and institutionalised locations, as discussed above). However, rather, through a central focus on care, the existence of the oppositions between autonomy and dependency is undermined and rethought, and space is created for understanding relationships of connection and interdependency as an integral part of human existence. None of us are fully autonomous, all of us are dependent in various ways, and we exist in relationships that entail fluctuating boundaries between, and responsibilities to, self and others in specific context. The practice of such connection and interdependency encompasses – at different and at the same times – relational issues of power, vulnerability, responsibility, intimacy, empathy, attentiveness, responsiveness, judgement, negotiation, control and conflict (see, for example, Sevenhuijsen 1998; Tronto 1993). Feminist theorisations of care can be subject to the criticisms that they are very much concerned with adult gender relations and women's position, and run the risk of regarding children only as those who receive women's care. Nevertheless, as I discuss below, this perspective is still of relevance to childhood studies.

To some extent, notions of interdependence underlie some analyses of childhood and children's lives. For example, some childhood researchers are careful to make the point that formulations of children as autonomous need to be understood in a context of generalised interdependence (such as Prout, 1999), and earlier mention of Leena Alanen and Magritt Bardy's (1991) idea of generational contracts and of Jens Qvortrup's (1985, 1995) argument that children participate in the societal division of labour point this way. It could be argued, however, that these concepts still retain an implicit and fixed separation between self and other, rather than seeing this as contingent.

Latterly some childhood researchers have begun more explicitly to explore how feminist theorisations of care and relational connection may be useful in illuminating children's lives – creating an under-traversed bridge between feminist and childhood studies. In some ways, this interest is not quite so recent, however. Carol Gilligan's (1982) study of girls' moral development, carried out in the USA, took issue with the dominant psychological depiction of such development as being towards a 'mature' autonomy, arguing that it masked a masculine ideal image of personhood. She identified an interconnected notion of care for self and others as a defining feature of women's moral maturity. Gilligan's arguments have been subject to criticism, notably that they are developmentally-rooted and essentialist. The interesting point for the present discussion, however, is that they have hardly been acknowledged or followed up as work within the field of childhood studies, even though her study is based on empirical research with girls and young women. Rather, its categorical placement as feminist work has meant that it has not crossed the bridge.

In a recent address, Barrie Thorne (2000) also identified a 'mutual eclipsing' between the adult-produced sociology of childhood and adult-centred feminist perspectives, and noted the benefits of drawing on and reworking feminist theories of care to bring into view obscured aspects of children's lives. In particular, she pointed to the ability to grasp 'the mutual subjectivities, relationality, and the dialectics of child and adult agency'. To this may be added that such reworking also provides a different perspective on child and child relationships.

Julia Brannen, Ellen Heptinstall and Kalwant Bhopal's (2000) work, carried out in Britain, is concerned with just these issues. It explores how children connect themselves to others in terms of the practice of social relationships at home and in school: between children and their siblings, their parents, teachers and peers. This perspective enables them to acknowledge that, as indicated above, there is more than one issue going on in these care relationships. For example, children can experience parents' care as control, a demonstration of connectedness, and as liberation at one and the same time, and can experience their own concerns and responsibilities towards family members and peers in the same complex ways. Mirroring Berry Mayall's (1993, 1994a and b) findings, however, they also found that children's ability to negotiate and practice care was more constrained in the context of the hierarchies and cultures of school.

Brannen, Heptinstall and Bhopal's study is a rare example of the exploration of children's connection and interdependency across the contexts of home and school. Other examples of a more recent traversing of the bridge between childhood and feminist studies, though, include Carol Smart, Bren Neale and Amanda Wade's (2001) identification of ethics of care, fairness and respect in how children experience and understand shared care after parental divorce. Tom Cockburn (1998) proposes a social model of citizenship that emphasises the ways in which people are interdependently connected to each other (rather than individualised autonomous beings) that will enable the active location of children within society, as against conceptions of them as dependents 'squeezed' into the 'unproductive' activities of home and school.

CONTRIBUTIONS TO THIS BOOK

The chapter contributions to this collection draw and expand on the variety of ways of conceptualising the relationship between children, home and school that are outlined in this introduction in diverse ways. What they all have in common, however, is that they centre on children as social actors who are actively negotiating the contexts of home and school, out of school or pre-school institution.

Priscilla Alderson begins the collection with a focus on children's civil rights in British schools. She reviews notions of rights, autonomy, respect and trust, and the ways that children and young people can be excluded or marginalized in political formulations and discussion. In particular, Alderson is concerned with issues of autonomy, connection and regulation in the generation of mutual trust and mistrust between actors in schools (staff and students) as communities, and set in wider local communities. She explores such issues by drawing on an empirical study of students' views about their rights in UK schools, focusing especially on a group discussion between children in a school in a disadvantaged area. The sense of mutual respect and connection between the children taking part in the group and in their discussion of civic rights contrasts somewhat with their accounts of the ways that their own and other children's access to space and facilities was restricted in their school and in the neighbourhood because of adult mistrust of their competence and/or motives. Children's lack of civil rights in education in particular is also demonstrated in Alderson's discussion of the UN Rapporteur on Education's report on education in England. Nevertheless, Alderson also points to good practice in some schools in promoting children's civil rights, and she concludes that such local initiatives are important in showing the way forward for respecting and trusting children's autonomy and sense of community.

Lack of children's rights to a voice is also a feature of Lise Bird's account of recent education reform in New Zealand, along with their institutionalisation through expert discourses. Bird focuses on children's 'needs' and the ways in which these are ascribed to children as dependencies to be met by adults. She shows how unexamined assumptions about innate children's needs underpinned New Zealand's overhaul of the management, structuring and funding of education provision. In contrast to policy discussions, Bird then uses material from her participant observation in a primary school to demonstrate how children's discussion of what they 'need' to learn was far more complex and, importantly, could be negotiated with other children and with teachers. She also shows how teachers can simultaneously impose and negotiate children's needs with children, including through constructing connections between their own and their pupil's needs. It is the moments of negotiation of needs between children especially, and sometimes between children and teachers, that Bird sees as pointing to the ways in which children could escape institutionalised discourses and express their views about education provision.

The previous contributions having examined education policy and provision in terms of children's (lack of) rights and participation, Fiona Smith and John Barker explore out of school care in Britain from a spatial perspective. They chart the growth of children's institutionalisation in this intermediary form of provision, which involves significant conceptual shifts for children attending them, especially given that the majority of it is school-based. Smith and Barker's research into out of school clubs took a 'child-centred' approach, with children themselves participating in defining the research agenda. This is in some contrast to their lack of involvement in the development of out of school services. Their findings reveal overlaps and tensions between education and play, and school and home, for both the children and their playworkers. Children contested some attempts to institutionalise clubs as an educational space, attempted to negotiate others, and accepted some aspects of the structures and boundaries spilling over into the clubs from the school environment. The clubs were also subject to familialisation in terms of reproduction of domesticity and feminisation. Children often resisted domestification of the club environment, but could themselves draw on 'mothering' imagery in relation to the playworkers and home-based ways of contesting adult control. Barker and Smith conclude that children want out of school clubs to be a different form of institutionalisation, transcending both school and home in a unique way.

Mairian Corker and John Davis' chapter explores issues of individualisation in their multi-voiced ethnographic portrait of Callum, a disabled child. They reject the dependency model dominant in expert educational discourses, which institutionalises disabled children, in favour of a social model of understanding focusing on agency and collectivity in disabled childhoods. This allows them to trace the relationship between autonomy and regulation in Callum's experience of bullying at school and also in his home neighbourhood. Corker and Davis draw attention to this relationship over time, before and after Callum is labelled as having Attention Deficit Hyperactivity Disorder and prescribed Ritalin – a drug negatively affecting his agency. In their illustrative example, they show how a constitutive feature of disabled childhood is that school and home are both institutionalised by expert discourses and practices in ways that affect and regulate children's privacy and autonomy.

The focus on children's individualisation and agency is continued in Kjersti Ericsson and Guri Larsen's chapter. They explore the strategies that Norwegian children may use in the context of school-home links, drawing on in-depth interviews with children and observation of parent-teacher meetings. Ericsson and Larsen characterise a closer relationship between school and home as producing possibilities for both increased regulation and control, and agency and autonomy, on the part of children. While teachers and parents can collaborate to exercise tight control of a child, children can also mobilise their connective relationship with these people to address self-identified problems. They can also exercise agency to resist the involvement of parents in efforts for autonomy and self-protection. Ericsson and Larsen see these possibilities, contained in and produced by the meshing of institution-alisation and familialisation, as a feature of contemporary childhood.

Cleopatra Montandon similarly regards tensions between regulation and autonomy as a feature of contemporary childhood, occurring in a context of an increasing social emphasis on their individualisation. She addresses such issues through an in-depth study of the views and experiences of a group of Swiss children. At home the children expected connective support from their parents, including their (longed for) autonomy, but even more so experienced through regulation. In school, they similarly expected fair regulation, although of a less personalised nature. For the most part they conformed to both familialisation and institutionalisation but could also subvert it, and finding more scope for negotiation at home. In contrast, peer relationships were experienced as a collective working towards autonomy, and were an important feature of their experience of institutionalisation.

Pam Alldred, Miriam David and Rosalind Edwards also examine the meanings that children and young people attach to 'school' and 'home', and their negotiation of the two settings, this time in the British context. School was understood as an institutionalised setting and home posed as a place of agentic familial connection. These meanings underpinned children's experiences and understandings of the 'gaps' and connections between the two. Alldred, David and Edwards use in-depth case studies of three children to explore the concrete ways that gender and ethnicity especially can shape children's negotiation of home–school relations, as they both encounter and create separations or connections between the two spheres. They conclude that the mix of institutionalisation and familialisation contained in home–school links initiatives enters into particular, but broader, social meanings and issues interacting in children's lives, and which are largely unacknowledged in policy terms.

Broader social circumstances impacting on the ways that individualisation is experienced is an issue in William Corsaro and Katherine Brown Rosier's account of pre-school African-American children's experience of the transition from home to school. Taking a revised and extended approach to socialisation, they use a longitudinal ethnographic approach to understanding 'priming events' in the lives of children attending a Head Start centre. These events focus children's attention on consequential choices and constraints, and are embedded in the everyday language and cultural routines in which children actively participate in family, school and peer group – an aspect of their individualisation. Corsaro and Rosier detail the ways that the children's mothers attempt to prepare and motivate their children for education and schooling, and to encourage attitudes and values that will counter challenging peer and neighbourhood influences. Priming events are also observed in the Head Start classroom, as part of an institutional curriculum that stands outside of, but is tempered by, the challenging circumstances of the children's lives. These circumstances are also engaged with and enacted in the children's peer group play. They argue that children do not merely and individualistically absorb, but actively and collectively appropriate and apply, priming experiences into their conceptions of themselves and their lives in a severely constrained environment.

Mano Candappa and Itohan Egharevba's chapter is also concerned with children in challenging circumstances. Using both qualitative interview and large scale survey data, they explore the tensions that refugee children who have come to live in Britain face at home in relationships with parents and at school in relationships with their peers. Candappa and Egharevba draw on the concept of generational contract to understand the former, and extend this from inter- to intra-generational contract to illuminate the latter. The conventional power relations embedded in the inter-generational contract (and in familialisation) were disrupted for these children as they related interdependently to their parents both as child and as carer, especially in acting as language brokers for parents less competent in English than themselves. The children were in a weak position in the intra-generational contract, however, where conversely their relative lack of English language competence proved a source of stigma, racist bullying and barrier to entry into peer groups. The children also faced tensions in negotiating social and cultural norms between the home and school, manifested in dress and behaviour, but with home cultural values being dominant. Home–school relations thus take on different implications in the face of renegotiated generational contracts.

Elisabeth Backe-Hansen addresses issues of age in viewing home–school relations as a landscape of different arenas or contexts that provide possibilities and constraints for young people as social actors. She draws on a large scale longitudinal study of teenagers, their parents and teachers in Norway, to explore issues of autonomy, connection and regulation. Backe-Hansen draws attention to the complex ways these issues interact and are bound together at the time of adolescence. Both a pre-supposed connectedness and a negotiated autonomy were facets of the young people's views of good parenting, along with some regulation. Schooling, however, was experienced and enacted as negotiating some autonomy in a regulated setting, and which could impact on the young people's motivation. Collaboration between home and school in terms of parent–teacher relations, was shaped by these issues. Backe-Hansen concludes that more attention is needed to the particular circumstances of young people's lives, rather than blanket home–school relations policies.

The following chapters thus reveal the different ways that children are active in and negotiate their regulation, autonomy and connection within home–school relations. A summing up of similarities and differences between the contributions is contained in the Afterword.

NOTES

1 In the following discussion the term 'home' often overlaps with or implicates the terms family, parents and household. Similarly, 'school' invokes education and teachers, policy and practice. Further complexity is introduced if we take into account that 'home', as well as 'family', 'mother' and 'father' can become ambiguous, lived, concepts for children of separated and divorced parents, and/or living in step and/or same sex families.

2 While some countries in other welfare regime types may have forms of child advocates, this is most often at the local, rather than nation state, level – for example, New Zealand.

REFERENCES

Alanen, L. (1998) 'Children and the family order: constraints and competences', in Hutchby, I. and Moran-Ellis, J. (eds) *Children and Social Competence: Arenas of Action*, London: Falmer Press.

Alanen, L. and Bardy, M. (1991) *Childhood as Social Phenomenon: National Report for Finland*, Eurosocial Report, Vienna: European Centre.

Andenaes, A. (1996) 'Challenges and solutions for children with two homes in the Nordic countries', in J. Brannen and R. Edwards (eds) *Perspectives on Parenting and Childhood: Looking Back and Moving Forward*, London: SBU/ESRC/IoE.

Ball, S. (1994) *Education Reform*, Milton Keynes: Open University Press.

Beck, U. (1992) *The Risk Society: Towards a New Modernity*, London: Sage.

Beck, U. (1999) *World Risk Society*, Cambridge: Polity Press.

Beck, U. and Beck-Gernsheim, E. (1995) *The Normal Chaos of Love*, Cambridge: Polity Press.

Bernstein, B. (1967) 'Open schools – open society', *New Society*, 14 September, 351–353.

Bernstein, B. (1977) *Class, Codes and Control*, Vol. 3, London: Routledge and Kegan Paul.

Bourdieu, P. (1986) *Distinction*, London: Routledge and Kegan Paul.

Boyden, J. (1991) *Children of the Cities*, London: Zed Books.

Brannen, J., Heptinstall, E. and Bhopal, K. (2000) *Connecting Children: Care and Family Life in Later Childhood*, London: RoutledgeFalmer.

Brannen, J. and O'Brien, M. (1995) 'Childhood and the sociological gaze: paradigms and paradoxes', *Sociology*, 29, 729–737.

Bühler, E. (1998) 'Economy, state or culture? Explaining regional differences in gender inequality in Swiss employment', *European Urban and Regional Studies*, 5: 1, 27–39.

CERI (1997) *Parents as Partners in Schooling*, Paris: Organisation for Economic Co-operation and Development.

Cockburn, T. (1998) 'Children and citizenship in Britain: a case for a socially interdependent model of citizenship', *Childhood*, 5: 1, 99–117.

Crozier, G. (1998) 'Parents and schools: partnership or surveillance?', *Journal of Education Policy*, 13: 1, 125–136.

Dahlberg, G. (1996) 'Negotiating modern childrearing and family life in Sweden', in J. Brannen and R. Edwards (eds) *Perspectives on Parenting and Childhood: Looking Back and Moving Forward*, London: SBU/ESRC/IoE.

Dalley, B. (1998) *Family Matters: Child Welfare in Twentieth-Century New Zealand*, Auckland: Auckland University Press.

David, M.E. (1993) *Parents, Gender and Education Reform*, Cambridge: Polity Press.

Deacon, A. (2002) 'Paternalism, welfare reform and poor families in the United States', in A. Carling, S. Duncan and R. Edwards (eds) *Analysing Families*, London: Routledge.

Duncan, S. (1995) 'Theorising European gender systems', *Journal of European Social Policy*, 5: 4, 262–284.

Duncan, S. and Edwards, R. (1999) *Lone Mothers, Paid Work and Gendered Moral Rationalities*, Basingstoke: Macmillan.

Edwards, A. and Warin, J. (1999) 'Parental involvement in raising the achievement of primary school pupils: why bother?', *Oxford Review of Education*, 25: 3, 325–341.

Edwards, R. and Alldred, P. (1999) 'Children and young people's views of social research: the case of research on home–school relations', *Childhood*, 6: 2, 261–281.

Edwards, R. and Alldred, P. (2000) 'A typology of parental involvement in education centring on children and young people: negotiating familialisation, institutionalisation and individualisation', *British Journal of Sociology of Education*, 21: 3, 435–455.

Edwards, R. and David, M. (1997) 'Where are the children in home–school relations? Notes towards a research agenda', *Children and Society*, 11: 3, 194–200.

Elshtain, J. (1981) *Public Man, Private Women: Women in Social and Political Thought*, Princetown NJ: Princetown University Press.

Epstein, J.L. (1992) *School and Family Partnerships (Report No. 6)*, Baltimore: John Hopkins University.

Epstein, J.L. (1995) 'School/family/community partnerships: caring for the children we share', *Phi Delta Kappan*, 76: 9, 701–712.

Esping-Andersen, G. (1990) *The Three Worlds of Welfare Capitalism*, London: Polity Press.

Esping-Andersen, G. (1999) *Social Foundations of Industrial Economics*, Oxford: Oxford University Press.

Frazer, E. and Lacey, N. (1993) *The Politics of Community: A Feminist Critique of the Liberal-Communitarian Debate*, London: Harvester-Wheatsheaf.

Giddens, A. (1992) *The Transformation of Intimacy: Sexuality, Love and Eroticism in Modern Societies*, Cambridge: Polity Press.

Gilligan, C. (1982) *In a Different Voice: Psychological Theory and Women's Development*, Cambridge MA: Harvard University Press.

Hallgarten, J. (2000) *Parents Exist, OK!? Issues and Visions for Parent-School Relationships*, London: Institute of Public Policy Research.

Hendricks, H. (1994) *Child Welfare: England 1872–1989*, London: Routledge.

Hockey, J. and James, A. (1993) *Growing Up and Growing Old: Ageing and Dependency in the Life Course*, London: Sage.

Holloway, S. and Valentine, G. (2000) 'Spatiality and the new social studies of childhood', *Sociology*, 34: 4, 763–784.

Hutchby, I. and Moran-Ellis, J. (1998) 'Situating children's social competence', in I. Hutchby and J. Moran-Ellis (eds) *Children and Social Competence: Arenas of Action*, London: Falmer Press.

James, A. (1993) *Childhood Identities: Self and Social Relationships in the Experience of the Child*, Edinburgh: Edinburgh University Press.

James, A., Jenks, C. and Prout, A. (1998) *Theorizing Childhood*, Cambridge: Polity Press.

James, A. and Prout, A. (eds) (1997) *Constructing and Reconstructing Childhood: Contemporary Issues in the Sociological Study of Childhood,* London: Falmer Press.

Jensen, A-M. (1994) 'Feminisation of childhood', in Qvortrup, J., Bardy, M., Sigritta, G. and Wintersberger, E. (eds) *Childhood Matters: Social Theory, Practice and Politics,* Aldershot: Avebury.

Jensen, A-M. (2001) 'Property, power and prestige – the feminization of childhood', in M. du Bois-Raymond, H. Sünker and H.H. Krüger (eds) *Childhood in Europe: Approaches, Trends, Findings,* New York: Peter Lang Publishing.

Klein, E.L. (1988) 'How is a teacher different from a mother? Young children's perceptions of the social roles of significant adults', *Theory Into Practice,* 27: 1, 36–41.

Leira, A. (1994) 'Combining work and family: working mothers in Scandinavia and the European Community', in P. Brown and R. Crompton (eds) *Economic Restructuring and Social Exclusion,* London: UCL Press.

Lewis, J. (1992) 'Gender and the development of welfare regimes', *Journal of European Social Policy,* 2: 3, 159–173.

Mayall, B. (1993) 'Keeping healthy at home and school: it's my body so it's my job', *Sociology of Health and Illness,* 15: 4, 464–87.

Mayall, B. (1994a) 'Children in action at home and school', in Mayall, B. (ed.) *Children's Childhoods: Observed and Experienced,* London: Falmer Press.

Mayall, B. (1994b) *Negotiating Health: School Children at Home and at School,* London: Cassell.

McLaughlin, E. and Glendinning, C. (1994) 'Paying for care in Europe: is there a feminist approach?', in L. Hantrais and S. Mangen (eds) *Family Policy and the Welfare of Women,* Cross-National Research Paper 3, European Research Centre, University of Loughborough.

Morgan, D.H.J. (1996) *Family Connections: An Introduction to Family Studies,* Cambridge: Polity Press.

Morrow, V. (1994) 'Responsible children? Aspects of children's work and employment outside school in contemporary UK', in B. Mayall (ed.) *Children's Childhoods: Observed and Experienced,* London: Falmer Press.

Moss, P., Dillon, J. and Statham, J. (2000) 'The 'child in need' and 'the rich child': discourses, constructions and practice', *Critical Social Policy,* 20: 2, 233–254.

Nasman, E. (1994) 'Individualisation and institutionalisation of children in today's Europe', in Qvortrup, J., Bardy, M., Sigritta, G. and Wintersberger, E. (eds) *Childhood Matters: Social Theory, Practice and Politics,* Aldershot: Avebury.

Norwegian Ministry of Children and the Family (1996) *The Ombudsman for Children and Childhood in Norway,* Oslo: Ministry for Children and the Family.

Oakley, A. (1994) 'Women and children first and last: parallels and differences between Children's and Women's Studies', in Mayall, B. (ed.) *Children's Childhoods: Observed and Experienced,* London: Falmer.

Oldman, D. (1994) 'Childhood as a mode of production', in B. Mayall (ed.) *Children's Childhoods: Observed and Experienced,* London: Falmer Press.

Pateman, C. (1988) *The Sexual Contract,* Cambridge: Polity Press.

Pfau-Effinger, B. (1998) 'Gender cultures and the gender arrangement – a theoretical framework for cross-national gender research', *Innovation,* 11: 2, 147–66.

Pringle, K. (1998) *Children and Social Welfare in Europe,* Buckingham: Open University Press.

Prout, A. (ed.) (1999) *The Body, Children and Society,* Basingstoke: Macmillan.

Prout, A. (2000) 'Children's participation: control and self-realisation in British late modernity', *Children and Society,* 14, 304–315.

Qvortrup, J. (1985) 'Placing children in the division of labour', in P. Close and R. Collins (eds) *Family and Economy in Modern Society*, Basingstoke: Macmillan.

Qvortrup, J. (1995) 'From useful to useful: the historical continuity in children's constructive participation', in A.-M. Ambert (ed.) *Sociological Studies of Children Vol. 7*, Greenwich, CT: JAI Press.

Qvortrup, J., Bardy, M., Sigritta, G. and Wintersberger, E. (eds) (1994) *Childhood Matters: Social Theory, Practice and Politics*, Aldershot: Avebury.

Reid, J. (1995) 'Young carers', *Highlight 37*, London: National Children's Bureau.

Rose, N. (1990) *Governing the Soul*, London: Routledge.

Sanders, M.G. and Epstein, J.L. (1998) *International Perspectives on School-Family-Community Partnerships Special Issue: Childhood Education*, 74: 6.

Scott, S., Jackson, S. and Backett-Milburn, K. (1998) 'Swings and roundabouts: risk, anxiety and the everyday worlds of children', *Sociology*, 32: 4, 647–663.

Sevenhuijsen, S. (1998) *Citizenship and the Ethics of Care: Feminist Considerations on Justice, Morality and Politics*, London: Routledge.

Smart, C., Neale, B. and Wade, A. (2001) *Changing Childhoods, Changing Families*, Cambridge: Polity Press.

Smith, D. (1998) 'The underside of schooling: restructuring, privatisation and women's unpaid work', *Journal For a Just and Caring Education*, 4, 11–29.

Solberg, A. (1994) *Negotiating Childhood: Empirical Investigations and Textual Representations of Children's Work and Everyday Lives*, Stockholm: Nordic Institute for Studies in Urban and Regional Planning.

Thorne, B. (2000) 'Children's agency and theories of care', ESRC Children 5–16 Research Programme Final Conference, London, 21 October.

Tronto, J. (1993) *Moral Boundaries: A Political Argument for an Ethic of Care*, London: Routledge.

U.S. Department of Education *Goals 2000: Education America Act*: http://www.ed.gov/legislation/GOALS2000/TheAct/

Vincent, C. and Tomlinson, S. (1997) 'Home–school relations: "the swarming of disciplinary mechanisms"?', *British Educational Research Journal*, 23: 3, 361–377.

Walkerdine, V. (1985) 'On the regulation of speaking and silence', in C. Steadman, C. Unwin and V. Walkerdine (eds) *Language, Gender and Childhood*, London: Routledge.

Woodhead, M. (1997) 'Psychology and the cultural construction of children's needs', in A. James and A. Prout (eds) *Constructing and Reconstructing Childhood: Contemporary Issues in the Sociological Study of Childhood*, London: Falmer Press.

Wyness, M.G. (1999) 'Childhood, agency and educational reform', *Childhood*, 6: 3, 353–368.

Zelitzer, V.A. (1985) *Pricing the Priceless Child: The Changing Social Value of Children*, New York: Basic Books.

1 Students' rights in British schools

Trust, autonomy, connection and regulation

Priscilla Alderson

This chapter considers meanings of respect for and trust in rights and rights-holders in small communities especially schools. Contradictory and complementary concepts of autonomy, linked to formal and informal trust and mistrust are reviewed in the context of the 1989 UN Convention on the Rights of the Child (the Convention). Reported views of British students about trust and respect in their schools are presented, and linked to the themes of autonomy, connection and regulation. Finally, implications for future policy and practice in relation to respect, trust and students' rights are considered, with the possibility of increasing connection and reducing social exclusion by thinking in new terms of addressing statal exclusions through participation rights. The concept 'statal' acknowledges political dimensions in exclusions which are too often blamed on the personal failings of excluded people. Statal refers to the formal structures in society, which discriminate against disadvantaged groups by denying them equal rights, opportunities and legal entitlements, and which can be clearly defined and acted upon.

RESPECT FOR AND TRUST IN RIGHTS AND RIGHTS HOLDERS

Modern meanings of rights developed less than 400 years ago in Locke's work (1690/ 1959) on the inalienable rights of man. These earliest rights to autonomy as self-rule, privacy, self-determination and freedom from interference moved away from feudal trusting subjection to the monarch and state. As confidence in individual's judgment and independence rose, trust conversely fell in any intrusions from strangers or the state. Kant (1796/1972) believed that only rational, property-owning man was qualified to make his own decisions. He divided relationships into respect between persons as ends in themselves, and legitimate disregard which treats non-persons (women, children and servants) as property and as the means towards other people's ends (Mendus 1987). Mill (1971) added that even if men and women cannot make wise personal decisions, their liberty is too precious for others to infringe it. These two concepts of autonomy are partly contradictory when they mean either Kantian wisdom to make correct choices or Millean resolve to take risks and to stand by uncertain best guesses.

Autonomy combines further contradictions. It may be seen as a stable inner capacity or an outer entitlement that is granted or withheld, such as when Russian intellectual refuseniks were treated as incompetent psychiatric cases. Children's autonomy may be respected as their capacity to take some responsibility, or as the rationale for regulation by adults: 'we will protect your future adult autonomy until you are mature enough to exercise it.' Autonomy may be regarded as safeguarded by lonely Kantian detachment, or fulfilled through human connection; as pure disembodied Kantian reason, or an identity that is strengthened through bodily experiences and knowledge. Some analysts respect autonomy which is separate from and unpressured by social circumstances; others believe that personal agency can only be realised within complex structures, pressures and choices. These contradictions resonate with uncertainties about children's autonomy and rights, as discussed later.

Respect and trust are closely linked in that both see the other person as reliable, reasonable, well intentioned, and sharing some similar values to one's own. Individualistic notions of property-owning rights and lonely, self-interested autonomy, raise immense problems for attempts to live with mutual respect, trust and intimacy in communities ranging from states, to schools, to families. Socialist 'left-wing' visions of rights as equal entitlements conflict with liberal 'right-wing' unequal individualistic rights to obtain and defend personal property and status (as debated, for example, by Andrews *et al.* 1991). Cockburn (1998) notes how children are ignored in these debates. These conflicting views especially leave children in an ambiguous position in liberal societies which link citizenship with owning property but deny this right to children (O'Neill 1994). Do children then count as persons or as their parents' property? Do they inevitably lack Kantian autonomy and wisdom as well as Millean resolve to bear responsibility and potential blame when making risky decisions? Adults may make self-destructive decisions, but decisions which affect children must respect their best interests (Children Act 1989; UN 1989), which are usually defined by adults. It is then often assumed that because children and young people do not have absolute rights to self-determination they have none at all (Ross 1998; Phillips 1997), although everyone's rights are limited by respect for law and order.

Bourdieu's concept of social capital (Bourdieu 1977) is valuable in analysing social inequalities. Yet the concept raises problems for young people and their rights if it implies that social capital such as behaviours, skills and knowledge are preordained and timelessly valued commodities passed on by adults who 'socialise' relatively passive children. It denies how children may generate and evaluate different kinds of social capital. 'Capital' also carries overtones of an investment which, especially for children who cannot legally own or dispose of property, waits to be drawn on in their adult future. Putnam (1996) further analysed social capital in useful terms of communities and networks but he ignored young people. For example, Putnam traced the decline in community trust and voluntary activities by the reported fall in leaders of Red Cross and scout groups (adults). He does not mention the young people concerned, or offer reasons why adults might be discouraged from sharing activities with them (such as rising mistrust in Britain and the United States about paedophilia and liability for accidental injuries). Putnam relies on public records, and identifies trust with activities and views linked to the public sphere of life and formal organisations. He

AUTONOMOUS RIGHTS HOLDERS IN SMALL AND LARGE COMMUNITIES, FAMILIES AND SCHOOLS

Attempts to resolve contradictions between individualistic autonomy and personal relationships include excluding friendship and family intimacy into the 'private' unexamined sphere (Seidler 1986). A second course is to grant householders rights over the rest of the family, but this reduces children to a property-like status. Complications arise if they are unwilling to accept this lower status, and also if the state intrudes into family privacy when children are thought to be abused. A third approach reconceptualises autonomy, no longer as detachment (Kohlberg 1981; Erikson 1971), but as expanded through connections which increase awareness of self and others (Gilligan 1982; Apter 1990) and through rational moral emotions such as trust (Alderson 1990).

The Convention (UN 1989) takes this view of rights which promote mutual respect in 'the spirit of peace, dignity, tolerance, freedom, equality and solidarity' (Convention Preamble, article 29). The Convention's 54 articles record broad, sometimes aspirational, children's rights to provision (of necessities and services), protection (from neglect, abuse and discrimination) and participation (versions of adult autonomy rights). The Convention is the first treaty to respect children's civil rights.

Provision and protection rights can equally well be considered in less controversial terms of welfare, needs or best interests, and many adults still confine children's rights to these two types. This is illustrated by the Commonwealth Teachers' Report on Education and Human Rights which has eight sections about children's provision and protection rights in education, but children's participation rights do not appear even to occur to the authors. In marked contrast to the rest of the report, section four speaks of teachers' civil rights, with 'every other citizen' (except children), to vote, contest elections, join political organisations and trade unions, speak and write on political issues and be free from victimisation. Teachers 'should be involved through consultation and negotiation in forming educational policies at every level' (NUT 1997) although nothing is said about pupils' or parents' involvement. Children's rights are similarly disregarded in recent government reports on citizenship education (QCA 1998, 2001), despite the growing literature on the crucial importance, the advantages and the rewards when schools practise what they preach, so that students are able to take seriously their education about democracy, respect, health, trust and citizenship (Jeffs 1995; Mayall 1996; Griffith 1998; Hammarberg 1997; Nairn 2000).

Whatever levels of mutual trust and respect children experience in their family, when they join schools and playgroups they have to adapt to different kinds of trust and rights, moving from informal (personal, private, intimate) trust towards more formal (impersonal, public, institutional) trust. Teachers *in loco parentis* have to control pupils in crowds and not as one or a few individuals as parents do. Communities of relative strangers must rely on some degree of formal regulation which is a symbolic and practical expression of mistrust, such as school rules. Schools try to teach students how to form appropriate levels of trust/mistrust in public and private life through

countless explicit and implicit messages, from norms for individual friendships to implicit and explicit rules for games, for classes and for the whole school.

The dilemma for staff and students is how to ensure appropriate safeguards against potential betrayal, exploitation and disorder, without simultaneously undermining latent and developing trust, goodwill and confident autonomy in pupils and staff, thereby inciting the very problems they aim to prevent (White 1996: 60). A solution is to achieve as high a level of willing connection (the spirit of community) and as low a level of overt coercion/resistance (the letter of regulation) as possible. Mutual trust and respect between individual teachers and students however are affected by many complications, from the nature of each relationship, and the differing levels of trust each student expects to have, to the school's ethos and national structures such as the government's national curriculum which implies mistrust in teachers and students' ability to plan their own learning. There are also regular powerful messages of mistrust in children and teenagers from the mass media, public opinion and child development experts which increase the risk teachers feel that they have to take if they are to trust pupils. The next section reports the research project on civil rights in schools.

REPORTED VIEWS OF BRITISH STUDENTS ABOUT TRUST AND RESPECT IN THEIR SCHOOLS

The research reported in this chapter arose from questions about the practical impact in schools of the contradictory meanings of rights, autonomy, trust and treating people as ends in themselves. The survey began by contacting every local education authority and scanning schools listed on the Internet to compile a purposive sample of 250 schools. Although only 58 teachers replied to the single sheet teachers' survey, and 49 agreed to conduct the pupils' survey, 2,272 completed questionnaires were received from schools which included primary, middle and secondary schools, comprehensive, selective and special, local authority, grant maintained and private, mixed and single sex, secular and religious, and schools in cities, towns and semi-rural areas with pupils from a range of socio-economic and ethnic backgrounds, across the UK.

The survey investigated students' views about their rights in UK schools based on the Convention's participation rights, phrased as questions about everyday matters of central concern to students aged seven to 17 years. A shiny green cover, for each student to detach and keep, briefly explained the research and the Convention's participation rights which were paraphrased as:

> your rights: to respect for your worth and dignity; to express yourself and to develop your skills and talents fully; to be heard and to have your views taken seriously in matters which affect you; to share in making decisions about your life; to have all kinds of useful information and ideas; to freedom of thought, conscience and religion; to learn to live in peace, tolerance, equality and

friendship; to privacy and respect and to fair discipline; to work together for rights and to see that these are shared fairly in your school.

A single 24-page questionnaire for all ages worked well, with 88 per cent of the youngest group saying it was interesting or very interesting, and 80 per cent of the eldest ones. There is not space here to report the survey replies (see Alderson 1999a,b, 2000; Alderson and Arnold 1999) except to say that many students reported feeling that teachers did not listen to them very much, or take account of their views, or trust them to make decisions and arrange meetings and help to run the schools. Many students appeared to feel mistrusted although, as psychodynamic social research has shown, this is an extremely complicated area to research. Research has found that nurses tend to mistrust those junior to them, and to resent feeling mistrusted by staff who are senior to them (Menzies Lyth 1989). This pattern applies to many institutions, perhaps especially to schools where the age discrepancies are so great.

We also visited 16 schools to conduct 34 small group discussions usually lasting half an hour. The schools we visited varied immensely in how much the students were trusted and involved by teachers; primary schools in disadvantaged areas were among the best in this respect. Before and during the rights in schools project, related projects in other schools assisted in the design, piloting and interpretation of the survey through detailed knowledge of actual practices in schools (Alderson and Goodey 1998; Highfield 1997; Cleves 1999). This chapter concentrates on one of the group discussions which has been picked at random and examined for themes linked to autonomy, connection and regulation. In the group were three boys and three girls aged nine years old. The school was in a disadvantaged city area with high-rise housing.

The interviewer began by asking the group what they enjoyed most at school or what they might change in the school if they were the head teacher. The group immediately began discussing activities, usually listening carefully to each other and talking in a shared, almost overlapping manner (as the punctuation attempts to indicate). Their manner of talking so spontaneously together suggests their sense of mutual respect and connection, and their trust in the interviewer whom they had not met before. (Each star denotes a new person speaking.)

* we had some little balls and Miss said we couldn't play with them and so we asked to go into the hall and we couldn't…
* we'd like to have our own climbing frames cos you can, like, climb on them instead of always doing games on the floor
* because we get a bit bored
* like swings
* in the playground
* yeah
* yeah but they stopped them once because someone fell off one and that's why they stopped them
* other schools have them
* yeah a school in —— has one and they're near the park

* if we did have a climbing frame we should have that surface on the ground
* like carpet underneath
* we had it at our park we have it this kind of carpet
* green
* yeah green carpet

The group went on to say how swings and seesaws were removed from their park which had a hard ground cover unlike the 'green carpet'. They showed high awareness of their safety (protection rights) and adults' concern about these. Yet the 'rights' ended in a loss of amenities for the children and, though they did not mention this, the driving motive may well have been the authority's desire to economise and reduce the risk of litigation following accidents.

* I'd like goal posts and rugby posts then we could have a game of football with proper posts
* because most of them argue because they say if it's over [higher than the goal top bar would be] it depends how high you are and that's not really fair
* we used to have goal posts but they took them down
  (Interviewer) why?
* I don't know
* they just took them down
* they was falling down really but they never really gave us any new ones
* well what we'd like is a net with them because if it [the ball] does go too high it always goes down in the ditch
* we have to use our coats [as goals nets]
* yeah and when we have to go in [the ditch] there's all stinging nettles down there and some people when they do it they're fighting who is going to get the ball out of the ditch and some people get pushed in …

The children's games might be seen by parents and teachers as irresponsible, fighting in the ditch and getting their coats muddy, and requiring tighter regulation. Another view would see the children as eager to connect and play together, to solve problems such as lack of goal nets, and to continue the football game across boundaries created by the lack of a proper pitch.

The children had to contend with problems caused by teenagers who also appeared to lack local amenities. The lack of concern in their community meant, in terms of the UN Convention, disrespect for children's and teenagers' rights to freedom of expression (article 12), association and peaceful assembly (article 15), an adequate standard of living (article 27), education for responsible life in a free society in the spirit of understand, peace, equality … and friendship (article 29) and to leisure, recreation and cultural activities (article 31). In practice, these rights mean being able to meet and play with their friends in public spaces. The group's comments implied that teenagers possibly protested more, and were more alienated by the lack of adult concern for their interests.

★   cos outside there's not very much to do there's a basket ball court and sometimes
    there's bigger people there, and younger ones like us can't go in there
★   and they pick on us
★   there's nowhere to play we just wander around or stay inside
[They go on to talk about graffiti, rubbish and broken benches in the park for which
they blamed the teenagers]
★   the older ones just snap off the benches
★   the people who live near they just watch them do it, they don't tell them off
★   when we're in our houses it would be nice to have something, maybe a friend
    or a pet because I've got a few pets, so if you have a pet you have some attention
    on that
★   it's a bit horrible at (at home) on sunny days when you can't go out because you
    know they're going to come up
★   there was a sign saying 'no one over 12' but they rubbed it out and put '21'

The phrase 'you have attention on that' mentioned above suggests loneliness and
boredom for children who cannot walk freely around their neighbourhood and
meet their friends, and who live in high rise flats with little space to have friends
round to play. When asked if they thought that children have different rights from
adults, the group replied:

★   yeah because adults swear and we're not allowed but some children swear
They add that adults drive cars dangerously, and do not signal when they are turning
'so they waste your time' while you wait to cross a side road in case any from the
stream of cars turns into it.
★   like you're going along on your bike and somebody will come roaring up,
    burning past in a really fast car and they'll almost knock you off, often that
    happens
★   well adults say not to argue with anyone or have rows but they have arguments
★   well only adults can have a say then, children don't get a say in it

Someone in the group whose house had been burgled said that adults rob houses,
and the group went on to talk about adults getting drunk and how people who run
pubs could prevent this. Later, they talked about possibly having keys to public
telephones to prevent them being vandalised and they discussed the pros and cons of
this idea for some time. On each occasion they suggested new ideas, then someone
else would point out a flaw, and together they would try to think of another solution,
showing close connections as friends and a collective sense of worry and responsibility
about their neighbourhood and a wish to improve matters.
    In many of the groups we spoke with, students said how much they enjoyed the
chance to talk together and to be listened to by an adult. All the groups were rational,
friendly and expressed responsibility and concern for others. Adults who sometimes
found some of the children hard to manage might well comment that 'they are
putting on an act, pretending to be far more mature than they really are', but it is

hardly possible to pretend to be more sensible and aware than you are capable of being, at least sometimes. Another concern that their teachers might have about the groups is that the children who were critical exaggerated and even invented problems in their lives, and saw the group session as an opportunity to grumble. Their tone of voice, however, was matter-of-fact not complaining and they tended simply to report incidents and not to use descriptive or judgemental words; the other children tended to confirm and not to question the examples or incidents mentioned.

Interviewer: Should adults have different rights from children?
★   Yeah because, like, if adults want to smoke they should do because they're old enough and they know what they're doing but children don't
★   I don't smoke
★   Well adults know what they're doing, smoking is very addictive, because well it's, you think you might, if you start smoking you'll be able to stop easily but you can't after a few cigarettes, you'd be addicted to it

The group said that adults were 'old enough' and 'know enough' to have more rights than children, yet they gave examples of adults being irresponsible and did not question the mismatch between their stated views, which may well repeat adults' statements, and their own observations and experiences. The group talked about how adults should ban cigarettes that give adults cancer and make the children's asthma worse when their parents and grandparents smoke, and also ban drugs 'that wash your brains out'. Some of the group began to say that they thought adults and children should have similar rights.

★   Cos civil rights are sensible for children and they're sensible for adults as well
Interviewer: For example?
★   Like um – like
★   to have the rights to do something as long as you don't get into trouble, yeah like go for a bike ride but be careful where you go
★   yeah parents just say that you can't go they say you can't be trusted but they don't give you a chance
They talked about needing cycle lanes
Interviewer: Do people in school respect your rights?
★   Yeah
★   Most of the time
★   Yeah but the dinner ladies …

They gave examples of disagreements with dinner ladies, then someone said the school should have security guards at the entrance, because three girls had run away from school, and everyone began talking, unusually at once, about how they needed metal instead of wooden fences. They implied that they believed schools' attention to security, following the fairly recent incident in Dunblane, Scotland, when children in a nursery class were shot and injured or killed, was to keep the children in rather than to keep intruders out. Their talk suggested again that they had quite deeply internalised the belief that adults are responsible and children are not, so that they interpreted incidents such as the new security measures in the school to fit their deeper beliefs about irresponsible, volatile children, even though they knew about dangerous adults and mentioned Dunblane.

The group moved on to talk about wanting a bigger playground and how an empty classroom (in their unpopular under-subscribed school) might be used as a leisure and pool table room. They repeated that children could not be trusted as much as adults to have rights, and the interviewer asked several times what was the danger in respecting children's rights, but the group ignored the questions and went on talking about how they would like to improve the school, until one boy said:

★   well I was going to cut me hand there, and me stomach
★   yeah he keeps trying to cut himself
★   I didn't really cut me hand
★   you tried to
★   you tried to before
★   cos there weren't no teacher around so he tried to cut his self
★   and he got a rope and he tied it round his neck and he was like pulling it

Someone then went on to talk about another boy who swore, interrupted games and lessons.

★   and he's actually getting to hurt other people, and stop their education
★   cos he always gets into moods and spoils the game or in rounders he says it's not fair, but it is fair because we did it equally

Everyone seemed to know about the first boy's self-harming and he did not appear to be ashamed or boastful but, like the others, accepting of this and other unhappy events like the drunk adults, vandalism and burglaries. The children seemed to manage the events and the conversation about them thoughtfully and with dignity trying, as they said, to be fair, equal and inclusive. Their concerns about community and friendship were also shown when they talked about how they might share in deciding which school they attended. They talked of wanting to keep in touch with friends, to avoid long bus journeys and to be at a school where they could 'feel comfortable'.

Interviewer:	Okay, last question, do you think children should have the right to say how their school is run, and share in making decisions?
★	Yes
★	Yeah
★	Every child, every child would have an opinion to say, that they form a group in a circle just like
★	maybe they could have a vote on what is being wanted the most
★	the whole school should get involved in what they're doing because some people might think it's not very fair

The groups wrestled with the dilemmas of proportionality, of being fair to everyone while making allowance for some children who have extra difficulties and trying to expect reasonably high standards from and for all. The children's sense of rights, emphasised fair, equal and mutual respect rather than selfish individualism. While playing football, the children were also playing the more complicated games of renegotiating rules which were designed for properly equipped pitches, of making do within economic deprivation, and of managing sometimes stressful relationships. Analysis of play between much younger children aged three and four years has shown how intensely aware they are of playing out emotions and power in their relationships, while their adult carers assume that they are simply doing constructive play with bricks (Danby and Barker 1998).

Painful contradictions in their lives, discussed earlier by the group, possibly contributed to the self-harming behaviour. The boy who said, 'if adults want to smoke they should do because they're old enough and they know what they're doing but children don't', hinted at contradictions in autonomy noted earlier, Kantian wisdom or Millean liberty. Are adults somehow less prone to addiction than children are, or more able to weigh the risks and benefits of smoking and to make a rational choice, or are adults entitled to make potentially self-destructive choices about smoking, drinking and driving which children may not make simply because they are not adults? Kantian wisdom involves rising into the realm of pure reason free from contingencies and bodily desires and inadequacies; man is entitled to rights in so far as he has autonomous, moral self-control (Kant 1948: 84, 1964). The advantages of such calm, disinterested reason are complicated by its underlying contempt for human bodies and interdependence (Grimshaw 1986: 31; Mendus 1987) which ultimately led to moral validation of Nazi extremes of inhumanity (MacIntyre 1966: 208; Gouldner 1977: 505; Seidler 1986: 120: Williams 1972, 1985). And Mill's liberty, when unconstrained by self-control or concern for others, is increasingly linked to utilitarian free choices for adult consumers. These unresolved contradictions about autonomy are exacerbated for children and teenagers by the deep ways in which they are age related in adult/child, reason/emotion dichotomies which are illustrated by numerous examples, including ones by the pioneers of childhood studies (James, Jenks and Prout 1998:198).

> Children offer living exemplars of the very margins of [social] order, of its volatility and, in fact, its fragility. On a momentary basis children exercise anarchic tendencies and sociality up to the limits of adult tolerance and often beyond, hence their temporal and spatial confinement in 'childhood' ... They are unstable, systematically disruptive and uncontained, so that, as individual manifestations of 'childhood', children are cognitively managed, though barely, under a variety of different rubrics: children's 'creativity', 'self-expression', 'primitiveness', 'simplicity' or just 'ignorance' ... For adults to celebrate such conduct beyond celebration or intoxication would be to invite the categorization of eccentricity at best (Hockey and James 1993), or, at worst, insanity: [and they quote Foucault 1967:123] 'madness does not represent the absolute form of contradiction, but instead a minority status, an aspect of itself that does not have the right to

autonomy, and can live only grafted onto the world of reason. Madness is childhood'.

Disadvantages of gender and ethnicity can become multiple jeopardies when an assumed helplessness of childhood is imposed on children, when adults who then claim to protect children cannot do so, when some adults set examples of helpless or selfish incompetence, so that children and teenagers are left feeling even more helpless and hopeless than the adults they observe and are likely to become. Melissa Butler noted similar contradictions between the received beliefs of the seven-year-old black children she taught in Chicago, who said 'we'll never deal drugs, or carry guns or join gangs,' and the subtle pressures all around them which would lead the boys as they grew older to do just that (Butler 1998; and see also Corsaro and Rosier, this volume). The children lived within contradictions between the simple instructions they heard about how to be good and to trust adults, and their regular experiences which severely challenged these. Butler and her class talked critically and logically through the contradictions, to see the immense pressures on black children, teenagers and adults, so that the children were able to move on from blaming them, and to work, as they said, for peace and justice.

Students are helped in some schools to retain the optimism and goodwill which they showed in their discussions, and their connections with their community, and to make sense of contradictions between adults' instructions and their examples. They are able to work with adults on creating more just and peaceful communities through actively solving problems on discrimination, bullying and mistrust (Highfield 1997; Hannam 1998; Davies and Kirkpatrick 2000). One example in a school we visited was the right to a free press. The *Guardian* newspaper had published a complimentary report about a disadvantaged junior school's achievements but these were disparaged in the local newspaper. The editor refused to publish a reply so every child in the school wrote a letter, and the school started to fax them to the editor. After his fax had been jammed for some hours the editor agreed to print their response. The head teacher believed that this was education in citizenship, a political version of the peaceful conflict resolution practised through the school. The final section considers a theoretical approach to rights and to social exclusion which explains and justifies practical approaches to citizenship in schools.

NEW APPROACHES TO RIGHTS, CONNECTION AND REGULATION

The British Government invited the UN Special Rapporteur on Education to conduct a Mission to review education in England. In her report (Tomasevski 1999), the Rapporteur praised the Government's foreign policy commitment to giving 'social, economic and cultural rights the same weight as civil and political rights' and to 'using its influence to seek the realisation of the social and economic rights contained in the Universal Declaration for all the people in the world' (Foreign and Commonwealth Office and Department for International Development 1999:11,15).

Yet she said that for English families 'silence prevails about domestic rights'; parents are seen as the consumers of education but cannot send their child to a particular school, or have non-discriminatory access to local schools. Britain's plans to spend five per cent of Gross National Product in 2001–2 on education still leave the UK lowest in the OECD ranking (OECD 1998: 37) and, at home, the Government sees social and economic rights as 'programmatic objectives rather than legal obligations' (UN 1997: 12.12.10).

Rights-based policies accept people's rights to make personal decision for themselves.

> In education, this entails balancing the rights and freedoms of relevant adults (primarily parents and teachers, alongside the main state actors) against the rights and best interests of the child. Young people are given a formal right to decide for themselves only after they become adults. The shift to rights-based education promises a long over-due change.
>
> (Tomasevski 1999: 8)

Despite reports which use a rights-based approach (Department for Education and Employment 1999a) and see education in the acquisition of skills and knowledge as a principal means towards eradicating poverty, English education law does not use rights language. Schooling is seen as a 'contract between school and parents' which does not include children (Department for Education and Emplyoment 1999b, paragraph 7). The recommendation of the UN Committee on the Rights of the Child that children should have the right to appeal against exclusions (UN 1995, para 32) has been ignored. Parental rights clearly fail when local authorities have parental rights for children in care (Tomasevski 1999: 11) in that three quarters of these young people leave school without qualifications (Department for Education and Employment 1999b: 12) thus showing the need for children to have rights to education.

The Special Rapporteur criticises 'social exclusion' which has not been defined beyond being a 'shorthand term for what can happen when people or areas suffer from a combination of linked problems such as unemployment, poor skills, low incomes, poor housing, high crime environment, bad health, poverty and family breakdown' (Social Exclusion Unit 1999, introduction). Like concepts such as 'ethnic minority' (which merges race, colour, ethnicity, provenance, religion, language and social origin), the term social exclusion hides more than it reveals. It tends towards blaming the victims and is not clearly related to social policies or solutions. The Special Rapporteur prefers the concept of 'statal exclusions', defined above, which can be clearly defined and acted upon. For example, ethnicity could then officially be recorded and the rights of the 12 per cent of British pupils who belong to ethnic minorities could be monitored (Tomasevski 1999: 12).

Human rights to education make schools not simply available, as at present, but also accessible, acceptable and adaptable. This would move on from the 'very English phenomenon' of having schools with widely differing standards which has been exacerbated by the following government activities: naming, shaming and blaming schools; setting up the quasi-market in which schools compete for pupils and resources (1988 Education Act); the use of output ranking instead of process ones so that schools are assessed by test and exam results regardless of the background and abilities of the pupils, instead of by the quality of education within the school; institutionalising competition between schools and learners by publishing league tables and exam results. Glossy brochures and parents' (shareholders') meetings 'would seem incomprehensible to those who define education as a public service and/or a public good' and who see the best interests of each child as the guiding principle for schools (Tomasevski 1999: 13–14). There are conceptual conflicts between the Government's aims to eradicate child poverty in 20 years but also to raise poor children's educational achievements now, and between the old language of parents' and children's duty to attend school and the current lack of excluded and other children's right to access to education. Local authorities can 'slip in discrimination' against race, ethnicity, gender, religion, language, social origin and disability because these are not defined or measured or reportable as discrimination issues, though they are linked to the 12,300 official exclusions in 1997/8 (Social Exclusion Unit 1998: 2.1) when black pupils are four times as likely to have special educational needs and 84 per cent of excluded pupils are boys (Department for Education and Employment 1999c).

Some matters will improve with the Human Rights Act, implemented from October 2000, and the Disability Rights Commission, established in April 2000. Yet the Special Rapporteur is 'concerned about the image of human rights' in Government policy on citizenship education (QCA 1998) which are:

> perceived as different from and alien to the rights and freedoms that learners will recognise in their everyday lives – their rights to education, and as future employees, as future parents or voters to equal opportunities ... Individualism and competitiveness as root values clash against solidarity and community. Parents' concerns ... easily lead to ability-based screening and consequent exclusion [which] become accentuated and exacerbated, not perceived as a human rights issue that ought to be addressed so as to familiarise children to accepting and assisting their peers, but rather as legitimate differentiation enhancing individualism and competitiveness. This has created a paradox: schools are expected to instill values of solidarity and competitiveness at the same time.
>
> (Tomasevski 1999: 25)

The UN Convention is 'a particularly well suited beginning as it offers learners from the youngest age a clear and easy identification with its spirit and wording and the immediate possibility of its translation into practice through the creation of human-rights friendly schools' (p. 25). Then school can show how 'children are citizens rather than citizens-to-be'. Through citizenship education, learners can build conceptual bridges between the inter-relatedness of the human rights and duties, freedoms and responsibilities of all the relevant actors, the causes and effects of discrimination and the individual and structural means of redress and inclusion through everyday issues they can easily identify with (Tomasevski 1999: 25).

Evidence from our research supports the Special Rapporteur's analysis of English schools. Government plans for citizenship education (QCA 1998, 2001) divorce instruction from practical activities in schools, and divorce rights from citizenship. Instead, national and school curricula could define democratic communities as those which actively defend the citizens' agreed, equal rights which everyone can understand and rightfully claim to enjoy. These rights include freedom from assault, arbitrary detention, or attacks on their honour and reputation, the right to express views in matters which affect them, and to enjoy peaceful association and a reasonable standard of living. Some British schools show how well this can be achieved, through promoting appropriate levels of informal trust (connection) and public mistrust (regulation). These schools also help to reduce the dangers of multiple jeopardy when imposed childhood helplessness adds to other disadvantages, through respecting and trusting children's and teenagers' autonomy and sense of community.

ACKNOWLEDGEMENTS

I am very grateful to all the school students and staff who helped with the Civil Rights in Schools research, to Sean Arnold my co-researcher and Kaye Stewart who conducted some of the group sessions, to the Children's Rights Office Education Group for discussing the first plans for the research, to Karen Nairne and Ros Edwards for helpful comments on the paper, and to the ESRC for funding the project no. L129251002.

REFERENCES

Alderson, P. (2000) 'School students' views on life at school and school councils'. *Children and Society*, 14: 121–134.

Alderson, P. (1999a) 'Human rights and democracy in schools: do they mean more than "picking up litter and not killing whales"?' *International Journal of Children's Rights*, 7: 185–205.

Alderson, P. (1999b) 'Civil rights in schools: The implications for youth policy'. *Youth and Policy*, 64: 56–72.

Alderson, P. (1990) *Choosing for Children: Parents' Consent to Surgery.* Oxford, Oxford University Press.

Alderson, P. and Arnold, S. (1999) ESRC Children 5–16 Briefing no. 1. *Civil Rights in Schools.* Swindon, ESRC.

Alderson, P. and Goodey, C. (1998) *Enabling education: experiences in special and ordinary schools.* London, Tufnell Press.

Andrews, G. (ed.) (1991) *Citizenship.* London, Lawrence Wishart.

Apter, T. (1990) *Altered Lives: Mothers and Daughters During Adolescence.* Hemel Hempstead, Wheatsheaf Harvester.

Bourdieu, P. (1977) *Outline of a Theory of Practice.* Cambridge: Cambridge University Press.

Butler, M. (1998) 'Negotiating place: the importance of children's realities'. In Steinberg, S. and Kincheloe, J. (eds) *Students as Researchers: Creating Classrooms that Matter.* London, Falmer: 94–112.

Cleves School (ed. P. Alderson) (1999) *Learning and Inclusion; the Cleves School Experience.* London, David Fulton Publishers.

Cockburn, T. (1998) 'Children and citizenship in Britain'. *Childhood*, 5 (1): 91–117.

Danby, S. and Barker, C. (1998) 'What's the problem? Restoring order in the preschool classroom'. In Hutchy, I. Moran and Ellis, J. (eds) *Children and Social Competence: Arenas of Action.* London, Falmer.

Davies, L. and Kirkpatrick, G. (2000) *The Eurodem Project: A Review of Pupil Democracy in Europe.* London: Children's Rights Alliance for England.

Department for Education and Employment (1997) *Excellence for all Children: Meeting Special Educational Needs.* Green Paper. London, DfEE.

Department for Education and Employment (1999a) *Learning Opportunities for All: A Policy Framework for Education.* London, DfEE.

Department for Education and Employment (1999b) *Social Exclusion: Pupils' Support.* London, DfEE.

Department for Education and Employment. (1999c) *Permanent Exclusions from Schools in England 1997/8 and Exclusion Appeals Lodged by Parents in England SFR11/7.* London, DfEE .

Erikson, E. (1971) *Identity, Youth and Crisis.* London, Faber.

Foreign and Commonwealth Office and Department for International Development (2000) *Human Rights Annual Report for 1999.* London, FCO/DfID.

Foucault, M. (1967) *Madness and Civilisation.* London, Tavistock.

Gillick v W Norfolk & Wisbech AHA [1085] 3 All ER 423.

Gilligan, C. (1982) *In a Different Voice.* Cambridge MA, Harvard University Press

Gouldner, A. (1977) *The Coming Crisis in Western Sociology.* London, Routledge.

Griffith, R. (1998) *Educational Citizenship and Independent Learning.* London, Jessica Kingsley.

Grimshaw, J. (1986) *Feminism and Philosophy.* Brighton, Wheatsheaf.

Hammarberg, T. (1997) *A School for Children with Rights.* Florence, Innocenti.

Hannam, D. (1998) Democratic education and education for democracy through pupil/ student participation in decision making in schools. Gordon Cook Foundation Conference, University of Strathclyde, May.

Highfield School (ed. P. Alderson.) (1997) *Changing our School: Promoting Positive Behaviour.* Plymouth, Highfield School.

Hockey, C. and James, A. (1993) *Growing Up and Growing Old: Ageing and Dependency in the Lifecourse.* London, Sage.

James, A., Jenks, C. and Prout, A. (1998) *Theorizing Childhood.* Cambridge, Polity Press.

Jeffs, T. (1995) 'Children's educational rights in a new ERA?' In Franklin, B. (ed.) *The Handbook of Children's Rights.* London, Routledge.

Kant, I. (1796/1972) 'Groundwork of the metaphysic of morals'. In Paton, H. *The Moral Law.* London, Hutchinson.

Kant, I. (1964) *Metaphysic of Morals* part 2 trans Gregor, M. London, Harper Row.

Kohlberg, L. (1981) *The Philosophy of Moral Development.* New York, Harper Row.

Locke, J. (1690/1959) *An Essay Concerning Human Understanding*, part 1. New York, Dover

MacIntyre, A. (1966) *A Short History of Ethics.* New York, Macmillan.

MacNamara, S. and Morton, G. (1995) *Changing Behaviour.* London, David Fulton.

Matthews, H., Limb, M. and Taylor, N. (1999) Reports of their ESRC Children 5–16 Project, Exploring the Fourth Environment: Young people's use of place and views on their environments. Northampton, Nene College.

Mayall, B. (1996) *Children, Health and the Social Order.* Buckingham, Open University Press.

Mendus, S. (1987) 'Kant: an honest but narrow-minded bourgeois?' In Kennedy, E. and Mendus, S. (eds) *Women in Western Political Philosophy.* Brighton, Harvester, 1–20.

Menzies Lyth, I. (1989) *Containing Anxiety in Institutions.* London, Free Association Books.

Mill, J. S. (1971) *On Liberty.* Harmondsworth, Penguin.

Morrow, V. (2000) '"Dirty looks" and "trampy places" in young people's accounts of community and neighbourhood: implications for health inequalities'. *Critical Public Health,* 10 (2): 141–152.

Nairn, K. (2000) 'Young people's participation in their school environment'. Symposium on Children's participation in community life, June, Oslo.

NUT - National Union of Teachers (1997) *The Stoke Rochford Declaration of Commonwealth Teachers. Education and Human Rights.* Presented to the 13th Commonwealth Conference of Education Ministers, Gaborone, Botswana. London, NUT.

OECD (1998) *Human Capital Investment. An International Comparison.* Paris, OECD.

O'Neill, J. (1994) *The Missing Child in Liberal Theory.* University of Newfoundland.

Phillips, M. (1997) *Corruption of Liberalism.* London; Centre for Policy Studies.

Putnam, R. (1996) 'The strange disappearance of civic America.' *The American Prospect:* 24: 34–48.

Qualifications and Curriculum Authority (1998) *Education for Citizenship and the Teaching of Democracy in Schools,* the Crick Report. Final Report of the Advisory Group on Citizenship. London, QCA, DfEE.

Qualifications and Curriculum Authority (2001) *Personal, Social and Health Education and Citizenship.* London, QCA.

Ross, L.F. (1998) *Children, Families, and Health Care Decision-making.* Oxford; Clarendon Press.

Seidler, V. (1986) *Kant Respect and Injustice.* London, Routledge.

Social Exclusion Unit (1998) *Truancy and School Exclusion Report.* London, SEU.

Social Exclusion Unit (1999) Report to the Prime Minister. London, SEU.

Tomasevski, M. (1999) *Report of the Mission on the UK,* October 1999 by the Special Rapporteur on the Right to Education. Geneva, UN.

UN (1989) *Convention on the Rights of the Child.* Geneva, UN.

UN Committee on Economic, Social and Cultural Rights (1997) *Concluding Observations: UK and NI, UN Doc.E/c.12/1/Add. 19.*Geneva, UN.

UN Committee on the Rights of the Child (1995) *Consideration of Reports Submitted by State Parties under Article 44 of the Convention: Concluding Observations: United Kingdom and Northern Ireland. Geneva, UN, Convention/C/15/Add.34.*Geneva: UN.

White, P. (1996) *Civic Virtues and Public Schooling: Educating Citizens for a Democratic Society.* London, Teachers' College, University of Columbia.

Williams, B. (1972) *Morality: an Introduction to Ethics.* Cambridge, Cambridge University Press

Williams, B. (1985) *Ethics and the Limits of Philosophy.* London, Fontana.

Young, A. (1990) 'Moral conflicts in a psychiatric hospital'. In Weisz, G. (ed.) *Social Science Perspectives on Medical Ethics.* Kluwer, Dordrecht, 65–82.

2 Educational reform in New Zealand

Where were the children?

Lise Bird

Many countries have gone through radical changes in their educational policies over the past decade, perhaps none so astonishingly comprehensive as those in Aotearoa/New Zealand. Reforms to school administration, curriculum and assessment were carried out in every sector of education in moves that allowed the state to reduce its financial and administrative responsibility for education.

While the ostensible focus of the reforms was to improve schools and thus to better cater for students' learning needs, the diverse voices of New Zealand children were largely silent in the policy debates throughout this period. This chapter reviews some of these debates, and questions the tardiness of New Zealand educational policies in moving to make children participants in the process. Active participation would mean that children are consulted about their own educational needs rather than being silent beneficiaries of care from more remote (if well meaning) adults.

To demonstrate some issues of policy at ground level, comments from key documents are contrasted with remarks of children in a small New Zealand primary school at the start of the reform process. Children's talk about 'needs' contrasts in interesting ways with the direction and goals identified in policy documents. This chapter suggests that there could be a clearer recognition of the complexity of the issue of 'children's needs' given, on the one hand, the diversity amongst children and the parameters of expected performance set by government-sanctioned curricula on the other. Comments from children and their teachers point to ways that children and policy makers could enter more dialogue about education, within the power dynamics that define relations between children and adults.

CHANGES IN POLICY ACCOUNTS OF 'CHILDREN'S NEEDS'

Patrons of a generic childhood

New Zealand educational policy has long been concerned with serving the needs of children. A decade ago Martin Woodhead (1997) criticised the focus on 'children's needs' in policy documents, arguing that these are notoriously difficult to define. Rising concern about child welfare at the end of the nineteenth century had helped to create childhood as a distinctive period of the lifespan, identifying this particular age-group as especially vulnerable and in need of protection. Along with critics of child development (see James and Prout 1990; see also James, Jenks and Prout 1998), Woodhead expressed concerns about the presumed universality of a middle-class conception of childhood grounded in particular nuclear family structures and Western/European cultural values.

Many policy documents of the 1980s attempted to distinguish 'objectively' between physiological and psychological ('welfare') needs, and assumed a congruence between the child's wants and needs. Woodhead (1997) made a further distinction between needs ascribed to children by others and the child's own wants or demands. In both cases the term implies some lack in the child or their accoutrements which could be filled or overcome. A discourse about children's needs positions 'the child' as vulnerable and incompetent, awaiting adults who will provide care in 'appropriate' ways. Childhood thus defined becomes 'a period of dependency, defined by protectionist adult–child relationships in which adults are dominant providers and children are passive consumers' (Woodhead 1997: 78). This process makes the ascription of needs to children invisible, as though by an omnipotent and impartial observer, and implies that there is consensus amongst knowledgeable adults about normative requirements for children. However there is a diversity of viewpoints about cultural norms, as can be seen in debates about the appropriate ages of consent for children making personal decisions about schooling, place of residence or consumer purchases.

Woodhead contrasted the view that need is a universal, human characteristic with a social constructionist perspective that defines need as a normative, or just desirable, requirement for adaptation to a particular culture. Policies written with a social constructionist take on the issue of need were considered less patronising towards children. Some pitfalls emerge when educational policies centre on the unexamined notion of 'children's needs', as outlined in the feminist work below.

Needs in child-centred pedagogy

The 'child-centred' movement has been described by Walkerdine (1984) as part of a subtle process of control in which adult power over the child is hidden in a liberal rhetoric of protection. The movement, linked to 'progressive education' with roots in the work of Rousseau, proposed that children learn best if provided with a setting for their own exploration and discovery learning rather than with the authoritarian regulations of the traditional religious classroom (Burman 1994). Children's needs are described as one of the foundations of child-centred learning; the child is to be allowed to develop 'naturally' and spontaneously, meeting both the universal, biological and more unique individual requirements of each child. Walkerdine (1984) pointed to the hidden work of mothers and teachers in providing the structure and background support for such seemingly spontaneous learning activities to occur. She also pointed out the greater opportunities for middle class mothers to meet such needs as unpaid caregivers. Burman (1994), following Walkerdine, pointed out the hidden assumptions involved in the teacher's assessment of the child's developmental 'readiness' to learn particular things.

Apart from the general uncertainty about how to recognise when a child is 'ready', and how to determine a child's 'needs', it would seem that middle-class children are more 'ready' than working-class children since they are more prepared and familiar with the skills needed to engage with schooling.

(Burman 1994: 166)

Such a class distinction is alluded to in some New Zealand documents mentioned below. Given the difficulties involved in simple definitions of children's needs, the stage was set, in New Zealand and elsewhere, for greater consideration of children's rights.

The 1990s: a shift from needs to rights

Reflecting on his critique of the 'needs' issue a decade later, Woodhead (1997) noted the changes to reframe concerns into more discussion of children's rights rather than their presumed needs. The change was part of an international shift that led to the introduction of the UN Convention on the Rights of the Child (UNCROC: UN 1989). UNCROC outlines two kinds of rights based on needs ascribed to children by adults acting on their behalf: (1) the child's right to be provided for in terms of minimal standards of care and education and (2) the child's right to be protected from abuse, discrimination and conflict. In addition, UNCROC outlines a third category of children's participation rights, based on children's self-defined needs for access to information, for consultation and for space to express (and to be listened to regarding) their personal views on issues of concern to them (Lansdown 1994; see also A. Smith 2000).

Recently Handley (2000) has written about the connections between needs and rights in the area of disability studies, a field that shares issues of advocacy and caregiver support with childhood studies. Handley argued that the shift from needs to rights is underpinned by a change from ascribed to self-defined needs. Further defining the 'wants' mentioned by Woodhead (1997), self-defined needs are those chosen and expressed by persons acting on their own behalf.

In New Zealand, as in many countries, the voices of children have become stronger in a number of areas of social policy, particularly in legal cases involving custody or protection from abuse (Henaghan 1996). However, economic policies have sometimes worked against an increase in participation rights for children. The move away from state provision of services towards greater financial responsibility of families has affected many policies in education and welfare and has in many ways sat uncomfortably with other changes in social policy related to UNCROC. Henaghan (1996) has argued that the balance between the responsibilities of the state, families and children in implementation of UNCROC is not working well in New Zealand at present. Consequently, he points out that the 'child's viewpoint is underdeveloped and often non-existent in New Zealand', putting Article 12 of the Convention (participation rights) under threat (Henaghan 1996: 173). There are also notable difficulties in New Zealand in challenging a traditional view that children's rights are subsumed under those of their parents. An added complexity has come with the greater recognition of rights of indigenous Maori during the past two decades. This has been associated with greater recognition of extended family rights regarding decisions about children's care, protection and surveillance within the family rather than to greater consideration of individual children's rights. A brief history of these educational policy changes will set the scene for a discussion of issues at the school-based level.

THE EDUCATIONAL REFORM PROCESS IN NEW ZEALAND

In the past decade New Zealand has undergone one of the most comprehensive overhauls in the world of its management, structuring and funding of educational provision. These educational reforms created something of a 'laboratory' of extremes made possible by the global push towards public-sector managerial reform. The Prime Minister, David Lange, introduced the most radical reforms in educational adminis-tration that the country had ever seen, set out in a policy document entitled, *Tomorrow's Schools*. These reforms restructured education from a centralised authority to one in which individual schools would be governed by a Board of Trustees with 'control over their educational resources – to use as they determine, within overall guidelines for education set by the state' (Lange 1988: 1) and the power to appoint staff. Boards were to be composed of a majority of elected parent representatives, the school principal, one staff member and, for secondary schools, a student representative. Each school was to develop its own policies via a 'school charter' setting out its objectives which would 'reflect the particular needs of the community in which the institution is located', within national guidelines (Lange 1988: 1). The original document also pointed to the creation of a set of national curriculum objectives (Lange 1988: 35), and there has been a complete revamping of curriculum content into seven key areas in the 1990s, a process near completion. A reform of assessment and qualifications has also been undertaken during the past decade and is still continuing. Alongside the reforms has arisen a wealth of critical commentary, focusing particularly on problems with bringing a 'market' approach to education (see e.g., Butterworth and Butterworth 1998; Fiske and Ladd 2000; Lauder, Hughes and Watson 1999).

It should also be noted that in practice the reforms have not always been executed as consistently as might appear on paper. Students' voices were silenced quite early in the reform process. After public debate about the suitability of student seats on the boards of trustees, the Education Act was quickly amended to allow secondary schools to dispense with having a student representative (Henaghan 1996: 177).[1] Clearly, the change to a more client-centred approach was oriented towards parents as the consumers of educational services, rather than towards their children, the students. In contrast to this, members of the Picot Taskforce whose report under-pinned *Tomorrow's Schools*, believed that 'the school existed to serve the child, and that the child's interests should be paramount', guided by the principle that the reforms should 'obtain the best value for the education dollar for the learner' (Butterworth and Butterworth 1998: 81). *Tomorrow's Schools* signalled that 'community education forums' were to be set up to allow exchanges of views to provide 'a voice for all those who wish to air their concerns – whether students, parents, teachers, managers or education administrators' (Lange 1988: 2). The issue of student involvement in community forums has not been specifically researched, so it is not known whether student input was influential in some areas. Each school's charter was to address 'the particular interests of students and potential students' (Lange 1988: 3). Though students were the professed concern, their involvement was for the most part taken for granted.

The focus on parents seems another indication that '[l]egal policy in New Zealand is based largely on the married two-parent family' (Henaghan 1996: 167). In being asked to write something about children's perspectives on these reforms for this chapter, I realised that I had had the unusual experience of having been an observer in one primary school during the upheavals of the reforms, including the very week the legislation came into effect. I was also taken back in time to my feelings of exclusion at the time since, as a non-parent, I had no place in the 'local community' surrounding each school which was to provide Board of Trustees which would run each school.[2] I also remember having been dismayed by the concentration of public discussion on implications of the reforms for parents rather than children as the 'consumers' of education, but, as a 'non-client' and hence an 'outsider', I had kept this disquiet to myself.

An ostensible policy focus on 'children's needs'

It is apparent that the goal of meeting children's needs was a key consideration of the New Zealand reforms. Yet direct assessment of these needs from children themselves has received little attention in the past decade. The effects of the reforms over the first decade have been monitored by the New Zealand Council for Educational Research, mainly via surveys and interviews of primary and intermediate school principals, trustees and teachers. The final report indicated that the most important perceived reason for the curriculum changes (a reason chosen by two-thirds of teachers) was 'children's needs' (Wylie 1997: vii).

The Ministry of Education itself pointed to the central importance of children's learning needs in a recent document setting out guidelines for a formal stock-taking of the reforms. Further improvement to schools was being sought by surveying the same 'key figures' of the original reform process: 'We need the input of parents, trustees, teachers and principals. Children only get one shot at a good education. We must ensure we get it right' (Smith 1999: 4). Though children were not, it seems, to be consulted as part of this revisioning process, the discussion document assumed that the needs of children were the main driving force behind change. 'Excellence in education is about meeting diverse student needs' (MoE 1999: 9).

The key phrase 'meeting diverse student needs' appears as something of a mantra through many documents. There has been little analysis of the way such needs will be defined and by whom. It is as though there exists a social consensus about what is best for students, that their needs are obvious and uncontroversial.

The task of defining needs more explicitly was taken up by the Education Review Office (ERO), a unit created by *Tomorrow's Schools* to monitor schools' effectiveness. ERO monitored the first National Administration Guideline, which stated that Boards of Trustees, working through the school staff, would be required to: 'analyse barriers to learning and achievement; and develop and implement strategies which address identified learning needs in order to overcome barriers to students' learning' (ERO 1997: 3). Their influential reports described these barriers as negative ones, focusing on what a child has to avoid or overcome in order to achieve well at school. One *Barriers to Learning* report (ERO 1997) defined the diversity of needs as including 'a wide range of abilities', 'diverse social, cultural and economic backgrounds' and 'multiple educational and behavioural difficulties' (1997: 9). The students with high needs had been earlier defined by ERO as those 'at risk of educational failure', facing barriers such as overcrowded homes, low family income, speaking 'a language other than English at home', and 'parents who were unsuccessful at school' (ERO 1996: 15). Though the language of the document attempts to avoid a 'discourse of disadvantage' (Jones and Jacka 1995), it is clear that there are particular educational difficulties faced by indigenous Maori and Pacific students. By focusing on more negative aspects of diversity ('difficulties'), the report fits Woodhead's (1997) description of needs as involving some lack which, if not met, could result in harm to the student. There is also an assumption that such needs are unproblematic and consensual.

There is a further problem with the analysis of students' needs in the ERO reports: the assumption that various needs form a hierarchy: 'In some cases schools may need to provide for students' basic physical and emotional needs before they can address their learning needs' (ERO 1997: 39). Students facing many of the barriers defined by ERO were described as having 'complex learning needs' which include the need for language skills, sensitive and knowledgeable student–teacher interactions and hence for 'high performing teachers who have all the skills to meet those needs' (ERO 1996: 15). Needs of transient students would include both learning needs such as remedial reading and English for speakers of other languages and social needs such as for 'counselling and anger management' (ERO 1997: 14). The result of this analysis is to imply that students from backgrounds posing fewer barriers have much greater learning needs. Given the report's focus on concerns about disadvantage experienced by students from minority groups which have traditionally had low school completion rates, something of a class division appears in the sorts of student 'needs' to be catered for by schools. An implication of the above passage would seem to be that schools in poorer areas should focus on 'basic' needs such as for nutrition and social support, while schools in more middle class areas may move on (in the sense of Maslow's 1968 needs hierarchy) to 'higher' cognitive or academic needs of students. This has clear resonances with the discourse of child-centred learning (Burman 1994) referred to earlier, which tended to position the middle class child as more 'ready' than poorer children to advance in their learning.

CHILDREN'S TALK ABOUT NEEDS

To move from the concerns about children in these policy documents to the sampling of views of children below may seem an abrupt move. Yet the differences cross many social institutions, pointing to a large gap between worlds of policy writers and those of children at school. Given the incommensurate issues and approaches in these two settings, the leap may seem forced. Perhaps it is that very gap that shows some of the problems involved in applications of policy, especially in order to include participation rights in education.

To paraphrase Freud, what do children really want, or need? In my field observations at a small New Zealand primary school, I recorded a number of spontaneous discussions between children in which they expressed a 'need' explicitly.[3] This was not a word used in conversation on a daily basis. Many other conversations could have been analysed for their reference to issues of need. By focusing explicitly on the word 'need' here my analyses are limited in what they can propose about children's views of their needs. However the material does provide an appropriate contrast with the writings on policy which use the word 'need' explicitly, providing the basis for further reflection on problematic issues of needs and rights under discussion here.

Children's conversations with each other

Two different kinds of comments about need emerged in the examples given below. Both have direct relevance for the concepts outlined by the writers discussed above: self-defined survival needs and expressions of normative need for completion. There was also collaborative discussion of need amongst children themselves, a use of the term that suggested a surplus meaning beyond the child-centred pedagogy.

Children sometimes discussed needs related to their biological survival. In two examples of this that I observed, children seemed to be making comments on their own lives. This suggests self-defined needs, yet these needs could also be considered universal human requirements. The example from the Year 5/6 classroom below is concerned with survival in outer space.[4]

11:34 The teacher, Sharon, announces that students will work in groups on projects about 'space and time'. One table of five girls discusses various possibilities. Two girls discuss survival needs in outer space.

Barbara: (to Susan): If we lived in space we'd need a capsule. [pause] We'd need [pause] gravity, so we don't just float up.

Joy: (interrupting, from the opposite side of the table): I can't see when you're writing upside-down.

Barbara: So? Change desks!

It was not clear from this brief conversation whether these children had a clear idea of the requirements for survival in their capsule. While their attention to the 'grounding' of gravity fits the idea that humans need a certain physical environment, it did not seem to occur to any of these girls that reading in space might involve difficulties such as reading at different angles. Their discussion may have been concerned with self-defined needs, but these were described in a narrow hypothetical sense. Given the presence of two adults within earshot (their teacher and myself), it is possible that these girls were expressing a normative narrative of scientific understanding, locatable in the curriculum, as their own.

A second kind of self-defined need easier to consider a socially constructed desire occurred in a conversation I had with a 10-year-old during lunchtime play. Susan showed me her wrestling cards and said, 'I only need Brutus to finish the set'. This comment was similar to many comments by children in maths lessons when they referred to completion of sets of objects or to abstract numbers. For example, one 7-year-old boy said to children at a table near him, 'I need 4 to make 7'. This particular sequence of words could be seen as a common or normative phrase; the use of 'need' in such lessons seems a way to make maths more personal and relevant for connections to larger social constructions implicated in maths discussions. Conversations about sets can be seen as referring often to a search for missing items needed for completing the set, suggesting mastery and ownership (c.f. Walkerdine 1984). Susan's comment above also seems to add another dimension of desire or pleasure to the expression of need, since wrestling cards were highly valued at that time, and were collected mainly by boys. The ubiquitous use of the word 'need' in various lessons may frame the linguistic contexts in which needs are usually discussed at school. Susan's comment links the maths class with status in the peer group at play, bringing together the satisfaction of completion and pleasure of ownership.

Another conversation about 'needs' in a classroom of younger children seemed to offer a third possibility beyond the discussion of basic individual needs or rights. Children ascribed needs to each other in a way that helped to facilitate one child's goal of putting her art work up for display.

14:29 Year 2/3 children are putting their own art work, plastic cutouts made to look like translucent 'stained glass' patterns, on an external window of the classroom. John stretches on his toes to put a transparency on the glass of the window.

Betty: It covers mine up.

John: That's the only place I could put it.

Betty gets up and takes down the sheet, which is only leaning against hers, not stuck to the glass with tape as the others are. She tries to slide it up to stay up higher on the window.

Karen: You need tape.

Then Betty takes down her sheet. Later I see that it is stuck to the window in another place.

This discussion seems to indicate a normative social interaction, in which helpful others respond to a situation in which their experience provides an alternative course of action. These children were capable of working cooperatively to juggle competing needs for display of their art-work. These were not, of course, generic 7- and 8-year-olds, but two 'working class' Anglo/Pakeha girls and a boy working collaboratively, despite previous altercations that I had observed during their interactions. This suggests that these children could converse about their own 'needs', despite their (and perhaps helped by) their similar ethnicity and class background. The needs defined by the children here were concerned with immediate, tangible requirements rather than the hypothetical issue of life in space mentioned by the older girls. Nonetheless, these children might have made some interesting comments about the goals of the reform process, had they been given a chance to comment.

Given the cultural complexities involved, the needs expressed above by children at Moana School might seem irrelevant to policy-makers or parents. Perhaps the infrequent discussions of need in the conversations I observed might suggest that this issue is not of importance to children. With a much larger frame, it is possible to indicate ways that children's comments were explorations of their imagined and experienced needs as part of ongoing negotiations with each other and, especially, with the adults around them. To make this story clearer, though, I need to bring in the expert voice of the adult who most often negotiated needs with children at the school: their teachers.

Adult shaping of children's talk about needs

Most conversations about children's needs were expressed as part of a complex interaction of need-analysis with teachers. These conversations highlight the ways that comments of children seemed to be congruent with the agendas of the adults working with them. Most comments by children at school about their needs were made in the presence of their teachers, who seemed to be subtly shaping the classroom to give space to children for the expression of their needs.[5]

One kind of classroom interaction seemed to be designed to encourage children to express, as their own, certain needs ascribed to them by adults. For example, two days after the introduction of the reforms in the Year 2/3 classroom, the teacher, Anne, led a discussion with children seated on the mat before a reading lesson on 'why children need to learn to read'. During this discussion Danny raised his hand to say that reading is needed in later life: 'people need to read stop signs'. This may be a common way for teachers to motivate children to learn particular skills. This boy's comment seems to be a reference to the dangers of road crashes and injuries for people who do not heed stop signs, though it could also refer to the expected behaviour of a good driver (or backseat driver assisting an adult). This statement also seemed to me to show the voice of the child taking on the adult concern about safety. It seemed to be a child's version of an adult expression such as that of a male teacher on another day: 'everyone needs to wear their helmet for the [cycling] demonstration'.

The process by which children learn to express as their own certain requirements of classroom life is part of child-centred pedagogy. The unfolding of this process seemed most visible in the older classroom. Sometimes children were encouraged to express certain needs within the circumscribed boundaries of an activity. At the beginning of a number of activities the teacher might ask students an open question so that children could express what they required to complete the activity. (Again, this shows the normative importance of completion for many classroom activities.) Students often responded by calling out the names of particular resources or actions. Later the teacher might point to further needs for the children to keep in mind, and/or the students might point to certain needs for materials specific to their current activity.

An example of this process of needs-expression can be seen in the older classroom. One day began with a discussion of the 'learning and teaching cycle'. Sharon pointed to a chart on the board with the following phrases written in a square: 'find out', 'what knows', 'activities', 'and needs'. The last phrase had an arrow drawn back to 'find out'. The rest of the board listed the schedule for the day, including the 'Class Meeting', under which was listed, 'what do we need?' These phrases fit within a framework of discovery learning, part of the child-centred curriculum. The issue of defining children's learning needs was central in the discussion below about plans for the day.⁶

9:15 *Sharon:*   Are there people who need handwriting help?
At this four girls and a boy raise their hands.
[Fifteen minutes later] There is much talking as small groups work on writing stories.
Sharon: No need to talk about it. You just need to do it.
[Forty minutes later]
Sharon: Return to the mat please to share stories. [pause] You need to be sure you
            publish a story every so often, [at least once a fortnight].
Kirsty: I need help with my story, with the artwork.

Kirsty's expression of need was not a direct response to Sharon's comment about the need to complete a story carefully; Kirsty seemed to be expressing her view that her story needed improvement to make it more artistic, pointing to a culturally desirable goal, perhaps, rather than an obvious lack. This kind of statement from a child was common in such discussions and shows the way that students were encouraged to take individual responsibility for their work. This was especially notable whenever the teacher asked children to call out requests for resources needed to created 'learning corners' for mathematics and art. In one of the fieldwork excerpts above, a small group of Anglo/Pakeha children discussed each other's 'needs' in a concrete collaborative process. This assertion of self-defined need was not the province only of Pakeha children; amongst the older children it was Kirsty, a girl from the indigenous Maori culture, who spoke most often in class discussion to clarify her requirements for completing a task.

The classroom discussion above was structured by the adult authority, the teacher, as an acceptable place in which to call out requests for particular resources. There was a clear connection between need and its fulfillment by the completion of a learning task. The 'filling' of a need for a concrete item allowed the writing task to be attempted, and allowed the student to perform as a 'good student' by expressing their involvement through participation in an activity with a clear end-point.

This work of teachers in getting students to articulate particular needs for help is consonant with a teaching strategy reported in a study of New Zealand primary school teachers' reactions to changes in assessment practices through the reform process (Hill 1999). Some teachers kept track of individual children's progress on a daily basis to help in planning their work with children, such as in maths. As one teacher reported:

> I work with the children on the floor doing work with them and we'll go over the work ... I'll get their book and then afterwards find out how they have gone, if they understand it then I can move them on, if they don't I'll get them back and see them. So that's a way of finding out where they're at and that's on

a daily basis and that's extremely effective because you cater for the children's needs.

(Hill 1999: 182)

Though this comment suggests a more global assessment of 'needs' using the ubiquitous rhetorical phrase, the need mentioned seemed to be a specific lack of skill. Another teacher's comment showed a reflective interlinking of her teaching needs with students' learning. 'It's need, I need to know before I can move to the next stage, have they got that? So it's got to be done, ongoing the whole time. Otherwise how would I know what to teach next?' (Hill 1999: 183).

This latter statement is interesting for highlighting the ways that needs of adults and children are constructed as interlinked, suggesting that the good teacher identifies what children need. The more interesting feature in Sharon's classroom above was that she did not simply infer children's needs but actively organised class discussion so that children would express such 'needs' themselves, at first with prompting but later without, since there were no sanctions for unprompted callouts. The larger parameters of the classroom interaction are of course set by the state, which has clear objectives for levels of understanding within the curriculum, and by teachers who must attempt to implement these. Hence the needs called out by children are only partially self-defined, since the completion towards which children and teachers are moving is already anticipated by other adults such as curriculum writers.

The classroom interactions above could be considered a classroom management strategy in which the teacher expresses her professional 'needs' as a 'softly, softly' way to coerce children into particular actions. Sharon sometimes described a desired action from children as something she herself needed. This was often the way she introduced activities in which nominated children were chosen for an activity or as choosers of other children to join with them on a task. Gender was often mentioned as one of the structural constraints on choosing, as she delegated the choice to particular students, as shown in the example below.

11:00 Sharon chooses two children to leave class to go to the library to choose books to read, after which another two will be chosen.

Sharon: Susan, you can go. I need to choose another person who hasn't gone.
Bob: (to class) She has to choose a boy!
Sharon: No, I don't have to choose a boy.

Sharon's reference to her 'need' to choose a child was a common way that children in this class were chosen for different activities, one in which there was often an alternation of genders. Use of the word need here also suggests an articulation of the adult's responsibilities as a good teacher, that the teacher 'needs to be fair', for example. This seems a common strategy of covert control that adults use with children. It would be interesting to research whether it might be easier to use this strategy with primary school children than with secondary school students, who might be less likely to volunteer help to an adult who simply expresses a need.

Sometimes a teacher could be more directive in telling the children what they needed, especially with regard to normative ideas about good student behaviour or actions. For example, during Sharon's feedback comments to individual children during class discussion about improving stories, she sometimes intervened to direct the content of a story, in the direction of a story towards one more socially desirable or more sensitive to other students. This tended to override the ostensible purpose of the writing exercise that students would write stories to their own satisfaction.

9:58 Peter reads his story to the group.
Sharon: Why do you have suicide in your plot?
Fiona has her arms crossed firmly across her chest and wiggles her legs, looking perturbed.
Sharon: (to Peter) Your story doesn't need the suicide; it's not important for the plot.

The comments made by Sharon to children ascribed certain needs to their stories and sometimes overrode their own expressed narratives. This did not stop children's expression of their needs; children readily volunteered to express their own needs in further conversations about their writing. In this way the children seemed to be guided in this classroom towards expression of needs within boundaries which had been constructed for them by the teacher. Yet, at the same time, these ascribed needs formed a launch-pad for expanded expression of their own self-defined needs (such as for help with editing). One could of course question whether these needs were really children's self-defined needs; but then, the same question could be asked regarding the teacher, who was also carrying out a task constrained by many social practices and expectations. The needs of children, parents and teachers are interlinked in the joint enterprise in schooling.

The fieldwork excerpts above suggest that in the child-centred classroom the teacher directs the child to an expression of socially desirably needs and that children eventually express these as their own. The teacher, too, may express teaching needs as her own, though the wider goals have been set by curriculum and policy writers. The creativity of discussion shown in these classrooms further suggests that policy makers could benefit from discussion with children about their learning needs. The setting could provide for an illuminative conversation about curriculum and assessment from which both children and adults might learn. The outcome of such conversations cannot be predicted, but are likely to veer beyond the paths set by discourses such as child-centredness.

OVERVIEW AND REFLECTION

A key rationale for the extensive educational reforms in New Zealand over the past decade was to meet the presumed needs of the (generic) child. These needs were inferred by policy-makers and by parents and teachers about children in their care, rather than by engagement with children themselves. This focus on needs seems today to have been a rather backward-looking stance, given the shifting policy climate in Europe and North America from an exclusive focus on children's needs to a consideration of children's rights (see Woodhead 1997). In Aotearoa educational policies have also been out of step with policies in justice and welfare, which have moved further to include children's participation in decision-making. The voice of the child can now be heard in the courtroom and in healthcare settings concerned with the management of their medical treatments. It is difficult to understand the reason that there has been so little consultation with students in New Zealand about making education work for them, to meet their self-defined needs. Sadly, it seems that hardly anyone (including myself) considered asking children, the main recipients of the reforms, what they made of it all at the time.

Children's viewpoints were missing in documents monitoring the reform process, as in the policy documents that preceded the research. Children's voices seem to have been unintelligible or unworthy of serious attention in the eyes of researchers monitoring the effects of the reforms. One 'off the record' comment from such a researcher highlighted problems in providing relevant survey questions for younger respondents, as well as difficulties with sampling. This comment showed little understanding of the strides made in recent years in the field of child-participant methodologies. Fortunately the field of child development has been active for over a century in dealing creatively with, though not in overcoming, methodological difficulties (see Alldred 1998). Though problems with sampling responses of children are different to those encountered in sampling adults, there are not, by themselves, good reasons to avoid including children in policy-related research.

In this chapter policy documents were contrasted with some children's comments, at the beginning of the reform process in New Zealand, about issues of 'need'. Many conversations amongst children that I observed seemed to have a normative shape, as though children had taken as their own the comments of teachers who were implementing curriculum requirements. Children were encouraged by their teachers to explore and express their individual resource and skill requirements ('needs') for a task in particular ways. This suggested that much of the discussion of needs in the classroom was part of a subtle process of coercion to create behaviour expected of good students, within a child-centred pedagogy. However, there seemed to be occasional moments when a group of children talking to each other created a collaborative effort that went beyond the expected script for expressing individual learning needs. These seemed to me to be the moments in which these children might have been able to talk about their needs and aspirations outside the usual discursive boundaries.

It seems timely to allow the voices of a diversity of children to help us to understand what the reform process has done and has not done. One of the policy statements discussed earlier (ERO 1997) suggested, problematically, that schools cater to assumed needs of students according to a Maslovian hierarchy, by attending to poorer children's 'basic' needs while more affluent children could be given more advanced academic work. Encouragingly, my fieldnotes showed little evidence of such a bias at the school observed. The classes with children from a range of backgrounds (though none highly affluent) indicated a considerable amount of collaborative discussion about intersecting requirements of different children. The negotiation of needs and rights in these multi-ethnic classrooms, each with at least one child with a disability, was no doubt far more subtle than what I have been able to describe here.

Hindsight is always excellent. Consultation with 'local communities' in *Tomorrow's Schools* did not explicitly refer to input from students who were the objects of the reform process, and so, it seems, children became invisible members of their communities, represented only by the voices of their parents. Entirely inappropriate was the early elimination of the seat for a secondary student on each school's Board of Trustees. It would have been in keeping with Article 12 of UNCROC to give students more of a voice in the creation and monitoring of the reform process. The format of the 'class meeting' in the school described above has possibilities for framing such a dialogue between adults and children. There are also encouraging signs in emerging research, such as on the study of secondary students' understanding of their rights at school (Nairn 2000).

A shift from a consideration of children's needs to their rights is unlikely, however, to be a panacea for all that is wrong with children's lives at the moment. Woodhead (1997: 80) noted that 'children's "rights", like their "needs" remains a very Western way of constructing child-adult relationships'. The diversity of competing cultural perspectives on terms such as 'family', 'rights' and 'needs' remains hidden within universal formulae which assume that the persons who are the object of these terms are generic individuals. In New Zealand we might also move beyond the false dichotomy which pits indigenous cultural rights against individual children's rights. Policies and practices which put schoolchildren into the 'too hard' basket, behind other groups negotiating for recognition, serve no one well.

There has been a lack of analysis of the complexities involved in considering rights that are based on self-defined needs (Handley 2000). If the diversity of views, lacks and wants of people with various disabilities, ages and cultures is fully acknowledged, the range of expressed needs could be infinite. How then would competing claims for rights be debated? A relativistic view that all self-defined needs are valid seems a poor platform for allocation of limited state resources. In children's worlds an extreme focus on individual agents acting autonomously is out of kilter with the interdependence that defines lives in family groups. Further, such a view of childhood assumes that children form a homogeneous group, with all the problems that have been identified by such essentialism that positions Western childhood as proper, normative and universal (c.f. Burman 1994).

In the classroom conversations I observed, there was not much discursive opportunity to engage with 'learning needs' in ways that allowed children participation in setting the agenda for the topic or the group process. There were glimpses, in the collaborative interactions between children on their own, of discussion that might move beyond the expectations of curriculum statements within child-centred pedagogy. Such talk could provide some welcome insights for struggling teachers and policy makers as well as school students and their parents. Education that truly serves 'children's needs' surely must be based on the capacities of children to participate in the shaping of their futures as well as on of the ability of adults (whether parents, teachers, policy makers, community members) to hear what children have to say.

Making national curriculum goals clearer to children as well as parents presents a new challenge. In keeping with UNCROC, children may benefit from working with adults who anticipate and augment the needs they may have trouble communicating. At the same time, we adults could also be more reflexive about practices at home and at school that expand or limit opportunities for children to express their views – even contradictory ones – in ways that they find effective.

NOTES

1 Currently there are moves to reinstate secondary student representatives.
2 Boards of Trustees have widened their membership considerably since the initial reforms.
3 At the end of 1989 I spent 4 months in a small, predominantly 'working class' primary school in an urban area of New Zealand, taking fieldnotes during class sessions in two classrooms, a combined year 2/3 class of 6- to 8-year-olds and a combined year 5/6 class with 9- to 11-year-olds (see Bird 1992).
4 Some comments were recorded verbatim by the interviewer who took fieldnotes in the classrooms. Other comments were recorded in note form and reconstructed later; these are noted in square parentheses.
5 I am grateful to Joanna Higgins and Carol Hamilton for these reflections on the use of the word 'need' in contemporary classroom practice in New Zealand.
6 A student teacher was assisting that day, which may have made the teacher elaborate on routines that were already well established in this class by the third term.

REFERENCES

Alldred, P. (1998) 'Ethnography and discourse analysis: Dilemmas in representing the voices of children', in J. Ribbens and R. Edwards (eds), *Feminist Dilemmas in Qualitative Research: Public Knowledge and Private Lives*, London: Sage.

Bird, L. (1992) 'Girls and positions of authority at primary school', in S. Middleton and A. Jones (eds), *Women and Education in Aotearoa 2*, Wellington, New Zealand: Bridget Williams Books.

Burman, E. (1994) *Deconstructing Developmental Psychology*, London: Routledge.

Butterworth, G. and Butterworth, S. (1998) *Reforming Education : The New Zealand Experience 1984–1996*, Palmerston North, New Zealand: Dunmore.

Educational Review Office (ERO) (1996) *Addressing Barriers to Learning, No. 6*, Wellington, New Zealand: Author.

Educational Review Office (ERO) (1997) *Students at Risk: Barriers to Learning, No 7*, Wellington, New Zealand: Author.

Fiske, E.B. and Ladd, H.F. (2000) *When Schools Compete: A Cautionary Tale*, Washington, DC: Brookings Institution.

Handley, P. (2000) 'Trouble in paradise – a disabled person's right to the satisfaction of a self-defined need: some conceptual and practical problems', *Disability and Society*, 16, 2, 313–325.

Henaghan, M. (1996) 'New Zealand and the United Nations Convention on the Rights of the child: A lack of balance', in M. Freeman (ed.), *Children's Rights: A Comparative Perspective*, Aldershot: Dartmouth.

Hill, M. (1999) 'Assessment in self-managing schools: Primary teachers balancing learning and accountability demands in the 1990s', *New Zealand Journal of Educational Studies*, 34, 1, 176–85.

James, A. and Prout, A. (eds) (1990) *Constructing and Reconstructing Childhood: Contemporary Issues in the Sociological Study of Childhood*, London: Falmer.

James, A., Jenks, C. and Prout, A. (1998) *Theorizing Childhood*, Cambridge: Polity.

Jones, A and Jacka, S. (1995) 'Discourse of disadvantage: Girls' school achievement', *New Zealand Journal of Educational Studies*, 30, 2, 165–176.

Lange, D. (1988) *Tomorrow's Schools: The Reform of Education Administration in New Zealand*, Wellington, New Zealand: Government Printer.

Lansdown, G. (1994) 'Children's rights', in B. Mayall (ed.), *Children's Childhoods: Observed and Experienced*, London: Falmer.

Lauder, H., Hughes, D. and Watson, S. (1999) 'The introduction of educational markets in New Zealand: Questions and consequences', *New Zealand Journal of Educational Studies*, 34, 1, 86–98.

Maslow, A.H. (1968) *Toward a Psychology of Being*, New York: Van Reinhold.

Ministry of Education (MoE) (1999) *Legislation for Learning: A Discussion Paper on Making the Education Act Work Better for Students*, Wellington, New Zealand: Author.

Nairn, K. (2000, June) 'Young people's participation in their school environments'. Unpublished conference paper presented at the Symposium on Research on Children's Participation in Community Life, Norway: University of Oslo.

Smith, A.B. (2000) 'Children's rights: An overview', in A.B. Smith, M. Gollop, K. Marshall and K. Nairn (eds), *Advocating for Children: International Perspectives on Children's Rights*, Dunedin, New Zealand: University of Otago Press.

Smith, N. (1999) Forward. *Legislation for Learning: A Discussion Paper on Making the Education Act Work Better for Students*, Wellington, New Zealand: Ministry of Education.

United Nations (UN) General Assembly (1989, Nov. 17) *Adoption of a Convention on the Rights of the Child*, New York: Author.

Walkerdine, V. (1984) 'Developmental psychology and the child-centred pedagogy', in J. Henriques, W. Hollway, C. Urwin, C. Venn and V. Walkerdine, *Changing the Subject: Psychology, Social Regulation and Subjectivity*, London: Methuen.

Woodhead, M. (1997) 'Psychology and the cultural construction of children's needs', in A. James and A. Prout (eds), *Constructing and Reconstructing Childhood: Contemporary Issues in the Sociological Study of Childhood*, London: Falmer.

Wylie, C. (1997) *Self-Managing Schools Seven Years On: What Have We Learnt?*, Wellington: New Zealand Council for Educational Research.

3 School's Out?

Out of school clubs at the boundary of home and school

Fiona Smith and John Barker

INTRODUCTION: CHANGING GEOGRAPHIES OF CHILDHOOD

Geographers have recently begun to make an important contribution to the new social studies of childhood by exploring how 'place' is significant both to the everyday experience of children and to the ways in which the concept of childhood is socially constructed (Holloway and Valentine, 2000). Research has, for example, illustrated that the conceptualisation of childhood as a time of dependency in the 'North' (Aldridge and Becker, 1995; Stables and Smith, 2000), which is heavily drawn upon by policy makers in the development of out of school care in the UK, does not necessarily provide an appropriate context for work with children in the 'South' (Robson and Ansell, 2000). Moreover, Katz's (1993,1994) research with children living in Sudan and New York has emphasised the importance of recognising significant variations in the ways in which children have access to and use space in different parts of the world.

At the national, regional and local scale another important and growing body of work focuses on the 'everyday spaces' of childhood: the school, the home, the playground and the street (see Holloway and Valentine, 2000). As social scientists from other disciplines have made clear, home and school are the two most significant environments in British children's lives (James, Jenks and Prout, 1998; Edwards and Alldred, 1999). Geographers working in these settings have been keen to explore the role they play in the reproduction and contestation of children's identities. Aitken (1994), for example, has highlighted the ways in which the institutionalised space of the school provides a social context for the control of children by adults and also an important spatial arena for the reproduction of racialised, gendered and class based identities. Other work in the home has focused on the domestic sphere as a site for the negotiation of power relations between adults and children (see Sibley, 1995). This work has been influential to those working in other spatial contexts (see Smith and Barker, 2000c) which is illustrative of the ways in which children's environments are inherently social spaces in which adults and children struggle for control.

The growing anxiety associated with children's access to and independent use of public space has been highlighted by a number of geographers including Valentine

(1997). One response to the increasing restrictions placed upon children in the public sphere has been the development of commercial, supervised playspaces (Matthews and Limb, 1999; McKendrick, Fielder and Bradford, 1999) providing parents with environments in which they believe their children will be able to consume a safe play experience. British children are increasingly 'placed' by adults within these bounded and supervised environments that supplement the key social settings of home and school (James, Jenks and Prout, 1998). Out of school care provides a pertinent example of such a bounded environment, creating another spatially segregated space in the contemporary geography of British childhood (Smith and Barker, 2000c).

As a number of geographers and other social scientists have noted, while children may be viewed as social actors in the various environments they inhabit, the way they experience and use different social settings is contingent upon the ways in which they are socially constructed by adults in different places. Thus as Mayall (1994b) has noted, children experience school and home in different ways, reflecting the different conceptualisations of childhood held by parents and teachers: 'Childhood ... is not experienced as one consistent set of relationships; rather its character in time and place is modified by adult understandings in these times and places of what children are, and what adult relationships with children are proper' (Mayall, 1994b: 116).

It is the aim of this chapter to build upon the growing body of work being developed by children's geographers and other social scientists working on the spatial aspects of children's lives to highlight the ways in which out of school clubs can be viewed as intermediary environments, connecting through time the spaces of home and school. Moreover, we aim to illustrate the ways in which the adults working in out of school clubs draw on both domestic and school-based discourses of childhood, reflected in the physical environment of the clubs and in the ways in which adults interact with the children attending them. By exploring how children feel about their clubs, this chapter will also illuminate the ways in which children make sense of, and negotiate the 'conceptual shifts' (Barrett, 1989) between home, school and the out of school club. It is to this specific spatial setting that our focus now turns.

SIGNIFICANT NEW SPACES FOR CHILDREN: THE GROWTH OF OUT OF SCHOOL CHILDCARE IN BRITAIN

Defined for the purposes of this research as providing childcare to groups of children aged 5–12 in settings offering opportunities for creative play, out of school care is provided by adult childcarers, usually called playworkers, who supervise children and organise activities before school, after school and during the school holidays. Most clubs use school premises, although they are also found in a number of other places including community centres and church halls. They tend to be provided by voluntary groups on a non-profit making basis, but are also run by local authorities and private businesses. On average clubs cater for 24 children per session. For children in full-time out of school care, this environment is arguably the third most important to them (after the home and school). The service thus significantly impacts upon the day to day temporal and spatial organisation of children's lives, increasing the amount of 'clockbound' time to which children are subjected (Mayall, 1996).

The out of school service is currently undergoing a period of rapid expansion throughout Britain. Successive Conservative and Labour Governments have, since the mid-1990s, made the development of the service an increasingly important part of national policy (see Smith and Barker, 1999a; 1999b). The 'Out of School Childcare Initiative' (1993) and 'The National Childcare Strategy' (1998) were implemented to support economic restructuring, the increasing number of mothers entering paid employment, local area regeneration and new welfare regimes (in particular the New Deal for Lone Parents). As a result of these national initiatives, delivered at the local scale, the number of out of school clubs in England and Wales rose from approximately 350 at the beginning of the 1990s to over 5000 at the end of the decade (Smith and Barker, 2000b). Moreover current investment of £220 million through the New Opportunities Fund Out of School Childcare Programme,[1] aims to create 865,000 out of school childcare places across the United Kingdom by 2003, providing out of school care for up to a quarter of the nation's primary school children (NOF, 1999). The impact of these recent policy initiatives are thus arguably the most significant outside of the formal education system currently directly affecting the lives of British children (Gill, 1999).

The 'child centred after school and holiday childcare' project

The research reported in this chapter sought to explore with children how they experience and feel about the sorts of environments being created by the policies described above. The chapter draws on data collected during a two year project, carried out in six counties in England and Wales which had distinct socio-economic and demographic profiles, and different levels and types of out of school care provision (for a detailed discussion see Smith and Barker, 2000c). The majority of clubs which took part in the research were located in schools, reflecting the type of environment in which the majority of British out of school clubs are located.

During the fieldwork phase of the project, approximately 400 children aged between 5 and 12 years were involved in the production of data. Underpinning the research was the principle that children are social actors, knowledgeful 'experts' actively involved in shaping the social spaces they inhabit, albeit within the wider constraints of the institutional environments in which they are located (Matthews, Limb and Taylor, 1998a; Smith and Barker, 2000c). This principle also informed the research design. In common with a growing number of geographers (see Matthews, Limb and Taylor, 1998b; Holloway and Valentine, 2000) we developed a 'child-centred' approach to this project by inviting 70 children attending out of school clubs in one urban and one rural area to define the issues that should be addressed by the research. They identified the following five themes as particularly important to children attending out of school clubs:

1 Activities available in clubs.

2 Playworkers (relationships with adults in clubs).
3 Friendships.
4 Rules.
5 Their ability to participate in decision making.

These children were also asked, if they were carrying out this project, how would they go about doing it? They suggested a number of both innovative and traditional techniques (Table 3.1), but stressed that the research must be appropriate to the particular setting in which it was to be conducted. As they overwhelmingly conceptualised the out of school club as a place for fun and play, they stressed that the techniques used should also be fun. Interestingly, they were adamant that methods associated with school, in particular those involving writing (including story writing and answering questions using the medium of a questionnaire) should be avoided.

The children were also clear that we should use a number of different techniques in each club as not all children would want to participate in the same activity. We took their advice, and invited children to take part in the activities of their choice during the week spent in each club.[2] Taking photographs proved to be the most popular method of data collection used, and also provided a useful tool to spark further discussion. These methods were supplemented by other techniques, including a questionnaire survey of parents to provide background socio-demographic information about the children taking part in the project and interviews with adults working in and running clubs (see Smith and Barker, 2000c for a more detailed discussion of these methods).

Staying on in school, after school

As indicated above, school premises including halls, gyms, classrooms and canteens are becoming increasingly significant sites for the provision of out of school care. Indeed, almost one half of all schemes are now based in schools and the fastest growing area of new provision is school-based (Smith and Barker, 2000b).[3] The spatial environment in which clubs are located has significant implications for the development of out of school care, as 'social space is never a mere issue of neutral location' (James, Jenks and Prout, 1998: 39). Of key concern to those currently developing out of school care is the impact of creating what has traditionally been a service to promote children's play in an educational setting. This has intensified the long standing debate concerning the educational benefits of childcare services (Holloway, 1999), dividing those who prioritise the welfare benefits and those who prioritise the educational impact (Statham, Dillion and Moss, 2000). As a growing number of clubs are promoting the educational benefits of the service (Holloway, 1999, Gill, 1999) the conceptual boundary between out of school education and out of school childcare is becoming increasingly blurred. Many of the clubs we visited explicitly promoted the educational benefits of out of school childcare (to parents) by providing opportunities (including specific space) for children to do their homework and take part in 'educational' activities. Such clubs were clearly responding to parental demand and drew heavily on educational and school-based discourses in setting the 'best' agenda

Table 3.1 Children's suggested research methods

Method	Comment
Photography of popular/ unpopular activities and places	Children suggested a Polaroid camera would be popular and enable them to discuss the photographs with researchers as soon as they had been taken.
Interviews (including adult led and child led)	Some stated that they would not want their interviews to be tape recorded. Other methods should be available to those children not wanting to take part in this activity.
Video filming their clubs	A number of children had reservations about this method, believing that some would show off in front of the camera whilst others might be camera shy.
Drawing pictures of their clubs	Some children suggested that they could draw pictures to indicate how they would like to see their clubs develop.

for children, reflecting government rhetoric extolling the benefits of 'homework clubs'. As one playworker described:

> There is pressure from parents and groups for homework clubs. The government's thrust is more about education, learning and work than it is about play ... play is the last thing on their mind.
>
> (Karen, Playworker, London)

Thus whilst '... day-to-day childcare is defined by local discourses, the larger needs of children are often defined by universal agendas that suggest certain kinds of development' (Aitken, 2000: 124).

However, the children attending these clubs did not simply accept homework as part of their out of school club experience. Only 6 per cent of children taking part in our research said they did their homework in the out of school club (Smith and Barker, 1999c) and we rarely witnessed any children using the rooms set aside for such purposes. As Mark explained:

> I hate it! I'm not going to do my homework at after school club. (sic)
>
> (Mark, aged 10, London)

For the overwhelming majority of children, homework was unpopular compared to the other competing play opportunities available. In general, children successfully contested the addition of homework as an activity in the out of school club, and were clear in articulating that the connection between out of school care and formal education was not a popular one. However, they had less control over other aspects of their clubs. Research has illustrated that schools are highly structured and regulated institutions that promote and (re)produce formal, hierarchical relationships between children and adults (Burgess, 1986; Alderson, 2000b). While children clearly contest adult-imposed spatial and temporal rules in schools (see for example, Mayall, 1994b; Wyness, 1999) power is placed firmly in the hands of teachers via the medium of 'school discipline', rendering children relatively powerless in the strict hierarchy of the educational institution. While a minority of schools have recently developed innovative initiatives to involve children in the creation of a more child centred and responsive environment (see Alderson, 2000b), these procedures are often tokenistic and fail to positively respond to or act upon the opinions of children. Thus children are rarely consulted about, or involved in, the decision-making processes that determine their school environments (Edwards and David, 1997). The 'spatial and temporal script' of schools are therefore largely defined and controlled by adults (Mayall, 1996; James, Jenks and Prout, 1998).

This type of highly structured and hierarchical environment is directly incongruous with that of the out of school club, which, in theory at least, endeavours to create a more informal relationship between child and adult (Petrie, 1994; 1996). Children attending out of school clubs have traditionally addressed their playworkers by their first name, and have had the freedom to use the toilet, eat and drink without regulation from adults. Conversely, the strict hierarchy within primary schools is maintained by insisting that children address teachers by their surname, and by enabling teachers to regulate children's personal habits (Mayall, 1994a). Moreover, while play is seen as one of the primary objectives of the out of school club, it is accorded a low priority in schools reflecting the formal educational demands of the National Curriculum. As Mayall comments 'playtime at school … is structured by a combination of adult control and neglect' (1996: 129). Therefore, the day-to-day practices of schools and out of school clubs have very different ideological bases.

However, a significant outcome of the increasing use of school premises for the provision of out of school care has been the development of out of school clubs which reflect the wider institutional environment of the school in which they are located (Smith and Barker, 2000a). It is increasingly common for school-based out of school clubs to, for example, insist that children address playworkers by their *surname* rather than *first name*. In these clubs it was interesting to note that children often referred to their playworkers as teachers and to the club as school:

> I like them … er … I like the teachers.
>
> (Mary, aged 5, Cheshire)
>
> The club is very good and all the teachers are lovely.
>
> (Darren, aged 7, Devon)
>
> It's like a whole little school … like a holiday school.
>
> (Sophie, aged 6, Cheshire)

As will be discussed in more detail later, children also draw on images of mothering when conceptualising and describing their playworkers. Moreover, while the space occupied by the out of school club changed its social significance for children throughout the day (for example, classrooms used for teaching activities before 3 p.m. became playspaces in the afterschool club) children often found it difficult to make sense of this 'conceptual shift'. A key way in which children seemed to negotiate the temporal transformation of their school into an out of school club was by importing behaviour associated with school playtime into the club. Thus, while playworkers tried to involve children in activities that were unique to the club (such as creative arts and drama), children regularly rejected their invitations in favour of playground style games such as football, 'bulldog' and 'it' (see Smith and Barker, 2000a for further discussion).[4]

Moreover, the play practices of children attending clubs held in schools are increasingly bounded, limited and contained, reflecting what the school considers to be acceptable behaviour. For a number of the clubs we visited, the school in which the club was located imposed rules, allowing premises to be used only on the condition that:

- Children's play does not interfere with or disturb the after school activities of staff (for example, teachers' marking and planning, the work of cleaners and caretakers).
- Children's behaviour does not contravene the strictly hierarchical adult–child relationship present within the wider school setting.
- The space used for play is not required for other purposes, such as parents' meetings, governors' meetings, or commercial use.

Thus whilst technically independent of the school, out of school clubs located in schools are subject to a complex web of power relations that promote the needs and interests of the educational institution above those of the club. The school regulates and controls the socio-spatial environment of the club in a number of ways. For example, playworkers often commented that they felt they were under surveillance from school staff, who regularly carried out after school duties within sight or earshot of the club:

> We have had ups and downs with the caretaker and members of staff saying the children are noisy, but that is all about understanding what play is about, and that after school is different … Because the children are noisy, they think we must be not looking after them properly … it seems busy, because the children are moving about, because they are not sitting quietly. There was a teacher who wasn't used to younger ones running around, she was used to them sitting down in rows. She forgets that it is not an extension of school.
>
> (Amanda, Playworker, Devon)

This quotation highlights the covert surveillance of the out of school club by school staff which places the club firmly at the centre of the panoptical gaze (James, Jenks and Prout, 1998) of the school. The threat of surveillance becomes internalised by the playworkers, a process Robinson (2000) defines as 'self subjectification'. Hence, adults working in out of school clubs become key agents in the regulation and control of the club, maintaining 'a watchful eye' over the children to ensure that the club adheres to the institutional structures and rules of the school (Smith and Barker, 2000c).

> We wanted a nice quiet place where we could sit and do our drawings and chat … so we sat on the stage, and the playworker came and said 'off'. If we sit on the steps we get told off, if we sit by the piano we get told off, by the equipment we

get told off, on the stage we get told off, on the floor we get told off, on the playworker's desk we get told off.

(Marcia, aged 7, London)

However, when self-surveillance fails to ensure strict regulation of school approved practices, school staff readily intervene during club hours to reprimand children whose behaviour violates that which is deemed acceptable during the school day (for example, children using loud voices or singing). Thus school staff explicitly regulate out of school clubs subject to the practices, hierarchies and philosophies of the wider educational establishment in which they are located, despite the fact that clubs are run outside of formal school hours:

There is one serious rule … you're not allowed on the stage, because (the head teacher) keeps coming in and complaining.

(Ruth, aged 9, London)

We used to use the school things, but we have to be very careful.

(Susie, aged 9, Berkshire)

Children were acutely aware of the connections between school and out of school, and the subjugation of the club by the institutional framework of the school:

The club has its rules, and then there's the school rules. The club has to obey the school rules as well.

(Daniel, aged 9, Berkshire)

For one child, the surveillance by teaching staff had tangible consequences for him during his next day at school:

The teachers are watching you. Mrs (Smith) is watching you, she just stares and watches you … she says 'why were you being stupid at the after school club?' And I say 'I wasn't', and she said 'you were because I was watching you, I know you did. I'll give you a detention'.

(Paul, aged 10, Berkshire)

Throughout the fieldwork phase of the research, it was clear that children observed and understood the power relationships that flowed between individuals in the school and the out of school club, clearly making sense of the 'hierarchy and boundary characteristics' (James and Prout, 1996) present. They were clear that teachers/the school were more powerful than playworkers/the out of school club. This is reminiscent of research which has highlighted the ways in which children make sense of the strict hierarchical structure of school, and the low status accorded to non teaching staff such as meal time assistants (Burgess, 1986; Sherman, 1997; Smith, 2000; Chazan, 1992). While children would regularly try to negotiate with playworkers and contest the rules they imposed, they rarely challenged the dominance of teaching staff. Thus children differentiated between those boundaries and limits that could be negotiated and those that were fixed. As the next section shows, children's friendship networks highlight one area where some of the boundaries associated with school were contested and renegotiated by children.

The impact of out of school clubs on children's school-based friendship networks

The ability to play with and make new friends was cited as one of the primary reasons children enjoyed spending time in an out of school club (Smith and Barker, 1999c). As Tina states:

> That's why I like coming here, there are friends you can play with.
>
> (Tina, aged 8, Cheshire)

With the increasing restrictions being placed upon children's access to playspace (Valentine, 1997), the out of school club provided a significant environment that enabled children to spend time in the company of friends outside of formal school time. Indeed, for many children in the study (in particular those living in rural areas), the out of school club provided the single most significant place to play in their local areas.

While many of the friendship networks observed in the clubs were pre-existing, reflecting networks already established in school, the out of school club also provided an opportunity for children to make new friends. The structure of most of the clubs we visited differed from other institutionalised children's environments (most notably the school) in that children were not segregated on the basis of age.[5] Children aged between 5 and 12 shared the same physical environment and played with children who they did not normally associate with in school.

> Sometimes I play with year 3 in the after school club, (and) year 5 or year 6.
>
> (Katey, aged 10, Berkshire)

Hence, the out of school club presented children with an almost unique opportunity to develop friendships that crossed traditional year groupings within a school setting. However, in most cases, children stated that this opportunity was limited to the out of school club and did not carry on once the children were back in 'formal' school. As James, Jenks and Prout (1998) argue, children's friendships are spatially variable, contingent upon and shaped by, the different social settings in which children spend their time. Thus, many children experienced 'situational' friendships that were initiated in, but did not extend beyond, the out of school club. One girl explained how she found this perplexing:

> That's the weird thing about it, when you're at school you never talk to them. I never talk to anyone (outside year 5), just year 5.
>
> (Hannah, aged 10, Berkshire)

However, while clubs provided more opportunities than schools to play with children from different age groups, they did little to break down barriers according to gender. Boys dominated outdoor playspace, primarily by playing football games from which girls were consciously excluded. The marginalisation of girls' play observed in school playgrounds (James, Jenks and Prout, 1998; Thomson, 1999) was thus replicated in most of the clubs we visited. While these processes are reminiscent of other work carried out in institutional settings (see for example Krenichyn's (1999) work on the gendered nature of school gyms in the USA), it should be noted that Jones' and Cunningham's (1999: 31) work on the prevalence of mixed gender play in non-institutionalised environments has led them to conclude that '(d)ifferentiation and segregation of children in play may therefore reflect inadequate play environments, or environments used beyond their environmental capacity, rather than an innate propensity' (see Smith and Barker, 2000c for further discussion). It is thus suggested that, while children do renegotiate friendship networks in clubs in ways that contradict what goes on in school, they are still subject to many of the structures and boundaries associated with the institutionalised environment of the school setting.

THERE'S NO PLACE LIKE HOME? THE REPRODUCTION OF THE IDEOLOGY OF DOMESTICITY IN OUT OF SCHOOL CARE

The home environment is popularly seen in the United Kingdom as the ideal setting for children's lives (Wyness, 1999; James, Jenks and Prout, 1998). As Holloway and Valentine (2000: 15) note:

> … childhood, for many in the North at least, has been increasingly domesticated over the course of the past two centuries. The process is not simply a material one, in the sense of children spending increasing amounts of time in the home, but is also ideological, in that there is a sense in which this is where children should spend their time.

As such, childcare for young children has tended to be located in the home (Richardson, 1993; Gregson and Lowe, 1995) and it is common for 'formal' childcare provision (including nurseries and daycare centres) to reproduce discourses traditionally associated with the 'ideology of domesticity' (Holloway, 1999). Many of the out of school clubs we visited made a conscious effort to create a domestic environment within the school setting by, for example, creating areas which replicated the home – with comfortable sofas and televisions. It is interesting that playworkers chose these particular objects, as watching television and sharing the sofa with parents and siblings has been cited by Christensen *et al.* (2000) as central to the way in which children represent time spent in the home with their families. These 'domesticated' spaces were explicitly promoted by playworkers as providing a 'home from home' environment, reproducing the sort of setting children with 'stay at home mothers' would have access to. In ways reminiscent of McKendrick *et al.*'s (2000: 114) work on commercial playgrounds, the domestication of out of school clubs represents a new and important way in which 'homespace is changing its position' from the private to the public sphere. It was apparent from discussions with playworkers that they felt clubs should replicate key elements of the idealised domestic environment. Previous research has also suggested that this is seen as a priority amongst parents who use formal childcare provision (Gregson and Lowe, 1995). Thus adults tried to connect home and out of school via the appropriation of domestic discourses that were reproduced and practised in many of the out of school clubs we visited.

However, this was often unpopular with the children. For example, 'home corners', created by adults to reproduce an idealised domestic space, were regularly deserted. Children stated that one of the key advantages of spending time in an out of school club was that it was not home – offering far more opportunities and resources for play and fun:

> [If I was at home] I'd just … watch TV and do nothing else, there's not much to do at home. But here, you just come down the stairs and it's all here, you can make things, it's really good.
>
> (Katy, 9, London)
>
> It's a good place to come after school. Home can be really boring, because of the TV, like BBC1.
>
> (Wilcott, 8, London)

Thus many children taking part in the study did not construct the space of the out of school club as a 'home from home' environment and many actively rejected a construction that drew upon and reflected discourses associated with the domestic sphere. Children appeared to enjoy the specificity and uniqueness of the out of school club, rather than its similarity with, or connection to, the home environment. However, as will be discussed in the following section, they did make connections between the out of school club and the domestic sphere when conceptualising play-workers.

The feminisation of out of school care

Although women's participation in the labour market is increasing, the domestic sphere is still strongly encoded as a feminine space (Laurie *et al.*, 1999; Rose, 1993), with the ideology of domesticity naturalising women's position and role in the home (Dyck, 1990; Leslie, 1997). Conversely, the development of formal, collectivised, organised and commodified childcare can be conceptualised as one of the key services that augments and transfers domestic tasks from the private sphere to the public arena (Gregson and Lowe, 1995). Thus, with a rapidly expanding collectivised child-care service, caring for children is undergoing a spatial shift from the private sphere of the unpaid mother, to the public sphere of the waged childcare worker (Dyck, 1990). However, although the location of caring for many families is moving from the home to the childcare institution, the practices of caring (for example, the nurturing and care of children) and those responsible for caring (predominantly women) remain unchanged.

Thus, in the out of school club, playworkers (the vast majority of whom in our study were women) reproduce a particular domestic representation of femininity, that draws upon ideologies of caring, nurturing and protecting children. The behaviour of these playworkers connects the institutional space of the out of school club with the domestic space and routine of the home. Their actions also reinforce the assertion that the world of caring is constructed as female (Mayall, 1996; Holloway, 1998). Many of the playworkers taking part in the study saw themselves as reproducing (and indeed substituting for) the role of mother during the out of school hours, mirroring what Dyck (1990) describes as 'mothering work'. It was also common for these women to be highly critical of the mothers they felt they were replacing. As Sarah states:

> You don't know why they have children. Why bother if you are going to give them to someone else to look after all day five days a week? I am more of a mother to them than she is.
>
> (Sarah, Playworker, Cheshire)

This comment is reminiscent of the campaign run by staff in Danish daycare centres in the early 1990s, which was critical of the amount of 'quality time' that parents who were in full-time employment spent with their children (see Christensen, 1999). Moreover, children's descriptions of their playworkers often reflected images associated with domesticity and motherhood:

> They're really nice, because when you hurt your head, they get a medical form and they help you if you're hurt, help you if you are stuck on your homework, they are just like a *mother and father* really.
>
> (Martine, aged 9, Bradford (emphasis added))
>
> They give us food, they really care for us, and they let us play. They are really like our *mums*, because they care for us.
>
> (Yvonne, aged 7, Berkshire (emphasis added))
>
> Some of them are kind ... some are nice, and some are loving, caring and considerate.
>
> (Meera, aged 6, London)

These descriptions are significant in that while a number of children called their playworkers 'teachers' as previously discussed, the way they conceptualised them also drew heavily on domesticated images of 'mothering'. This obviously has implications for the relationship between playworkers and children in the clubs. As Mayall (1994b: 116) argues:

> ... whilst children may be regarded as part of the group people (rather than outside the category people, or subsumed as part of the family as parental offspring) the critical and distinctive characteristics of the sub-group children's interactions with both other people and with daily settings depend not so much on their absolute powerlessness vis-à-vis adults, but on the precise nature of the

power-relationship between the children and the adults in any given setting. Thus I want to suggest that the level of their powerlessness varies according to how the adults in specific social settings conceptualize children and childhood.

A number of researchers have commented that children are more successful social actors, creating their own space and challenging adults' spatial hegemony in the home than in the school. Mayall (1996), for example, argues that children often gain 'negotiating power' in the domestic sphere and Wyness (1999) has noted the important contribution children make to the social life of the home. As an intermediary space between home and school, out of school clubs provide opportunities for children to actively contest adult control in ways which are reminiscent of the home, but rare in the physical setting of the school. Examples of this could be seen in clubs where children re-defined adult led activities on their own terms. As we have written about in more detail elsewhere, this included children turning what adults had meant to be an educational exercise about the Trojan Horse of Ancient Greece into a competition to see how long each person could spend in a cardboard box and children moving furniture from its designated position in the classroom to create dens in which the presence of adults was strictly prohibited (see Smith and Barker, 2000a; Smith and Barker, 2000c for more discussion). By re-defining activities and re-structuring the physical environment of the clubs, processes rare in the classroom during the formal school day, children were able to exert some ownership over part of the spatial environment of the schools in which their clubs were located.

CONCLUSION

In this chapter we have begun to explore out of school clubs as intermediary spaces, at the interface of home and school. Throughout the discussion we have highlighted some of the ways in which these spatially bounded environments draw heavily upon discourses that are located beyond their geographical and temporal limits. Just as the influence of the school extends beyond its confines through homework and home–school relations (Alderson, 2000a; Wyness, 1999), the concepts of home, care, education and school are intertwined within the social space of the out of school club.

The empirical evidence presented in this chapter suggests that the 'boundaries' between home and school are becoming increasingly blurred in the relatively new spatial setting of the out of school club in two key ways. First, the way the physical environment of the club is being developed reflects both educational discourses about the 'best agenda' for children (reflected in the development of homework rooms and 'educational' activities), and domestic discourses inferring that the home environment is the ideal setting for children (reflected in the creation of home-corners). Second, educational and domestic discourses also impact upon the way playworkers conceptualise the children they work with, and consequently, the relationship between adults and children in the clubs. Whilst the growing use of surnames for playworkers suggests an increasingly formal relationship between adults and children in some out of school clubs, playworkers taking part in our study also clearly saw themselves as taking on what Dyck (1990) has termed 'mothering work', inferring a more informal and caring relationship with children. It is interesting to note that children also drew upon these somewhat contradictory images in their conceptualisation of playworkers as both 'teacher' and 'mother' figures. What is also clear from this research is that children experience, and, perhaps more importantly, want to experience, out of school clubs as unique environments. The rejection, for example, of homework and 'home-corners', suggests that children do not want to spend time in clubs which simply replicate school or home. The children taking part in our study were clear that they want to spend their out of school hours in places which offer them the opportunity to play with their friends in ways in which they feel they have some control. In effect, they want the sort of freedom to choose what to do that most experience at home within the spatial setting of the school.

The current exponential increase in the number of children attending out of school clubs in the United Kingdom obviously has significant implications for the nation's children. As indicated earlier in this chapter, current government policy suggests that up to one million children will spend time in an out of school club by the year 2003, potentially making the development of out of school care the single most significant policy development currently affecting children outside of the formal education system. If clubs are to provide the sorts of socio-spatial environments in which children themselves want to spend time, it is imperative that policy makers and local providers take children's views and wishes seriously, and actively engage them in the process of developing a child focused service. As Franklin (1995: 19) argues 'Children must be allowed and encouraged to participate in decision-making especially in policy areas such as [out of school care] where they constitute the significant consumer group.'

However, despite powerful arguments in favour of consulting with children over the development of the services they use, our research in clubs suggests that at present, such a process is rare and, where it happens, is all too often tokenistic. While the 1995 United Nations Committee on the Rights of the Child recommended that the UK government 'consider the possibility of establishing further mechanisms to facilitate the participation of children in decisions affecting them' (p. 5), little progress seems to have been made at either the level of national policy or in individual clubs. While our research discovered notable exceptions to this rule, for example, the Camden Play Service in London and 'The Children's Participation Project' in Kirklees have developed appropriate 'participatory tools' which have enabled children and young people to influence the development of their clubs and government policy at the local level, we believe that the general reluctance to involve children is in part, at least, a response to the ways in which policy makers and adults working in clubs conceptualise childhood as a time of dependency. As noted earlier, this is generally indicative of the way children are currently conceptualised in the 'North'. Furthermore, considering the increasing number of clubs being set up on school premises, subject to the rules and regulations of the wider institutional environment in which they are located, it is questionable how far children's desire for a unique play environment over which they have some say will be met in the future.

NOTES

1 The New Opportunities Fund has been created by the Government to distribute profits from the National Lottery to projects focusing on health, education and the environment. It is intended to specifically target funding in areas of social exclusion and disadvantage. The out of school programme offers a one off opportunity to create new out of school childcare places in addition to money from Government sources. The key focus of the programme is the creation of out of school clubs.
2 Informed consent was obtained from all children, playworkers and parents before the researchers carried out any of the work in clubs. Priscilla Alderson's (1995) work on ethical practices with children informed this process.
3 The remainder of schemes make use of a variety of premises, including church halls and community centres, although a minority of clubs have their own purpose built premises.
4 'Bulldog' and 'it' are popular playground games in the UK where children have to try and catch one another.
5 A minority of clubs did provide children aged over 8 years with their own room. This was a response to the demands of older children for an environment which reflected their needs better than the rest of the club. For further discussion please see Smith and Barker 2000c.

ACKNOWLEDGEMENTS

The authors gratefully acknowledge the support of the ESRC which funded this research (project number L129251050) and the children, clubs, playworkers and parents who took part in it. We are also grateful to Ros Edwards for her comments on an earlier draft of this chapter.

REFERENCES

Aitken, S.C. (1994) *Putting Children in their Place* Washington, DC: Association of American Geographers.
Aitken, S.C. (2000) 'Play, Rights and Borders: Gender-bound parents and the social construction of children', in Holloway, S.L. and Valentine, G. (eds) *Children's Geographies: Playing, Living, Learning* London: Routledge.
Alderson, P. (1995) *Listening to Children: Children, Ethics and Social Research* London: Barnardos.
Alderson, P. (2000a) *Young Children's Rights: Exploring Beliefs, Principles and Practice* London: Save the Children/Jessica Kingsley.
Alderson, P. (2000b) 'School Students' Views on School Councils and Daily Life at School' *Children and Society* 14, 121–134.
Aldridge, J. and Becker, S. (1995) 'The Rights and Wrongs of Children who Care', in Franklin, B. (ed.) *The Handbook of Children's Rights: Comparative Policy and Practice* London: Routledge.
Barrett, G. (1989) 'A Child's Eye View of Schooling', in Barrett, G. (ed.) *Disaffection from School? The Early Years* London: Falmer Press.
Burgess, R. (1986) *Sociology, Education and Schools: An Introduction to the Sociology of Education* London: Batsford.
Chazan, M. (1992) 'The Home and the School', in Coleman, J. (ed.) *The School Years: Current Issues in the Socialization of Young People* London: Routledge.
Christensen, P. (1999) *Towards an Anthropology of Childhood Sickness: An Ethnographic Study of Danish School Children* Unpublished PhD thesis, Hull University, UK.

Christensen, P., James, J. and Jenks, C. (2000) 'Home and Movement: Children Constructing "Family Time"', in Holloway, S.L. and Valentine, G. (eds) *Children's Geographies: Playing, Living, Learning* London: Routledge.

Dyck, I. (1990) 'Space, Time and Renegotiating Motherhood: An Exploration of the Domestic Workplace' *Environment and Planning D: Society and Space* 8, 459–483.

Edwards, R. and Alldred, P. (1999) 'Children and Young People's View of Social Research: The Case of Home School Relations' *Childhood* 6 (2), 261–281.

Edwards, R. and David, M. (1997) 'Where are the Children in Home School Relations? Notes Towards a Research Agenda' *Children and Society* 11, 194–200.

Franklin, B. (1995) *The Handbook of Children's Rights* London: Routledge.

Gill, T. (1999) 'Play, Child Care and the Road to Adulthood' *Children and Society* 13, 67–69.

Gregson, N. and Lowe, M. (1995) '"Home" Making: On the Spatiality of Daily Social Reproduction in Contemporary Middle Class Britain' *Transactions of the Institute of British Geographers* 20, 224–235.

Holloway, S. (1998) 'Local Childcare Cultures: Moral Geographies of Mothering and the Social Organisation of Pre School Education' *Gender, Place and Culture* 5 (1), 29–53.

Holloway, S. (1999) 'Reproducing Motherhood', in Laurie, N., Dwyer, C., Holloway, S. and Smith, F.M. (eds) *Geographies of New Femininities* Harlow: Longman.

Holloway, S. and Valentine, G. (2000) 'Children's Geographies and the New Social Studies of Childhood', in Holloway, S.L. and Valentine, G. (eds) *Children's Geographies: Playing, Living, Learning* London: Routledge.

James, A. and Prout, A. (1996) 'Strategies and Structures: Towards a New Perspective on Children's Experiences of Family Life' in Brannen, J. and O'Brien, M. (eds) *Children in Families: Research and Policy* London: Falmer Press.

James, A., Jenks, C. and Prout, A. (1998) *Theorising Childhood* Cambridge: Polity Press.

Jones, M. and Cunningham, C. (1999) 'The Expanding Worlds of Middle Childhood', in Teather, E.K. (ed.) *Embodied Geographies: Spaces, Bodies and Rites of Passage* London: Routledge.

Katz, C. (1993) 'Growing Girls/Closing Circles: Limits on the Spaces of Knowing in Rural Sudan and US Cities', in Katz, C. and Monk, J. (eds) *Full Circles: Geographies of Women Over the Life Course* London: Routledge.

Katz, C. (1994) 'Textures of global changes: eroding ecologies of childhood in New York and Sudan' *Childhood: A Global Journal of Childhood Research* 2: 103–110.

Krenichyn, K. (1999) 'Messages About Adolescent Identity: Coded and Contested Spaces in a New York High School', in Teather, E.K. (ed.) *Embodied Geographies: Spaces, Bodies and Rites of Passage* London: Routledge.

Lansdown, G. (1995) *Taking Part, Children's Participation in Decision Making* London: Institute for Public Policy Research.

Laurie, N., Dwyer, C., Holloway, S. and Smith, F.M. (1999) *Geographies of New Femininities* Harlow: Longman.

Leslie, D. (1997) 'Femininity, Post-Fordism and the "New Traditionalism"', in McDowell, L. and Sharp, J. (eds) *Space, Gender, Knowledge: Feminist Readings* London: Arnold.

Matthews, H., Limb, M. and Taylor, M. (1998a) 'The Geography of Children: Some Ethical and Methodological Considerations for Project and Dissertation Work' *Journal of Geography in Higher Education* 22 (3), 311–324.

Matthews, H., Limb, M. and Taylor, M. (1998b) 'The Right to Say: the Development of Youth Councils/Forums in the UK' *Area* 30, 66–78.

Matthews, H. and Limb, M. (1999) 'Defining *An* Agenda for the Geography of Children: Review and Prospect' *Progress in Human Geography* 23 (1), 61–90.

Mayall, B. (1994a) *Negotiating Health: Primary School Children at Home and School* London: Cassell.

Mayall, B. (1994b) 'Children in Action at Home and at School', in Mayall, B. (ed.) *Children's Childhoods Observed and Experienced* London: Falmer Press.

Mayall, B. (1996) *Children, Health and the Social Order* Buckingam: Open University Press.

McKendrick, J., Fielder, A. and Bradford, M. (1999) 'Privatization of Collective Play Space in the UK' *Built Environment* 25 (1), 44–57.

McKendrick, J., Bradford, M.G. and Fielder, A.V. (2000) ' Time for a Party! Making Sense of the Commercialisation of Leisure Space for Children', in Holloway, S.L. and Valentine, G. (eds) *Children's Geographies: Playing, Living, Learning* London: Routledge.

NOF (1999) *Out of School Hours Childcare: Information for Applicants* London: New Opportunities Fund.

Petrie, P. (1994) *Play and Care, Out of School* London: HMSO.

Petrie, P. (1996) 'Standards, Regulation and Development of School-Age Day Care and "Open Door" Services' *Children and Society* 10, 225–235.

Richardson, D. (1993) *Women, Motherhood and Childrearing* London: Macmillan.

Robinson, J. (2000) 'Power as Friendship: Spatiality, Femininity and "Noisy Surveillance", in Sharp, J., Routledge, P., Philo, C. and Paddison, R. (eds) *Entanglements of Power: Geographies of Domination/Resistance* London: Routledge.

Robson, E. and Ansell, N. (2000) 'Young Carers in Southern Africa: Exploring Stories from Zimbabwean Secondary School Students', in Holloway, S.L. and Valentine, G. (eds) *Children's Geographies: Playing, Living, Learning* London: Routledge.

Rose, G. (1993) *Feminism and Geography: The Limits of Geographical Knowledge* Cambridge: Polity.

Sherman, A. (1997) 'Five Year Olds' Perceptions of Why We Go To School' *Children and Society* 11, 117–127.

Sibley, D. (1995) 'Families and Domestic Routines: Constructing the Boundaries of Childhood', in Pile, S. and Thrift, N. (eds) *Mapping the Subject: Geographies of Cultural Transformation* London: Routledge.

Smith, F. and Barker, J. (1999a) 'Learning to Listen: Involving Children in the Development of Out of School Care' *Youth and Policy* 63, 38–46.

Smith, F. and Barker, J. (1999b) 'From "Ninja Turtles" to "The Spice Girls": Children's Participation in the Development of Out of School Play Environments' *Built Environment* 25 (1), 35–43.

Smith, F. and Barker, J. (1999c) *Children Have Their Say: Children's Perspectives on Out of School Care* London: Kids' Clubs Network/Brunel University.

Smith, F. and Barker, J (2000a) '"Out of School", in School: A Social Geography of Out of School Childcare', in Holloway, S. and Valentine, G. (eds) *Children's Geographies: Living, Playing, Learning* London: Routledge.

Smith, F. and Barker, J. (2000b) *The Childcare Revolution: A Decade of Kids' Clubs* London: Kids' Clubs Network and Brunel University.

Smith, F. and Barker, J. (2000c) 'Contested Spaces: Children's Experiences of Out of School Care in England and Wales' *Childhood* 7 (3), 317–335.

Smith, R. (2000) 'Order and Disorder: The Contradictions of Childhood' *Children and Society* 14, 3–10.

Stables, J. and Smith, F. (2000) '"Caught in the Cinderella trap": Narratives of Disabled Parents and Young Carers', in Butler, R. and Parr, H. (eds) *Geographies of Disability* London: Routledge.

Statham, J., Dillion, J. and Moss, P. (2000) 'Sponsored Day Care in a Changing World' *Children and Society* 14, 23–26.

Thomson, S. (1999) 'Pupil's Playgrounds or Adults' Territory?' *Mind the Gap! Changing Boundaries of Childhood in the 1990s* Conference, Leicester University, 8 September.

Valentine, G. (1997) '"Oh Yes I Can." "Oh No You Can't.": Children and Parents' Understanding of Kids' Competence to Negotiate Public Space Safely' *Antipode* 29 (1), 65–89.

Wyness, M. (1999) 'Childhood, Agency and Education Reform' *Childhood* 6, (3), 353–368.

4 Portrait of Callum

The disabling of a childhood?

Mairian Corker and John Davis

INTRODUCTION

Within the 'new' sociology of childhood, there is an increasing emphasis on children as individuated social actors who have rights in relation to their parents and their home lives and, to a lesser extent, as 'pupils' and 'users' of organised services, and who can reflexively shape their selves. Home and school are often characterised as having crucial roles in producing children's individuated autonomous personhood. However, though mainstream accounts of childhood and children's lives acknowledge that childhood is socially, culturally and historically variable, there is in general a widespread neglect of approaches that integrate the experiences of disabled children *within* mainstream accounts. This reflects the tendency to position disabled childhoods and disabled children differently, in relation to other children, the family, and in relation to the structure as a whole (Priestley, 1998b), feeding into what James, Jenks and Prout (1998: 201) call 'the structural account' of childhood sociology. This presents polarised views of children as being 'relatively passive in respect of making the social', and of structure as 'a set of objective and external conditions which determines the conduct of societal members as they enter into different relationships or groups'.

Because it is disability, rather than disabled childhood, that ultimately defines this different position, accounts of disabled children's lives also tend to be depersonalised within the structural account and reduced to 'objective' structures. This is one result of the study of disability being very much dominated by the paradigms of medicine, science, 'special' education, the law, and psychology – paradigms that collectively constitute the *individual and medical models of disability*. These paradigms represent disabled children as deviant, (un)natural, passive, incompetent, and impaired – as what they lack rather than who they are. In order to counteract depersonalisation and objectification, disabled people and their organisations have concentrated on developing an oppositional body of knowledge and practice that views *disability*, like childhood, as socially, culturally and historically variable (Barnes, Mercer and Shakespeare, 1999). Disability is distinguished from accredited or perceived *impairment*, or 'physical difference', which itself becomes the focus for disabling practice. This alternative understanding of disability – *the social model of disability* – also incorporates the promotion of 'positive' representations of disabled people, or, as disabled feminist Jenny Morris writes, it uses 'pride against prejudice' (Morris, 1991). The social model places 'choice' in opposition to the 'control' that is seen to be characteristic of the individual/medical models, and in terms of outcomes, is focused on 'social action' and 'collective identity' whereas that of the individual/medical models emphasise 'individual treatment' and 'individual identity' (Oliver, 1996: 34).

These different accounts of disability highlight a number of issues. First, the social model and the individual/medical models, along with their different representations of disabled people and their visions of 'society', are in struggle in a climate where the latter continue to be privileged in social process. Second, and by corollary, this means that the relationship between them has to be conceptualised in terms of regulation or power and autonomy or resistance. As forms of social action that exist in a social relation with each other, both the exercise of regulation and of autonomy involve agency, and agency can manifest itself, for example, in transformative or consensual social practice. The 'regulated child' and the 'autonomous child'[1] can be seen as two possible *outcomes* of the struggle between these agencies, which in turn, and irrespective of impairment, directly impinge on the experience of disability.

In the UK, all of these issues impact on educational policy and practice relating to disabled children. 'Special' educational policy and practice hinges on the assessment of disabled children's *individual needs* in terms of school placement, curriculum and teaching practice and in relation to the aetiology *of their impairment*. This process of assessment, which is called 'statementing' in England and Wales and 'recording' in Scotland, begins from the moment impairment is diagnosed. In spite of this early emphasis on impairment, it is government policy that disabled children's needs should be met in mainstream schools 'wherever possible'. However, as mainstream education continues to debate the age at which 'formal' education should begin, it is often forgotten that disabled children have always experienced early intervention from educational and medical professionals, and this spans both public and private settings such as the home. Further, it is a 'fundamental principle' of the Department for Education and Employment's draft 'SEN Code of Practice' (2000), currently the subject of consultation, that 'parents have a vital role to play in supporting their child's education' (paragraph 1.3).[2] The Code of Practice also suggests that 'critical success factors' (1.4) in whether or not its fundamental principles are upheld can be found at different levels of the social and educational structure. The emphasis on individual needs is retained in the view that 'special education professionals [should] work in partnership with parents and take into account the views of individual parents in respect of their child's particular needs'. But we can begin to see the emergence of the social model in the statement that 'the culture, practice, management and deployment of resources in school or setting should be designed to ensure all children's needs are met'. However, the most common form of guidance takes a middle line between the two. For example, the statement 'those responsible for special educational provision should take into account the wishes of the child concerned, in the light of their age and understanding' alludes to children's choices but also leaves the door open to particular stereotypes about the competency of disabled children to make those choices.

This is important when we consider that though these 'principles' and 'critical success factors' are meant to drive how policy is put into practice, the document insists that there is scope for 'flexibility and variation in the responses adopted by schools, early education settings and LEAs' (1.5). In this chapter, we show how such flexibility can create tensions between 'individual' and 'social' understandings of policy and practice, when individual perspectives remain the dominant ideology in the manufacture of inequality. The chapter is based on a one year, detailed ethnographic study of a 14 year old deaf boy, whom we call Callum,[3] which is extracted from a larger study of disabled children that sought to examine their lives in a variety of contexts that included home and school.[4] During the study period, we had the opportunity to observe and interact with Callum on his own, with his peers (both deaf and hearing), with his parents and with a number of professionals. Through this, we were able to build a *multi-voiced account* of Callum's life that is rich in both contested and common positions. However, bullying was identified as an important theme. We were therefore particularly concerned with learning how the relationship between autonomy and regulation changed with respect to Callum's experience of bullying in different social settings and spaces, and at different times, and how the voices of other 'actors' were implicated in this relationship. A significant factor in this change was that during the time we spent with him, Callum was additionally labelled as having Attention Deficit Hyperactivity Disorder (ADHD). He was subsequently prescribed the drug Ritalin, an amphetamine type drug that is known to influence children's agency negatively. Callum's story, for us, raises significant questions about the emergence of ADHD as 'the disability of the twenty-first Century' and about policy and practice which seeks to label and regulate 'different' children who challenge the structures and cultures of 'special' education and 'able' parenting.

THE MULTI-VOICED ACCOUNT

As noted above, we have chosen to present Callum's story as a multi-voiced account, the cast of actors for which is given in Table 4.1. This choice was made because our involvement in the research process made us both acutely aware of how our own positions and interests, together with our own knowledge and lack of knowledge, could be imposed at all stages of the research (Corker and Davis, 2002, forthcoming). As a number of feminist writers have indicated, this at best risked distorting the data, at worst risked reducing it to a reflection of our authority and world-views (Harding, 1991; Smith, 1998). Offering the reader a number of perspectives in the final text has a number of advantages. First, it is an important way of both liberating the many voices of the researched (Corker, 1999) and of dispersing the researcher's authority (Davis, 2000). Second, multi-voiced accounts enable the reader to see how social relations are constructed, how particular social values become disabling, and how particular discourses become associated with cultural patterns of power and access (van Dijk, 1996) and the distribution of social and material resources (Gee, 1990). In other words, as Callum's mother interestingly puts it:

> The department that Callum goes to in his present school is not called a hearing-impaired unit. If it gets the word unit then it has to be extra funded. It's not called a unit … it's called hearing-impaired facilities (laughs). What the difference is I don't know, but that's, that's … that's the script.

Table 4.1 The cast of actors

Callum	14 years old, 'deaf', communicates orally.
Callum's family	HOME
Margaret	Callum's mother; has part time job
Peter	Callum's father; works full time
	(Callum also has two older siblings and a number of pets)
Callum's peers	SCHOOL
Ricky	'The best friend'; 'emotional-behavioural difficulties' (EBD); (mainstream – M)
Mike	'The chief bully'; 'dyslexia' and 'EBD' (M)
Nora	'The ally'; 'deaf'; ('special' unit – U & M)
Gill, Melissa and Kate	'The unit bunch'; 'learning difficulties' (U & M)
Andy, Jimmy	'Bullies'; not disabled (M)
Professionals	SCHOOL
Isobel	'The minder'; specialist teacher (U & M)
Janet	'The sympathetic adult'; specialist teacher (U & M)
Rob	Mainstream teacher
Reported voices	THE BACKDROP
Doctor X	'The American psychologist'
The mass media	'The Ritalin frenzy'
The researchers	BETWEEN HOME AND SCHOOL
Mairian	Deaf; feminist disability studies scholar; interest in language
John	Hearing; anthropologist; interest in children and sport

In this way, such accounts have the potential to create a bridge between 'micro-analysis' (Prout and James, 1990) or the worm's eye view, and macroanalysis (Qvortrup, 2000), or the bird's eye view. They help us to examine local structuration processes as well as some of the mutually constitutive relationships between 'situated activity' and, for example, 'demographic facts' (Giddens, 1976). Third, multi-voiced accounts incorporate a recognition that communication is not always direct and is a multi-layered patchwork of voices and silences. It is therefore important to read social interaction reflexively (Davis, Watson and Cunningham-Burley, 2000; Davis, 2000; Davis and Corker, 2002, forthcoming), and to interpret it intertextually (Kristeva, 1986) and over time. On a practical level, what this means is that, for example, when we interview someone, asking particular questions may invoke silence *in the interview context*, but the silence may be filled in a different context and in a different way at some other time. Equally, we may make intuitive observations in fieldwork that we interpret 'on the spot' from within our own world-view. Intertexual readings then help us to identify which interpretations are closest to and most distinct from the interpretations of those with whom we do research, and to build in prospective and retrospective commentary from the socially situated lives of local participants. In focusing on Callum's 'voices' and 'choices' over time and context, we want to show how multi-voiced accounts can yield significant information about how social change and transformation are or can be effected.

Portrait of Callum

This section initially presents a chronological set of 'snapshots' of social interaction and researcher observation in different contexts, both social and geographical. At this stage, we aim to encourage readers to read these snapshots intertextually, and to ask themselves what each snapshot tells us about autonomy and regulation as they relate to Callum's experience of bullying before and after he acquires the ADHD label. Researcher observations (fieldnotes) were either hand-written or typed contemporaneously into a small, hand-held computer. Social interaction was recorded on audio-tape and transcribed later by one of the project administrators in a way that retained the local dialects used by children and adults. Where colloquialisms are used, however, we have inserted an interpretation in italic type after the first usage. We have included examples from naturally occurring interaction that took place during periods of participant observation and from semi-structured or unstructured interviews.

April, School

A1 John's fieldnotes, Monday a.m., support unit

Mairian:	Is it (the support you get) OK?
Callum:	Aye … makes it easier
Mairian:	What about other kids?
Callum:	Nut they always shout at me an' that
Nora:	He gets a slagging *(criticised, insulted).*
Mairian:	What about you … do the other kids talk to you?
Nora:	Uhuh
Mairian:	Do you feel the same as Callum?
Nora:	Sometimes …

A2 John's fieldnotes, Tuesday, mainstream art class

Callum's told us he 'doesn't like art'. Rob (who is more interested in what we are saying than in what's happening in the class) thinks social integration works well, but not academic – at least in his class. [Is he against integration?] /…/

Callum has had his hand up for help for ages, and eventually Rob gets to him … Callum is baiting Andy by saying 'Punch me right now' – heckles Rob 'I'll get yi detention', and Jimmy says watch this and Callum punches. As he punches, both boys grass Callum up for kicking the table – what was friendly has become out of hand. /…/

Callum complains because Jimmy is trying to blow on his paper 'Jimmy stop it,' he says and tells Rob. But Rob tells Callum he'll be through next door in a minute if he doesn't watch it. Then Callum says to Jimmy 'Your face is gonny go through the window if you don't stop it – ye shite *(expression of contempt, like 'You piece of shit')* ye.' … Callum starts to complain to Jimmy again but Rob overhears him and chucks him out.

John: Why did Callum get sent out?

Andy: He was shoutin' and all that. (They're both smiling a lot – sort of
           victorious)

John: Did he deserve to? (they smile even more)

Boys: Yeah

John: Are you sure you never got him chucked out?

Boys: Nut *(Not likely)* (still smiling)

Rob says he feels Callum works better when he's isolated

Andy goes over and baits Callum a wee bit I can hear Callum saying 'Go
away' but Rob does nothing – rather surprising, because Rob has told us before
that you have to treat them all the same – no exceptions as it's not fair and also
you'd lose control eventually.

A3 John's fieldnotes, Tuesday p.m., support unit

Kate is really down. Callum's no help as he winds her up by saying to Isobel
'Why are you doing her work for her?' and Kate says to the teacher 'He's always
slagging me off and you don't do anything about it' … 'You're always blabbing
ba ba ba ba ba.' Nora who knows we are watching tells Callum to be quiet and
gives me a knowing look. Earlier Callum said to the teacher 'You've told us that
100 million times' and looked pointedly at me.

June, on a school trip

J1 John's fieldnotes, early Tuesday a.m.

Isobel tells me (in full earshot of the other kids) Callum was 'very lucky' to have
been seen by an American clinical psychologist, Dr. X … he was asked by the
school's psychologist to assess Callum. And he said that he has ADHD … Now
she's saying that yesterday Callum said, 'Look at all the ducks in the field'. But
they were actually cows. And so he got a bit of a slagging.

The children are now talking about Callum's mistake yesterday, about the
duck (Mairian: Again, they've overheard what Isobel said – is there no privacy?).
When it comes to the crunch, Ricky abandons Callum, and joins in. Isobel
takes this opportunity to intervene. Says, 'Ricky can you pick on someone else?'
It's not that she says stop it or it's completely unacceptable to slag them off. She
says, 'Can you pick on somebody else?' Then Gill says, 'Ricky, why don't you
slag yourself for a change?'

J2 Mairian's fieldnotes, Tuesday lunch-time

My feeling about Callum was that how at peace with himself he seems to be
today. He was very observant. I remember particularly for example, when we
were walking up to the place where the competition was, Callum had passed a

stall which had some peace plants outside and he noticed them, and the size of the flowers, which was exactly what was in my head at the time – it felt like a sort of bond between us. There was nothing really spoken. It was under the surface, but it was there. I also noticed Callum was interested in his surroundings … but Isobel keeps calling him into line and telling him to 'pay attention' to what she's saying … I think he wants to be on his own sometimes – to put space between himself and hearing people and to get away from the buzz, noise and irritation of them interrupting his thoughts all the time – so that he would give himself the opportunity to really take in what was going on round about him, as if it was very important to do that. I think that he's got this diagnostic label stuck on him – it changes some people's attitudes towards him, and he simply isn't getting enough stimulation from in school.

J3 John's fieldnotes, Tuesday lunch-time

Janet tells me that Callum since his diagnosis is going to be put on Ritalin and that she thinks that it's a disgrace. I tell her about my work in special schools and about the behaviour thing being a label and she says, 'Yeah, a girl came to us from a special school to us a while back. It took us two years to you know socially integrate her, to break the learned behaviour. It wasn't that there was anything wrong with her it was just that she hadn't had the possibilities to see how she might behave … In Callum's case it's really frustrating because he's not allowed to do CDT … and it's his favourite subject. Our school can't offer him what he needs and then they wonder why he goes crazy. And their answer's just to dope him up. Next they'll be saying that they have to move him to a special school because he can't function'

J4 Transcript of audiotaped discussion, Wednesday afternoon, on country walk.

37. *John:*   … [Your Mum] said it would keep you out of trouble. What did she mean?
38. *Callum:* Because I always fight and aw that.
39. *John:*   With the kids at [school]?
40. *Ricky:*   He always does.
41. *John:*   Have you got any friends at [school]?
42. *Callum:* Nup *(not only)*, … no really.
43. *John:*   No really.
44. *Ricky:*   He's only got me.
45. *John:*   So how … does it … kick off? What starts it?
46. *Callum:* [still referring to previous question] Am no bothered.
47. *John:*   But do you go out and play? Do some of the kids come up and hassle you or what?
48. *Callum:* Well like. They call me, like, geekie and all that. And ah just get sick o' it and ah just start ba'erin' them and then ah get inti trouble.

 49. *John:*   And how old are these kids?
 50. *Ricky:*   Same age as him.
 51. *Callum:*   Nup, younger. Right, there's a laddie that stays next door ti me that's only, say nine. And he makes faces and aw that.
 52. *John:*   And do they annoy anybody else?
 53. *Callum:*   Nup, they just always annoy me. /.../
 97. *John:*   Did they tell you why (you couldn't take CDT) Cal?
 98. *Callum:*   Well they thought because ah couldnae put em, use like the drills and things right, because mebbe ah might put ma fingers or somethin' and get it drilled.
 99. *John:*   But do you think that's the case? Has that happened before?
100. *Callum:*   Nup. It's just 'cause ah might of em hurt maself or something.
101. *John:*   Aha. Do you think that's a good reason?
102. *Callum:*   No.
103. *John:*   Do you think that's a oh? Do you think it's a true reason?
104. *Callum:*   Probably, yeah.
105. *John:*   Probably yeah. What about at home? Do you do anything with tools at home?
106. *Callum:*   Aye, right ah make things, like maybe climbin', you know the climbin' frame things?
107. *John:*   Yeah.
108. *Callum:*   Ah can make thaim.
109. *John:*   And what sort o' tools d'you use?
110. *Callum:*   Like saw and …
111. *John:*   Aha. Is it spanners and screwdrivers and all sorts?
112. *Callum:*   Yeah. A fix ma bike maself as well.
113. *John:*   And do you? Do you hurt yourself when you do that?
114. *Callum:*   Nup.
115. *John:*   So do you think? Do you think that?
116. *Callum:*   Ah 'tink it's no fair because ah didnae get ti dae it there. Ma mum said she does not want me goin' to another school to do craft and design. She said I've … I'm doing craft and design, 'He is doing it in this school'.
117. *John:*   So is that yet to be sorted oot then? Is she going to complain?
118. *Callum:*   Aye. Ma mum's gonni get it sorted oot before the summer holiday.

September, School (Callum is now taking Ritalin)

S1 John's field notes, Monday

Isobel tells us that Ricky's not part of Callum's gang now and says that now Callum's on Ritalin its 'not his fault' – it's other children winding him up. She tells us that Ricky's involved in Mike's gang though he had actually grassed Mike up when Isobel asked him what was happening. She says the children don't realise that Callum's changed.

S2 *Transcription of audiotaped conversation,* **Monday**

23. *Mairian:* Has Mike changed then?
24. *Callum:* He's done it since he came here, an he done it in his old school and now he's started it here. A wis just going into second year when he came …
25. *Mairian:* Has he hurt you before?
26. *Callum:* Aye he's punched me and kicked me
27. *John:* Does he have problems?
28. *Callum:* He doesna take anything, but he will no get away with it (diverts) Ma nose is all chipped wi breaking the concrete (referring to the job he's doing).
29. *John:* Is there children who take medicine?
30. *Callum:* Yeah to help 'em an that – cause ti keep them calm … Av started talking medicine.
31. *John:* How did that come about … medicine … do you know what it's called?
32. *Callum:* Nut
33. *Mairian:* How does it make you feel?
34. *Callum:* Eh … it keeps me calm – if a dinnae eat anything – then am sick. So av got to eat something (diverts) … We get Monday and Tuesday off next week
35. *Mairian:* (bringing him back) Before did you not feel calm?
36. *Callum:* Oh yeah, … a felt a wis goin' up and doon
37. *Mairian:* When we went [on school trip] last term … remember you seemed to go off to feel calm. Did you do that before?
38. *Callum:* Yeah sometimes …
39. *John:* Who was it … GP? Your Mum, the school … who said that?
40. *Callum:* It was ma Mum … she discovered a wis getting angry … am fine now cus av got a job … a work five to eight /…/
69. *Mairian:* What about your friend Ricky?
70. [Callum's face changes … he looks really angry]
71. *John:* A suspected Ricky had mebbe been lying …
72. *Callum:* No … a fell out wi him, am not friends wi him and a never will go back to being friends wi him.
73. *John:* What happened?
74. *Callum:* Well it's cos he was sticking up for Mike. Ricky wouldnae come near me again cause he's feared o me.
75. *John:* Did you fight him?
76. *Callum:* He had punched me and kicked me, so a got really angry and a just battered him and he went straight down to the ground, so he never comes near me now cos he's feared. He used to come near me before the summer holidays but not now.
77. *Mairian:* Does he go near Mike?
78. *Callum:* They get a big gang and follow me about.

79. *John:*　　What are they saying?
80. *Callum:*　A wis off all last week … because they just grabbed me and then [Isobel] … a wis scared to tell anyone, and [Isobel] said to Mike did you do that to Callum so he said no and she said 'Mike you're a liar you don't know how to tell the truth. [Isobel] phoned his Mum and then went to the Head. Nothing very much got done by the Head and nothing is gonny get done – I could press charges if nothing is done by Christmas holidays – a could make a statement eh?
81. *Mairian:*　Why do you think they pick on you?
82. *Callum:*　A lot of reasons … but they pick on everyone …

S3 Mairian's fieldnotes, Tuesday

Isobel thinks Callum's really coming on and that 'that boy is not stupid he really is intelligent … what a change'. John looks frustrated but doesn't want to alienate Isobel. He says 'Yeah but I have to say I'm not for the Ritalin … a'm really against drugs being used with children especially as in America it is used as an excuse to not put in proper funding to support children. I like the change that the drug has induced to some extent but I believe it could have been achieved socially.' Isobel responds, 'Yeah and there is a problem there with his social side because he has really matured on this drug and is actually moving away from his other friends but that means he is quite isolated'.

March, the following year, at Callum's home

(Callum is still taking Ritalin and has been moved to a different mainstream school)

M1 Transcript of audiotaped interview with Callum's parents, in Callum's presence

225. *John:*　　… just to get back to what you were saying about the bullying as well. So you found that basically there was safety in numbers.
226. *Margaret:*　Yeah, I think I think … no. I don't actually think it was safety in numbers. I think it was more a case of … well maybe it was … I think there was plenty staff to look out for them as well.
227. *John:*　　Oh right, yeah.
228. *Peter:*　　Oh aye, before we actually sent Callum to (his old school), the psychologist said that … (his old school) is too highly academic, you know, eh basically. And I'm saying to myself, but just because somebody's deaf doesn't mean they're stupid you know.
229. *Margaret:*　It's really annoying.
230. *Peter:*　　… And I mean I know quite a lot of people that are deaf who are totally deaf, and can't speak. I mean I've known them from I was like thon size. So I mean they're not stupid. They're quite clever.

231.	*John*:	(to Mairian) … We meet this on a daily basis in our work, don't we? … We see it everywhere we go. Is the children's ability not being recognised?
232.	*Margaret*:	… Isobel was one of the originals, and she always … she would fight. You know … she would really get into a verbal argument if she felt her children were being you know undermined.
233.	*John*:	Weren't getting their best, yeah.
234.	*Mairian*:	Well can I just quickly sort of get in there. When you used the phrase 'her children', how …
235.	*Margaret*:	That's how she looked at them.
236.	*Mairian*:	How do you actually feel about that?
237.	*Margaret*:	I, I was really. I felt that was. I felt I, my boy was going to school and I knew he'd be safe. It was like. Every mother's the same. You never think anybody else can look after your child as well as you can. Well I knew with Isobel that was different. You know, if there was trouble I knew she was there. I could phone. Now this is a thing you won't often find. I could phone Isobel at home and she was quite happy to sit and talk to me on the phone. And we become really good friends you know. And there was none more upset than Isobel at losing Callum, simply. Well to a degree I think she felt that we were helping the department to give up the unit … we probably did play right into the department's hands …

M2 *Transcript of audio-taped interview with Callum in the presence of his parents (at his request)*

378.	*Mairian*:	… if there's one room in the house where you want to go sometimes. When you're on your own would you go to your bedroom?
379.	*Callum*:	Aye.
380.	*Mairian*:	Why … why's that? Why is this important to you?
381.	*Callum*:	Because a need peace and quiet …
382.	*John*:	I'm interested in when he said I need peace and quiet. What … what happens if you don't get peace and quiet?
383.	*Callum*:	Mmm?
384.	*John*:	What happens if you don't get peace and quiet?
385.	*Callum*:	Em just be silly.
386.	*John*:	Is that right. So it's a kind of calming.
387.	*Callum*:	I like to keep myself calm. /…/
401.	*Mairian*:	What I'm wondering is now you've got somewhere you can go, when you want peace and you want to be by yourself. What happens when … you're at school and you feel you need peace and want to be by yourself? What do you do then?
402.	*Callum*:	I ask the teacher.
403.	*John*:	And where, where do you go?

404.	*Callum:*	Well there's a wee room that's getting done.
405.	*John:*	Uh-huh.
406.	*Callum:*	Yeah. Where other children go to get …
407.	*John:*	… where other children
408.	*Callum:*	… so they can get peace and quiet.

DISCUSSION

On reflection, we are conscious of the 'quietness' of Callum's voice and the way in which it is often drowned by the 'loudness' of the voices around him unless he asserts himself. However, in April and June, Callum demonstrates inquisitiveness (J2), mischievousness (A3), challenging behaviour (A2) and awareness (J2, J4). This was reflected in his interest in his surroundings (J2), and his desire to engage with John in particular (A3, J4), which we attributed to the fact that Callum's adult environment, and often his peer environment, was predominantly female. Indeed, if Ricky had not come on the school trip in June, Callum would have been the only male apart from John. There is no doubt, however, that Callum's reflexivity diminished after he was given Ritalin. His apparent willingness to allow adults to assume responsibility for his voice correspondingly increased the amount of time he spent with his adult 'minders' (Margaret's word), at least one of whom (Isobel) saw him as having 'matured on the drug' (S3). In September, his responses, when he gave them, seemed more ritualised, less considered and lacking in agency. In our final meeting, he wasn't really with us at all – his voice was almost monosyllabic. The reduction in Callum's agency coincided with him moving from being 'one of the crowd', jockeying for attention with his peers, to a position of isolation from his peers, including his 'only' friend Ricky (J4, S2).

Transcripts A1, A2, J1 and J4, in different ways, suggest that 'slaggin' and 'ba'erin' are very much part of the discourse, and often the social practice of Callum's peer group at both school and in his local neighbourhood. Though Callum initially feels that the bullies single him out (J4), he then says they 'pick on everyone' (S2). However, elsewhere, Callum implies that this neighbourhood bullying is usually related to his deafness, but how he is implicated in the social practice of bullying in school changes over time. From the moment we first meet him there are references to his being bullied (A1), but we frequently observe him giving as good as he gets both in terms of what he says (A2, A3, J4) and in terms of what he does (A2, S2). It is nevertheless clear that Rob, for example, singles out Callum's behaviour as 'deviant', and divorces it from its cultural roots. He then justifies Callum's exclusion by claiming that 'Callum works better when he's isolated' (A2), whilst failing to tackle the provocative behaviour of Callum's peer group. This is reinforced when Rob fails to intervene as Andy tries to bait Callum even after he has been excluded.

It is important, also, to link these episodes to Callum's observed and expressed need for 'peace and quiet' (J2, M2). While it may be that Rob is correct in his assessment of the effects of isolation, Callum's need for peace and quiet is too often shattered by the taunting he receives from his peer group and the demands of adults that he 'pays attention'. At the same time, when he does demonstrate agency, his peers label this as 'slagging' (A3) and adults suggest he's showing off. This has to be understood in the context that for most deaf people, listening and paying attention are never 'passive' and the constant mental activity required demands private space from time to time. Callum's story suggests that this space is often not available, and so has to be claimed. In this context, we note that there are many ways in which Mairian's voice is similarly silent and often reduced to reflexive observations, and that she and Callum make connections on a non–verbal level, for example in shared notions of the value of 'peace and quiet'.

The sea of voices in which Callum is submerged contain both discourses of regulation and of autonomy, but the power of the former is very evident when we look at the patterning of these discourses and how they seem to be reflected in Callum's responses at different times. For example, Margaret emphasises safety, implying that she sees Isobel as someone who 'can look after' and 'fight for' Callum, and talking about how upset Isobel was about 'losing Callum' when he moved schools. She doesn't object to Isobel referring to Callum as one of 'her children', and in describing Isobel as a 'friend' she indicates closeness, whilst blurring the boundaries between home and school (M1). Callum also indicates a similarity between his mother and Isobel when he describes them, on separate occasions, as being the ones who 'sort it out' (J4, S2). This ties in with Margaret's understanding of 'safety' as a function of the number of adults that are there to 'look after' Callum (M1), rather than as a function of the anonymity of the peer group. Neither Margaret nor Isobel question these regulatory adult structures (J1, S2, M1), though Margaret's 'closeness' to Isobel is tempered by her suspicion that Isobel's disappointment at Callum's departure is more linked to 'helping the department to give up the unit' (M1).

On the other hand, Janet (J3) and Peter (M1) tend to emphasise Callum's autonomy, arguing 'for' the development of his ability at CDT in spite of its perceived risks, for example, and rather less 'for' a focus on the regulation of his environment so that the risk elements are removed. Though Callum initially refers to regulation as being 'no' fair' (J4), and his attitude towards adults 'sorting it out' is more neutral (J4), he later makes an implicit association between Mike's problems and the fact that 'he doesna take anything' (S2). It is interesting to consider whose perceptions of Ritalin he is reflecting here. Though there are marked differences in the emotional loading of Margaret's and Isobel's accounts of the ADHD issue, Margaret demonstrates desperation, whereas Isobel publicly announces that she thinks Callum is 'lucky' to have found a solution to his 'problems' in the diagnosis of ADHD (J1). Only Janet (J3) and John (S3) express opposition to the use of Ritalin.

CONCLUSION

It has often been assumed in studies of children and childhood that 'home' and 'school' are themselves relatively autonomous in the ways in which they influence children's lives and shape childhood. Thus, though young people perceive 'home' and 'school' as distinct environments, and clearly differentiate the roles of 'teacher' and 'parent', adult roles are also viewed collectively in terms the balance they strike between regulation or discipline and autonomy or 'freedom'. We would refer to this balance as 'the dignity of risk'. This term has been used elsewhere in connection with the oppressive principle of 'normalisation' (Perske, 1972). However we take a different view of 'risk' here, one that sees risk as an increasingly salient feature of late modern society and its institutions (including education). This brings people into more active engagement with aspects of their lives, aspects that were previously the terrain of tradition of taken-for-granted norms (Beck, 1992). 'Risk' includes disability, and whereas non-disabled children have been/are subjected to risk on a fluid basis, disabled children are considered risky *per se*. This means that autonomy can itself be a measure of the individual's ability to deal with risk, which has important implications for children growing up in a risky world. Further, as government policy increasingly highlights parental involvement and visibility in schools, as reading or classroom assistants and parent governors, for example, and 'parent–professional partnerships', the relationship between home and school is destabilised, less predictable and more risky.

This relationship might now be characterised in terms of both the publicisation of private life and the breakdown of the social anonymity of childhood in school. We use the term 'anonymity' here because we view adolescence in terms of two parallel trends. It is clearly a time when young people are testing the water of 'special' relationships as they strike out for personal autonomy and individualisation. At the same time, there is a drive to be part of the anonymity of collective sameness – to be 'one of the crowd' – and this is socially enacted in what young people wear, the music they listen to, and so on. In this way, there is probably an element of all childhoods that is 'tribal' (James *et al.*, 1998). However, as was suggested in the introduction, the publicisation of private life has *always* been a constitutive feature of disabled childhoods. Disabled children and their parents become the objects of scrutiny and surveillance from the moment impairment is identified, and identification leads to separation in terms of policy and practice, irrespective of grand claims to inclusion. In this sense, the 'culture' of 'special' education is very much representative of a 'closed society' and, as Kirchhöfer (1998: 227) notes, 'the private space closes its doors to public behaviour in an open society, whereas in the closed society the private space leaves the door open to public behaviour'. Moreover, a visible impairment can act as a barrier to anonymity, and this reduces the availability of private space still further.

Thus, with one important exception, what this account demonstrates is a high level of continuity and cohesion between 'home' and 'school' particularly in the kinds of knowledge that are and are not in circulation. The exception, as we saw above, concerns Callum's exclusion from CDT at school on 'safety' grounds – part of the school's practice of structural regulation – when he clearly engages successfully in similar activities at home. This may be an example of teachers' fear of litigation resulting in their erecting barriers to inclusion (Davis and Watson, 2001). Importantly, continuity extends to perceptions of ADHD and the use of Ritalin. It is probable that ADHD has always been around, but it is certainly only in the last decade that it has been named. We cannot say whether this 'naming' has stimulated the huge increase in its identification, but what concerns us about Callum's story is that there are some forms of knowledge that have not reached 'home' or 'school'.

For example, Hindley and Kroll (1998: 65) note, citing Barkley's (1990) analysis of characteristic behaviours associated with ADHD, that clinicians should be cautious about using the hyperactivity disorder construct *with deaf children*. In particular it seems likely that the mechanisms Barkley describes 'can apply to deaf children in hearing families but as a consequence of language and communication differences and parental constructs of the child (Marschark, 1993) rather than as a biological disorder.' They continue:

> Apart from differences in diagnostic systems, the training of British child psy-chiatrists appears to place a greater emphasis on social and psychological aspects of child mental health than that of their North American colleagues and so, indirectly, discourages the use of medical diagnoses. However an increasing number of British clinicians, particularly pediatricians, are using DSM-IV as a guide and making the diagnosis of ADHD. More importantly, more parents are aware of the condition, so there is increasing pressure to diagnose and medically treat hyperactivity disorders in Britain.
>
> (Hindley and Kroll, 1998: 65)

To this, we would want to add, and to emphasise again, that we need to understand *how* parents become aware of the condition and whether this influences them to act in particular ways. We are aware, for example, that Margaret and Peter had been following the deeply polarised debates – the 'Ritalin frenzy' – in the national media. We would not want to diminish the struggles that families go through when faced with children who behave in difficult and unpredictable ways, nor do we want to point the finger of blame. However, as researchers working within a social model perspective, we were faced with the ethical problem of knowing that decisions were made on the basis of partial knowledge, and often driven by the dominant discourses and structures of the medical model. Further, it was clear that our interventions, like Janet's and Peter's, had little influence on these discourses and structures and this was the source of a great deal of frustration to us.

The advantage of the multi-voiced, temporal account we have presented here is that it shows that it is dangerous to fix our judgements in time and space. But we do want to point out the incongruity between an adult culture that on one hand so readily resorts to pharmaceutical solutions whilst, on the other, attempts to regulate children's autonomy in reaching out for their own solutions. Children's solutions, it has to be said, range from a need for 'peace and quiet' to their own substantially more risky pharmaceutical solutions such as Ecstasy. But because children's solutions are so often regulated, adults risk sending out very confusing messages. We feel that this 'Portrait of Callum' shows how the regulation of risk is implicated in the disabling of Callum's childhood, and this is compounded by the regulatory desire to maintain his dependency on adult solutions through a systemic cohesion that embraces home and school. As a disabled child, he is more likely to be seen to need protection from risk and to be incapable of autonomy. In the instability of the 'risk society', childhoods are changing in ways that require children to act unpredictably. Children constantly tell us this and ask us, as researchers, to be their advocates, but we remain on the horns of an ethical dilemma because policy-makers and practitioners, for the most part, fail to listen.

NOTES

1 We are aware of James *et al.'s* (1998: 206) helpful description of four 'new' discourses of childhood, which make the distinction between the 'socially constructed child', 'the social structural child', 'the tribal child' and the 'minority group child'. Though the frameworks and emphases are slightly different, there are some similarities between these discourses and the 'positions' described by Priestley (1998a) in relation to disability (Priestley works his framework around the four theoretical dimensions of materialism, idealism, individualism and collectivism).
2 This document refers to England and Wales. However, the points referred to in the ensuing discussion, and parents and children's participation are also embedded in Scottish legislation and guidance.
3 All names of people and places in this account have been changed in order to protect the identities of the researched.
4 This study was part of the *Lives of Disabled Children* project, a two year research project, co-ordinated by staff from the Universities of Edinburgh and Leeds. The project was funded by the Economic and Social Research Council's *Childhood 5–16 Programme* (award number L129251047).

REFERENCES

Barkley, R.A. (1990) *Attention Deficit Hyperactivity Disorder: A Handbook for Diagnosis and Treatment*. New York: Guildford Press.

Barnes, C., Mercer, G. and Shakespeare, T. (1999) *Exploring Disability: A Sociological Introduction*. Cambridge: Polity.

Beck, U. (1992) *Risk Society: Towards a New Modernity*. London: Sage.

Chouliarki, L. and Fairclough, N. (1999) *Discourse in Late Modernity*. Edinburgh: Edinburgh University Press.

Corker, M. (1999) 'New disability discourse, the principle of optimisation, and social change', in M. Corker and S. French (eds) *Disability Discourse*. Buckingham: Open University Press, 192–209.

Corker, M. and Davis, J.M. (2002, forthcoming) 'Shifting selves, shifting meanings, learning culture: Towards a reflexive dialogics in disability research', in D. Kasnitz and R. Shuttleworth (eds) *Engaging Anthropoligy and Disability Studies*. Berkeley: University of California Press.

Davis, J.M. (2000) 'Disability studies as ethnographic research and text: research strategies and roles for promoting social change'. *Disability & Society*, Vol. 15., No. 2, 191–206.

Davis, J.M. and Watson, N. (2001) 'Where are the children's experiences? Analysing social and cultural exclusion in "special" and "mainstream" schools'. *Disability & Society*, Vol. 16, No. 5, 671–687.

Davis, J.M., Watson, N. and Cunningham-Burley, S. (2000) 'Learning the lives of disabled children: developing a reflexive approach', in P. Christensen and A. James (eds) *Research with Children: Perspectives and Practices*. London: Falmer, 201–224.

Department for Education and Employment (2000) *Special Educational Needs Code of Practice Consultation Document*. London: DfEE.

DeGrandpre, R. (1999) *Ritalin Nation*. New York: W. W. Norton.

Gee, J.P. (1990) *Social Linguistics and Literacies*. New York: Falmer Press.

Giddens, A. (1976) *New Rules in Sociological Method*. London: Hutchinson.

Harding, S. (1991) *Whose Science? Whose Knowledge?* Ithaca: Cornell University Press.

Hindley, P. and Kroll, L. (1998) 'Theoretical and epidemiological aspects of attention deficit and overactivity in deaf children', *Journal of Deaf Studies and Deaf Education*, 3 (1), 64–72.

James, A. and Prout, A. (1999) Preface to the second edition, in A. James and A. Prout (eds) *Constructing and Reconstructing Childhood*. London: Falmer, ix–xvii.

James, A., Jenks, C., and Prout, A. (1998) *Theorising Childhood*. Cambridge: Polity.

Kirchhöfer, D. (1998) 'Veränderungen in der alltäglichen Lebensführung Ostberliner Kinder', *Aus Politik und Zeitgeschichte* B11(8): 31–45.

Kristeva, J. (1986) 'Word, dialogue and novel', in T. Moi (ed.) *The Kristeva Reader*. Oxford: Blackwell, 34–61.

Marschark, M. (1993) *Psychological Development of Deaf Children*. Oxford: Oxford University Press.

Morris, J. (1991) *Pride against Prejudice*. London: Women's Press.

Oliver, M. (1996) *Understanding Disability: From Theory to Practice*. Basingstoke: Macmillan.

Perske, R. (1972) 'The dignity of risk', in W. Wolfensberger (ed.) *The Principle of Normalisation in Human Services*. Toronto: National Institute of Mental Retardation.

Priestley, M. (1998a) 'Constructions and creations: idealism, materialism and disability theory'. *Disability & Society*, Vol. 13, No. 1, 75–94.

Priestley, M. (1998b) 'Childhood disability and disabled childhoods'. *Childhood*, Vol. 5, No. 2, 207–223.

Prout, A. and James, A. ([1990] 1999) 'A new paradigm for the sociology of childhood? Provenance, promise and problems', in A. James and A. Prout (eds) *Constructing and Reconstructing Childhood: Contemporary Issues in the Sociological Study of Childhood*, 2nd edition. London: Falmer Press.

Qvortrup, J. (2000) 'Macroanalysis of childhood', in P. Christensen and A. James (eds) *Research with Children: Perspectives and Practices*. London: Falmer.

Smith, D. (1998) 'Bakhtin and the dialogic of sociology: an investigation', in M. M. Bell and M. Gardiner (eds) *Bakhtin and the Human Sciences*. London: Sage, 63–77.

van Dijk, T.A. (1996) 'Discourse, power and access', in C.R. Caldas-Coulthard and M. Coulthard (eds) *Texts and Practices: Readings in Critical Discourse Analysis*. London: Routledge.

5 Adults as resources and adults as burdens

The strategies of children in the age of school–home collaboration

Kjersti Ericsson and Guri Larsen

This drawing adorns the title page of a recent Norwegian government report to the parliament on collaboration between home and school. Like a little princess, the child is being carried by her teacher and parents in something resembling a sedan chair. Looking at the picture, one is reminded of the description French researcher Philippe Meyer (1983: 40) presents of the modern child's position: 'The son or daughter of "good family", is an infant monarch, whose every move is watched, whose every word is treasured, upon whom all the family's hopes are concentrated, since he or she has absorbed almost all its energy'. Not only the hopes of the family, but also the hopes of the school, are concentrated on this infant monarch. However, it is not actually clear if the little monarch in the picture is powerful or powerless. Certainly, the child is the central figure, but the action is ascribed to the adults with the teacher seemingly leading the way. The parents are following, steadily supporting the sedan chair of education. The child is sitting, content, yet passive. Among the children interviewed for our research on the relationship between home and school, was seven-year-old Cecilie. She did not act like the child in the drawing at all. Here are some extracts from the interview:

Interviewer: Can you tell me what you do at school?
Cecilie: Mother has already told you that!
Interviewer: But I would like you to tell me as well.
Cecilie: No I won't. You're not supposed to hear from both of us.

Eventually, the interviewer manages to persuade Cecilie to tell him about her experiences at school. A little later, Cecilie once again questions his legitimacy:

Cecilie: Why do you want to know all this?
Interviewer: I think it's exciting.
Cecilie: Afterwards it's your turn to tell *me* something – I want you to tell me the story about the knight Bluebeard and the story about the expensive shoes.

Cecilie demands reciprocity. As she has told her stories, the interviewer should contribute his. After a few more questions, she once again takes control of the situation:

Cecilie: Now it's your turn to tell *me* something! Now I'm going to ask *you* questions!
Interviewer: Yes?
Cecilie: How many idiotic questions do you ask every day?

Cecilie certainly gets the better of the adult interviewer. She demands that the roles be changed. With the utmost clarity, she states her opinion of his questions. Suddenly, she climbs up to the top of a wardrobe, and continues the conversation from there. To establish eye contact with Cecilie in her exalted position just beneath the ceiling, the interviewer has to bend over backwards. It is almost as if Cecilie knows the old trick to establish dominance – placing the visitor in a low seat and oneself on high.

In the encounter with little Cecilie, something every teacher and parent knows is clearly demonstrated: more often than not, children have their own agendas and projects which may not coincide with those of adults. Children are not passive and pliable. The drawing of the girl in the sedan chair communicates *one* perspective on the role of children in their schooling. In our view, another perspective is also needed. Children have to be acknowledged as agents in descriptions and analyses of school matters, including in relation to collaboration between home and school.

In Norway fifty to sixty years ago, school and home were seen as separate worlds with almost no formal collaboration between the two. The first national regulations that mandated some degree of formal collaboration between teachers and parents were adopted in 1939. However, it took nearly two decades before they were implemented. Today, collaboration between home and school is regarded as an essential requirement for the social and intellectual development of children. Parents are expected to be extensively involved in their children's schooling.

Cederström (1995) interprets the increasing emphasis on home–school collaboration as a manifestation of floating and contested boundaries between the authority and competence of the two parties. In earlier times, cultural reproduction was taken for granted. The division of labour between home and school was clear, and the school's authority was undisputed. Teachers expected parents to deliver children who were ready for formal schooling. Parents expected teachers to teach the children whatever they needed to know. This division of labour and responsibilities is no longer self-evident. Hence, the need to collaborate and negotiate.

What consequences does this extensive collaboration have for the children? From our perspective, children are actively trying to cope with the many challenges linked to being a pupil. These challenges may be academic or social, and they may concern teachers, parents or peers. For children, the relationship between home and school may be entangled in a variety of battles: to be at the top of the class; to minimise the time spent on homework in order to save time for more attractive pursuits; the battle for autonomy; to be the peer group's coolest of the cool, or to overcome the role of social outcast in relation to other children. How does home–school collaboration influence children's scope for action and strategy options? Two main possibilities may be outlined:

1   On the one hand, as teachers and parents exchange information and make concerted efforts to influence children's schoolwork and behaviour, closer collaboration creates opportunities for more stringent control.

2   On the other hand, a possible blurring of the boundaries between school authority and home authority through extended home–school collaboration may give children increased influence. Through the enlistment of parents and teachers to support their demands, children may use adults as resources in efforts to change problematic aspects of their life at school or at home.

This chapter will explore these two possibilities, based on results from a recent research project, carried out in four schools in the city of Oslo. Our methods are qualitative interviews with forty-one children, their parents, and their form teachers. When interviewed, half of the children were in the first year of primary school (seven years old), and half were in the first year of secondary school (thirteen years old).[1] In addition we were present at twenty-four parent–teacher meetings, and eight parent meetings held by the schools.

The empirical illustrations presented in this chapter stem in part from observations of parent–teacher meetings with the child present, and in part from interviews with children. The interviews tell us something of the attitudes of children to home–school collaboration. In addition, they give us concrete examples of how children attempt to manoeuvre between home and school.

THE CHILD IN PARENT–TEACHER MEETINGS

In Norway, it is mandatory for schools to arrange parent–teacher meetings twice a year. At these, each individual child's development is discussed. Often the child attends with the parents. Sometimes the meeting is only for adults. The parent–teacher meeting may be regarded as the most central arena of collaboration between home and school. Parents who do not show up for this meeting, are often branded as neglectful by teachers.

Let us first take a look at the role of the child in this situation. Drawing on the two possibilities outlined above, we may ask: does the child primarily emerge as an object of concerted control efforts from teachers and parents? Or does the child emerge as an agent, able to voice his/her own concerns and press for changes, perhaps with support from one of the adult parties?

Some of the parent–teacher meetings give the impression of a child having to face not one, but two or three benevolent and well-meaning, though nonetheless overpowering, adults. Here is seven-year-old Peder Martin with his mother and teacher (Birger):

Birger:	(to Peder Martin) Listening isn't very easy for you. When you're bored you wander around the class room, talking to the others. Do you agree?
Peder Martin:	Yes.
Birger:	What shall we do? You're disturbing the class, both me and the others.
Mother:	(to Peder Martin) Do you have any suggestions?
	(Peder Martin says nothing)
Birger:	Perhaps I should give you extra work?
Peder Martin:	I have some kind of worksheet now.
Birger:	You have your own exercise book, is that okay?
Peder Martin:	Yes.
Birger:	He works in his exercise book until the others are finished. We can't have him wandering around in the classroom. But do you know what? The work you did, you did very quickly because you knew the answers, but it was messy. It is not always important to finish first. You've improved. Your handwriting looks better (they look at the exercise book, Peder Martin is panting slightly).
Mother:	You can do it if you want to.
Birger:	Exactly. Do you agree?
Peder Martin:	Yes (still panting).

Peder Martin pants and answers 'yes'. He does not appear very comfortable. However, parent–teacher meetings may also give a child the opportunity to formulate his/her own concerns and seek the help of adults. Sometimes teachers really make an effort to interact with children in a way that makes them visible as active participants. Here is a teacher named Vigdis in a parent–teacher meeting with seven-year-old Petter and his parents:

Vigdis:	Petter, I want to ask you something. I wonder if you sometimes think I am unfair. I may be. Maybe I do stupid things sometimes? If you think so, will you please tell me?
Petter:	Yes.
Vigdis:	So I don't go on doing stupid things. Will you do that?
Petter:	Yes.

Vigdis: I think this is important. You have to dare to tell me. You can come to me and say: Vigdis, what you did was a little stupid.

Petter: Yes, I am going to tell Liv (another teacher) now, because she's so strict.

Vigdis: Is Liv strict?

Petter: Yes.

Vigdis: In what way do you think she is strict?

Petter: In what way – I don't know exactly. (To his father) You know too, dad!

Father: It was only once. But you ought to tell her.

Petter: Yes.

Vigdis: And then, if you don't feel quite up to it, you can tell me and I will tell her. Liv wants to know too, if we tell her in an okay way.

Mother: Is she often strict?

Vigdis: (To Petter) No. Sometimes when you're in the gym. I think it is because you are a little wild when you are all together in the gym, and Liv becomes a little afraid that something may happen, that you may hurt yourselves.

Father: And her voice may sound a little different in the gym.

Vigdis: Exactly. But if you want, Petter, I will talk to Liv about this.

Petter: Yes.

Vigdis: But I think you should try to talk to her too.

Father: Can you do that?

Petter: Yes, I can.

Although the adults question Petter's perception of the gym teacher, they also take him seriously enough to promise to voice his concerns to Liv. They also signal his importance as a responsible participant by encouraging him to speak his mind and act on his own behalf. We have several observations of Vigdis (teacher) in parent-teacher meetings with children present. She consciously addresses the children, often succeeding in getting them to tell her what is bothering them. However, sometimes her efforts are frustrated. Here is the father of seven-year-old Kim, together with Vigdis (teacher). Kim is also present, although he is hardly audible:

Vigdis: Kim, do you think you have too much homework?

Father: No, I don't think so. But he sat a long time with his homework yesterday. You know, it said 'ruler', and he did not know what it meant.

Vigdis: No, that's understandable. (To Kim) Did that make you a little worried?

Father: Yes, he was a little worried.

Vigdis: (To Kim) But if there is something you don't understand when your father is not at home, I think you should just forget it, and then tell me what you didn't understand the next day. Then I'll try to explain it.

Father: Yes, because 'ruler', you know, may have different meanings.

Vigdis: Sure.

Father: I had to look twice myself.

Vigdis: Of course. (To Kim) But it is important that you don't just sit there being worried. Because it may happen that I forget to explain things.

Father: Yes. It's not as if he didn't want to do his homework, he didn't know how to do it.

Vigdis: Yes, I understand. (To Kim) Then it really is stupid that you should have to sit there and worry because you don't understand.

Father: He needs to improve his reading, then everything will be okay. He does well in maths, doesn't he?

Vigdis: Yes, very well.

Vigdis tries to bring Kim into the conversation, but his father is so eager to help that he mutes Kim, leaving the child little chance to speak and act for himself. Kim's father is an involved parent, doing his best to be supportive of his child's schoolwork. However, his best proves to be a little too much.

MORE STRINGENT CONTROL

The empirical illustrations from parent–teacher meetings point to variations in the child's position within home–school collaboration. One possibility is that the child becomes the target of more extensive control as parents and teachers join forces. This position is glimpsed in the parent–teacher meeting with Peder Martin. Older children have told us of similar situations. Aleksander has bad memories from the sixth form:

> I didn't do my homework, and I chatted with my class-mates during the lessons, and I was scolded for that. [Who scolded you?] First I was scolded in the parent-teacher meeting, and then my parents scolded me afterwards. ... [Has your teacher ever told your parents things that you wish he had not told them?] Mm, in the sixth form. I was rather messy, forgot to do my homework and things like that. I was hoping that the teacher would not tell my parents. But he did. [What did your parents say?] They said: Enough of this! Pull yourself together!

The teacher mobilises Aleksander's parents to work on making their son take his schoolwork more seriously. In the seventh form, we observed the parent-teacher meeting between Aleksander's mother and his teacher (Aleksander was not present). This time, his mother used the opportunity to mobilise the teacher. His mother wanted his teacher to demand more from Aleksander: 'He learns easily, but he does not put in much of an effort. I think, as a teacher, you could push him harder.' Aleksander's mother returns to this topic several times. Thus, Aleksander experiences several efforts to straighten him up. Some originate from his teacher who enlists his parents' help, some originate from his parents, who want his teacher to act.

An example of joint – and very stringent – parent–teacher control, is related to us by a teacher named Birger. He discusses a boy who constantly creates problems in class: 'He does so much mischief that he ought to get a prize for it'. In collaboration with the boy's parents, Birger now writes daily reports about everything that happens during the school day. At the end of each day, he has a conversation with the boy, reviewing successes and failures, acceptable and unacceptable behaviour, both in the classrooms and during breaks. Everything is written down. At the end of the week, the report is sent to the boy's parents. Each week Reidar's parents and teacher (Birger) have a telephone conference to fill in the details. This arrangement was decided on at a meeting with the headteacher and the school counsellor:

> Together, we arrived at the conclusion that the parents should receive daily reports on the boy. He has to understand that everything he does is registered. He cannot deny anything. I am very detailed in my reporting: what did he do in the first break, what did he do in the second? If something happened, I write it down. If everything went fine, I write that: no negative reports from this break. He cannot deny anything to his parents. Here it is, in black and white, what we have agreed on. I write the report together with him. When I have written the report, he has to answer to his parents.

This boy risks being transferred from his current school to some kind of special school for troublesome children. A tight control regime, exercised in collaboration between his teacher and his parents, keeps him in his local school, at least for the time being.

EXERCISING INFLUENCE

Collaboration between home and school may, however, offer children alternative positions: children may become recognised participants in their own education, entitled to an opinion, and empowered by the parents' presence. We glimpsed this position in a parent–teacher meeting with Petter, discussed earlier. Older children may have an impressive mastery of the arena of parent–teacher meetings. One example is thirteen-year-old Camilla, who we observed in a meeting with both of her parents and her teacher. Without a doubt, Camilla plays the leading role in the situation. Her parents blend into the background. Camilla negotiates on her own behalf, and she does so determinedly. She brings up the fact that some of her classmates are bullied by others, and she resists an attempt by her teacher to define the incidents as 'perhaps not very serious'. She tells her teacher that she is not very happy with the work group she has been assigned: she thinks it is unfair that she has been separated from her best friends, and besides, there are two pupils in the group who 'do not contribute'. The teacher promises to reconsider the composition of the groups before the next term. Camilla also protests against being labelled as dyslexic, as she 'knows what is wrong', and the teacher respects her refusal to see a speech therapist. For Camilla, the parent–teacher meeting serves as a channel for airing her views and attempting to influence everyday life in the classroom. Her parents' presence may be important. Even if they blend into the background, Camilla may feel their silent support.

In our material, there are many examples of children using their parents as valuable resources in relation to their school life. Many children actively use their parents in efforts to improve schoolwork. Most of the children we have interviewed often, or at least on occasion, take initiatives to activate the resources of their family when doing homework. Parents, older siblings and even grandparents are asked for help. Indirectly, this will also influence the child's experiences in the classroom. Children may also use parents in more direct attempts to accomplish changes at school. Parents may for example lend added authority to their complaints about teachers. Kaja, thirteen years old, mobilised her mother when she was dissatisfied with her maths teacher. Her mother took Kaja's complaint to a parents' meeting at the school. The other parents concurred, and the teacher was forced to mend his ways. Several clever girls are annoyed by having to act as extra tutors in group work with less diligent co-pupils. They rally for parental support of their desire to change to a 'better' group.

Children may use their parents for several purposes. In a parent–teacher meeting where seven-year-old Astrid was also present, we observed how little Astrid, too timid to voice her own concerns, whispered instructions to her mother. Her mother then explained that Astrid wanted to change to another desk, and why she wanted this. Supported by her parents, thirteen-year-old Anna complained to her teacher about being harassed in the school yard by a boy who called her a 'handicapped bitch' and other names she found offensive. The teacher made the boy apologise to Anna, and the harassment stopped. Anna seems to have a rather hard time among her peers. However, she copes as best she can by mobilising the resources she has at her disposal: her teacher and parents, as well as her own considerable mental strength.

Using teachers as resources to solve problems at home seems to be more difficult. We have hardly any successful examples. In one parent–teacher meeting, thirteen-year-old Ruth attempts to enlist her teacher's support against her mother. Earlier, in her interview with us, Ruth told us that her mother incessantly complains that she spends too much time watching television. In the parent–teacher meeting, the teacher praises Ruth's excellent schoolwork, and wonders how Ruth, who is an active tennis player and regularly takes piano lessons, finds time for it all. Ruth grabs the opportunity to try to make her mother see that her complaints about excessive television watching are meaningless. To Ruth's chagrin, her teacher allies herself with her mother – watching television is an unworthy activity which should be strictly controlled.

One teacher told us a story about a little boy who at least managed to be comforted at school after a traumatic incident at home. One morning the boy came into the classroom crying desperately. Between sobs, he said that 'mummy tried to kill daddy with a knife last night'. One little classmate told him to 'go and sit on teacher's lap while we talk about this'. The class used the whole school day to talk with the boy about what had happened. Afterward, none of the children said a word to anyone outside the classroom about the incident. The teacher had not asked them to keep quiet. She was both impressed and moved by the empathy and maturity her small pupils showed.

FIGHTING FOR AUTONOMY

Finally, there is the possibility that parents get so involved in their child's schoolwork that they more or less take over, as we glimpsed in the parent–teacher meeting with Kim and his father. Older children may resist this kind of behaviour. Thirteen-year-old Farid is ambitious, and has a thorough understanding of the importance of a good education. However, he regards his schoolwork and his relationship with his teacher as his own business. He resents his mother's interference. Farid wants to replace parent–teacher meetings with meetings solely between pupils and teachers. In his opinion, parents just mess things up: they take what the teacher says too literally, they pester their children with perpetual talk about homework and studying, and they demand top grades in every subject. When asked if he has ever wanted his mother to speak to his teacher about anything that she has not already raised, his answer is: 'No! She has talked to the school about everything. It's impossible to invent anything more!'

Thirteen-year-old Rakel also wants to keep her schooling as a parent-free territory. She never asks her mother for help with her homework, and she gets irritated and tells her mother to mind her own business if she tries to intervene. Rakel finds her mother 'too inquisitive', and she wants 'some private life'. Her mother is frustrated by Rakel's attitude. 'I try to help, but she will not allow me. Rakel is very strong-minded,' she says. Rakel's mother feels that the information she gets from the school is far too scanty. As Rakel will tell her nothing, she is dependent on the teacher to keep her up to date on her daughter's schoolwork. Rakel seems dutiful with home-work. The battle with her mother is not a battle about escaping schoolwork. Rather, it is part of a larger battle over autonomy. Rakel's project is to live an independent life, and this project colours her interaction with her mother, also in relation to schooling.

Children may try to escape both over-ambitious and intrusive parents. However, children may attempt to escape their parents' efforts to help because they fear that parental intervention may make things worse. In her interview, Camilla (thirteen) recalls an incident of harassment bordering on violence (at least in the context of the relatively idyllic Norwegian school yard). She feels that the teachers in part mis-interpret, and in part do not want to see, what is going on between the children. When girls are harassed by boys, the teachers see it as flirting. It is an interpretation Camilla angrily rejects. Telling one's parents is impossible. If the other children find out about it, one runs the risk of reprisals. Camilla's father senses that there is something very wrong in Camilla's life at school. Camilla and her brother, who attends the same school, are in the habit of suddenly falling silent if he enters the room and they are chatting about episodes in the schoolyard. Her father truly wants to help, but Camilla sees no viable way to use him as a resource to solve her school yard problem. Her main concern is preventing him from making things even worse by intervening. Hence, she tells him nothing of her problems.

'CURRICULARISATION' OF CHILDHOOD

The Swedish researcher Gunilla Halldén (1989: 13) makes a distinction between the conception of the *child as being* and the *child as project*. According to Halldén, the child as being is seen as belonging to the private world, and the home is regarded as a sanctuary for individuality. The conception of the child as a project stresses the child's development as a result of interaction between the child and its environment. The child's role as a social creature, and its relations to the world outside the home and family is underlined. Our conception of the child as project is slightly different from Halldéns, focusing on the assumption that children do not simply grow into adults, but have to be worked on, actively and consciously. The outcome is decided by the amount and quality of work that is 'put into' the child. This conception of the child as project is implicit in most of the current Norwegian public discourse on socialisation.

The drawing on the front page of the parliamentary report may be an expression of just this conception of the child: the most central and important project of adults. Sociologists of childhood emphasise the child as an agent, actively participating in the creation of both itself and society. This perspective is developed in opposition to the picture of the child as raw material for the process of socialisation (see Prout and James, 1997). It is indeed important to make the child visible as an agent. However, the child as a project is not only a *perspective*, to be replaced by another perspective. It is also a social reality, central to the constitution of contemporary childhood.

This social reality is very visible in our study. One possible outcome of extensive home–school collaboration may be a strengthening of the process which Judith Ennew (1994: 127) has termed 'the progressive "curricularisation" of non-school activities of childhood'. The life of the whole family may be 'curricularised' as it is drawn into the orbit of the school. In interviews, some parents relate the manner in which they are being actively socialised into the role of 'school parents' when their children start school: not only the children, but also the parents are given homework. The parents' homework may, for example, be listening to their children reading lessons out loud. When the task is finished, it is noted on a special sheet the child returns to school. Thus, the teacher can oversee whether both the child and the parent have done what they are supposed to do. Others tell how the school instructs them to act as speech therapists for their children – a service which the school cannot afford to provide because of budget cutbacks.

The modern ideal of the 'good childhood' has been a carefree, playful and protected period, unburdened by the work, duties and responsibilities of adulthood. This ideal has had (and still has) a stronger cultural impact in Norway than in many other countries with different educational traditions (see Martinson 1992). When the starting age for school was changed from seven to six in 1997, the reform was met with considerable resistance. However, this childhood ideal may be undermined if the child is increasingly conceived of as a project which must be worked upon system-atically and actively both at school and at home. The goal of the project is the acquisi-tion of the competence and cultural capital that are deemed necessary for a good start in an ever more competitive life. In her study of parental intervention in elemen-tary school, Annette Laureau notes a change in the parental role: parents are no longer merely expected to give their children love, intimacy and security and to safeguard their physical health and development. Now, they are also expected to stimulate and take responsibility for the intellectual development of their children. Mothers ought to be actively involved in children's school careers: 'corporations' expectations that upper-middle-class wives will be involved in their husbands' careers also are similar to teachers' expectations for parents' involvement in school' (1989: 172).

One possible consequence of extensive home–school collaboration could be that parents are turned into prolonged arms of the school – continuing the work of the teacher after school hours. Together with other initiatives to improve parenting (in Norway the government has advocated public courses to improve parental competence), this could produce a more professionalised interaction between children and parents. If followed, one example of suggestions we feel might lead to this development, is US researcher Carmen Simich-Dudgeon's recommendations on how 'LEP' (Low English Proficiency) minority parents should be trained to stimulate their children:

> Parent-as-tutor training, regardless of the academic area that is being reinforced (i.e. maths, language, arts, science), must include training of parents in verbal interaction techniques that promote cognitive and language development. A key component of this training should be teaching parents how to ask the right questions and how to follow up their children's responses. The following verbal interaction techniques can be used to train parents:
>
> a. Begin by factual recall and factual description questions about the activity at hand (e.g. 'What color is this?' 'How much is four times four?').
> b. Expand the interaction with questions that require the children to compare the characteristics or behaviour of the things being studied ('How is X different from Y?' 'How are they similar?') and/or make generalization from the facts:
>
> *   explain the conclusions reached ('Why do you think …')
> *   defend a point of view, provide justification ('How did you arrive at X conclusion?')
> *   paraphrase the children's responses ('Then what you mean is …')
>
> LEP parents must learn to allow their children to ask questions as well as respond to questions. Follow-up questions should be chosen over rejection or nonacceptance of their children's responses. LEP parents must be taught to allow their children plenty of opportunities to interact verbally and listen to what the children say and how they say it. Parents should allow their children time to organize and plan their responses and give them time to develop the appropriate response by discussing related topics and issues. Finally, parents must learn that students' responses should be followed by an evaluation (e.g. 'That was very good!' 'Excellent!' or repeating the answer or simply nodding and moving to the next question). By training parents in verbal interaction strategies, the teachers are actually socializing both the parents and their children to patterns of 'school talk'.
>
> (Simich-Dudgeon, 1993: 194)

Simich-Dudgeon's recommendations smack of educational totalitarianism. Even if suggestions like these still sound extreme to the Norwegian ear, the mentality is recognisable. An excerpt from a parent–teacher meeting between Birger (teacher) and Waseem's (a seven-year-old boy of minority background) father may serve as an illustration:

Birger: Waseem ought to speak grammatically correct. I believed he will improve little by little, but he still speaks Norwegian very poorly … You speak Norwegian well. It is important that you speak Norwegian at home. You can help him with his Norwegian if you, for example, point to the curtain and say the Norwegian word – build up his vocabulary. He did not know what string was, or twine. It is difficult, he does not understand some everyday words.

Mr. Farooq: His mother, she tries to speak Norwegian, but she is not very good. I do not have time to sit at home. I am working a lot at nights. I have to sleep in the daytime.

Birger has the best of intentions, and it is undoubtedly a problem to be a little boy in a Norwegian school without speaking Norwegian properly. Nonetheless, one has to wonder what impact interacting in a foreign language will have on the Farooq family. What will it do to Mrs. Farooq as a mother if she is forced to speak to her children, and have them speak to her, in a language she masters poorly? One may fear that the emotional richness and spontaneity of family life is in danger of being sacrificed to educational progress.

PROJECT OR SUBJECT?

One may well ask similar questions, not only about minority families, but about families in general. What happens in the wake of parents' increased responsibility for the intellectual development of their children? What happens if more of the interaction between children and parents are subjected to the 'speech-pattern of the school'? What happens if the conflicts of the classroom are transferred to the home, continuing there? What happens if parents, in their relationship with their children, continuously feel obliged to take intellectual stimulation into account?

In a worst case scenario, the results of extensive home–school collaboration could be that the child as being is completely superseded by the child as project, continuously worked on by ambitious adults, both at school and at home. Such a child would lead a thoroughly 'curricularised' life, moving in arenas which are all subsumed under one dominant, professionalised logic. In Norway, we are currently far from that situation. However, tendencies pointing in this direction emerge in our study.

Fortunately, other tendencies also emerge: we see children, empowered by the support of their parents, voicing their concerns in parent-teacher meetings. We see teachers genuinely trying to get children to speak their minds and act on their own behalves. We also see some confident children, taking their leading role in the parent-teacher meeting for granted, defining problems and negotiating solutions. We see children seeking, and getting, the help of adults to solve a variety of problems: difficult homework, the need to get teachers who are too strict to change their ways, conflicts with co-pupils, harassment in the school yard. (However, we also see children trying to get help, and failing.)

Finally, we see some children trying to evade, or limit, parent-teacher collaboration. For some, it is a question of not having to suffer the unpleasant experience of being doubly scolded for the same offences. For others, it is a question of exercising autonomy.

Which tendencies will prove the strongest? If the goal is a move away from the most dystopic vision, an important first step could be to reformulate the objective of home–school collaboration making the empowerment and agent-role of children central. Perhaps we should draw a new picture which replaces the image of the passive child in the sedan chair. In the new picture the child remains centre stage, but this time standing on his/her own feet, actively taking part in shaping his/her school experience. Let the adults retreat into more modest (but no less demanding!) positions, as accessible resources in children's struggles to cope with the many challenges of schoolwork and peer relations. The idea of totally child-monitored education may be utopian, but there are many constructive changes which are within our reach.

An ambiguous conception of the child surfaces in our study. On the one hand, we have the child as an individual in his/her own right – entitled to play a part in the creation of his/her own life. On the other, we have the child as a project into which adults invest time, money, hopes, dreams, and identity. This ambiguity may mirror a major condition of contemporary childhood, commented on by several researchers. Allison James, Chris Jenks and Alan Prout (1998) talk about the parallel tendencies of the child's increasing autonomy *and* the increasing control of the child. The Norwegian sociologist Ivar Frønes (1994) points to the combination of prolonged dependency and early maturing as the paradox of modern childhood. Both parents and society at large want to grant children more autonomy, while simultaneously controlling and protecting them. The balance between these two parallel tendencies is influenced by everyday practices that we often take for granted. One such practice is home–school collaboration.

NOTES

1 In Norway, the mandatory school period is currently ten years. Children enter elementary school when they are six years old, and remain there from form one to seven. They then enter secondary school for forms eight to ten. Before 1997, the mandatory school period was nine years, and children were seven years old when they first went to school. Form seven was the first form of secondary school. Our interviews were carried out in 1996, the last year of the old system.

REFERENCES

Cederström, J. (1995) 'Skal skolen lukke sig for at kunne åbne sig? – Om skolens interne avklaring som en forudsætning for en 'åben' dialog med forældrene,' ('Do the schools have to close in order to open up? The necessity of internal clarification as a condition for open dialogue with parents') in P. Arneberg and B. Ravn (eds) *Mellan hem och skola. En fråga om makt och tillit. (Between home and school. A question of power and trust.)* Stockholm: Liber Utbildning, 190–103.

Ennew, J. (1994) 'Time for Children and Time for Adults', in J. Qvotrup, M. Bardy, G. Sgritta and H. Wintersberger (eds) *Childhood Matters. Social Theory, Practice and Politics.* Vienna, European Centre. Aldershot, Avebury, 125–143.

Frønes, I. (1994) 'Dimensions of Childhood', in J. Qvortrup, M. Bardy, G. Sgritta and H. Wintersberger (eds) *Childhood Matters. Social Theory, Practice and Politics.* Vienna, European Centre. Aldershot, Avebury, 145–164.

Halldén, G. (1989) 'Barnen som tillhöriga privat eller offentlig sfär – historiska perspektiv på föreställningar om barn' ('Children as belonging to the private or the public sphere – historical perspectives on conceptions of children'). Unpublished paper presented at the NFPF conferenc in Uppsala 9–11 March.

James, A., C. Jenks and A. Prout (1998) *Theorizing Childhood.* Cambridge: Polity Press.

Lareau, A. (1989) *Home Advantage. Social Class and Parental Intervention in Elementary Education.* Philadelphia: The Falmer Press.

Martinson, F.M. (1992) *Growing up in Norway, 800 to 1990.* Carbondale: Southern Illinois University Press.

Meyer, P. (1983) *The Child and the State. The Intervention of the State in Family Life.* Cambridge: Cambridge University Press.

Prout, A. and A. James (1997) 'A New Paradigm for the Sociology of Childhood? Provenance, Promise and Problems', in A. James and A. Prout (eds) *Constructing and Reconstructing Childhood: Contemporary Issues in the Sociological Study of Childhood.* London: Falmer Press, 7–33.

Simich-Dudgeon, C. (1993) 'Increasing Student Achievement through Teacher Knowledge about Parent Involvement', in N.F. Chavkin (ed.) *Families and Schools in a Pluralistic Society.* New York: State University of New York Press.

6 Home and school constraints in children's experience of socialisation in Geneva

Cleopatra Montandon

INTRODUCTION

Children are increasingly considered as actors playing an important role in their own socialisation. The transformation of the way children are represented is noticeable not only among researchers and other specialists but also among teachers, parents and other educators. It is epitomised in the creation and recognition of children's rights and is given visibility in the media. This change is certainly not as prominent in all societies and all social groups. In some post-industrial societies, however, the discourses on children as well as the way they are treated reflect these changing representations. The question then arises whether the recognition of children as social actors means they are less constrained, less controlled in the main social contexts of their socialisation and whether they are given more opportunities to become more autonomous? This chapter will try to address this question by focusing on a group of children in Geneva and more particularly on how they themselves experience, negotiate and analyse the power relations in the main socialisation contexts in which they are involved. Based on data from in-depth interviews of 11- to 12-year-old children, it analyses the ways they deal with authority, their views on parental and teacher control, their emotional responses and strategies towards their educators' demands. It then highlights the role peers play in their socialisation, namely in the ways they cope with and negotiate institutional constraints.

THE RESEARCH CONTEXT AND THEORETICAL FRAMEWORK

Geneva has a population of 400,000. It is a cosmopolitan Swiss canton with a third of the population belonging to various ethnic communities. Over a third of the children up to age 4 go for part or the whole day to various day-care centres, kindergarten or similar institutions and from this age up the great majority enter the public school system. An important reform is being introduced in the primary schools, based on child-centred educational principles, attributing high value to the development of children's autonomy and initiative and encouraging 'partnership' between the school and the family. In the fields of education and leisure, children are offered a large number of opportunities. Autonomy is not valued in the school only.

Children have generally obtained a greater say in many other contexts of their social-isation. In their families child-rearing practices tend to allow for more negotiation (Kellerhals and Montandon, 1991) and in the fields of sports, cultural activities, and so on, children are able to exercise choice. At the same time, however, they are not necessarily less constrained and much more is expected of them. Their decision choices are made in contexts where competition is high and their lives are increasingly controlled and institutionalised. One third of the children who go to public primary schools are enrolled in various extra-curricular activities organised by the school system and an important number of schoolchildren (mainly middle class) have their time occupied by organised activities such as music and other lessons and sports. Their everyday experiences can be related to more global social processes. As in many other western cities individuals in Geneva enjoy an unprecedented freedom of movement together with new types of constraints (Büchner, du Bois-Reymond and Krüger, 1995).

The data presented in this paper concern the tension between the constraints and the freedom children experience in modern societies. They come from a study that took place in Geneva, the aim of which was to explore the children's point of view on their own socialisation both at home and at school. This research involved the participation of 68 11- to 12-year-old children – 35 girls and 33 boys – belonging to four sixth-grade classrooms located in four different areas of the city and representing all social groups. They were interviewed twice, both at home and school (in-depth interviews lasting 60–90 minutes each) (Montandon, 1997; 1998).

The theoretical approach to which this study subscribes is the sociology of childhood (Alanen, 1990; James and Prout, 1990; Waksler, 1991; Jenks, 1992; Mayall, 1994a; Qvortrup *et al.*, 1994; Corsaro, 1997). This means that children were considered as social actors who participate in interactions, activities, exchanges, negotiations and adjustments which contribute to the construction, perpetuation and trans-formation of their social world. Following a comprehensive, Weberian, perspective, the meaning children give to their experiences, the reasons they attribute to their actions and the interpretations they make of the various processes they are engaged in were considered as necessary elements for a sociological analysis. The children's experience, however, was not considered as occurring in a social vacuum, independent of social structures.[1]

The concept of *experience* is central in the study and consists of three main and interdependent dimensions: the *representations*, *emotions* and *actions* individuals or groups manifest as regards various social aspects of social reality. This chapter addresses these dimensions in dealing with the children's experience of parental and teacher authority and control. It will analyse their struggle for autonomy and the contribution of their peers in this process.[2]

CHILDREN'S EXPERIENCE OF PARENTAL AND TEACHER AUTHORITY

Children have many things to say about their relations with their parents and teachers and more particularly about the methods and means they use at home and school.

When encouraged to talk about their interactions with their educators, they give interesting details on the representations, emotions and actions that constitute their experience of control and authority as well as autonomy.

Experience of parental authority and desire for autonomy

Representations of parental control

The children interviewed in the Geneva studies give quite clear representations of the role of their parents. Quite interestingly, if they emphasise the encouragement of autonomy when they talk about their general expectations of their parents, they seem to be more control oriented when reacting to specific situations.

The majority generally expect their parents to provide *emotional support*, that is love, understanding and comfort. Half of them expect some kind of discipline. Their parents are supposed to see that they know how to behave in public and to provide enough *guidance* so that they may know how to control themselves. Some expect their parents to offer them *material support*, meaning food, a home, pocket-money, some others would like their parents give them *support for their schoolwork*, help them with their homework. But one fourth of the children explicitly mention that their parents should *stimulate their autonomy*: 'They should not do too many things for me, so that I start getting along by myself', says a girl. Another girl adds: 'because when I'm grown up, it's not my parents who will take care of me, I will have to take care of myself'.[3]

The children's representations of the parental role are more control oriented when they are asked to state what their own parents are supposed to do if they become aware they themselves have some specific problem: trouble with spelling at school, for example, or cheating during a test, or becoming increasingly shy, or starting having tooth caries due to eating too many sweets. Reacting to these situations, the children suggested various methods their parents should use:

a   *control*, applying surveillance, strict rules;
b   *motivation*, appealing to their reason, arguing the pros and cons;
c   *moralisation*, consisting of making reference to values and principles;
d   *emotional appeal*, that is showing they are disappointed, 'threatening' to withdraw their love;
e   *understanding*, that is listening to what the child has to say;
f   *coordination*, that is consulting other people who may know what to do.

The method that the children proposed more frequently was control. Eight children out of ten for example think that their parents should make them work harder and supervise them more closely in order to remedy their lower marks in spelling: 'My father', says a boy, 'should make me do spelling exercises. And if my spelling improves, he should make me do more difficult exercises and more often'. Seven children out of ten think that their parents should forbid them to eat sweets or should stop giving them pocket money if they have tooth caries due to eating too many sweets: 'Well, they should confiscate my money-box, my pocket money until I have no more caries!' declares another boy. Six children out of ten think that they should be punished by their parents if they cheat at school: 'They should tell me, "if you cheat you can't play outside any more", they should punish me', says a boy. A girl thinks that her parents should intervene: 'They should tell me, "if you cheat once more, we shall ask your teacher to make you sit all alone, at the back of the classroom"'. When the problem is relational, like shyness, fewer children suggest that their parents should use constraining measures. Three out of ten, however, think that their parents should oblige them to meet other children, as this girl says: 'They should make me meet other people, send me on courses, to holiday camps'.

Parental measures other than control, such as motivation, moralisation, or appeal to feelings are suggested much less frequently by the children. No doubt the measures they mention are related to the problem that has to be solved: they think more frequently that control should be used in the case of spelling difficulties or cheating, appeal to feelings in the case of shyness and motivation in the case of indulging in sweets. Generally speaking, however, control comes far ahead. Why do they ask for control in spite of the fact that when they name what they expect of their parents they insist on love, understanding, guidance and the encouragement of autonomy? One hypothesis could be that they distinguish what parents are supposed to be in general, from what parents are supposed to do when faced with a problem and want to correct or modify their child's behaviour. It could also be that children prefer that their parents take 'clear-cut' measures such as control, rather than make use of moralisation or appeal to feelings which are more fuzzy or costly from a psychological point of view. Spelling exercises may be less constraining than emotional work.

Another way to approach the children's ideas on control is to see what they say about effective control in their everyday life in the family and more particularly about punishments. One child out of four thinks that the control his/her parents exercise is loose and occasional: 'They are never on my back, they let me free', says a boy. 'Well, I think I'm darn free. I'm never told off by my parents', says a girl. Half of the children think their parents exercise 'normal' surveillance: 'They let me do things, but not *n'importe quoi* (just anything)'. For one child out of four, however, parental control is too strong and ongoing: 'If I go out, they want all the time to know where I am and with whom; it makes me nervous. I'm out with my friends and my mother she's out there on the balcony looking at me', says a boy. A girl reacts to her parents' control although she understands them: 'They supervise me a lot because I have grown up and I have my own life! They are too anxious and this should change'. In sum, the majority of the children of the study state that their parents control them.

Punishment can be considered as an indicator of parental control. Six children out of ten say that they have been punished at one time or other by their parents. It is interesting to note that children seem to accommodate this. Three out of four recognise that the punishment was deserved: 'It's a good thing in the end because if we do something really bad we won't do it again, we don't want to be punished twice for the same thing'. Some children seem to have developed or accepted a theory that justifies punishments: 'For me, those who never get punished, well it means that their parents don't care, they let them do anything', says a girl. Another one has a somewhat different version: 'I'm never happy when punished, but well they must educate us and if we don't follow the rules it is normal that we get punished. And then, when we go visiting friends, they say, "well, your children are very well brought up", and it is a pleasure, because then we see that the punishments were not useless'.

Some children, four out of ten, say they are never punished and almost all of them believe it is better this way. For them punishing a child is not a good child-rearing method. One boy said: 'I don't think punishments are effective. Anyway, most do the same thing again, it's no use; it's better to explain what is good or bad instead of saying "what you do is bad, you are punished", and then the children don't even know why they have been punished'. Some of the children who are never punished say they regret this, like this boy who thinks that he's not deterred enough: 'Sometimes they should punish us depending on what we do; perhaps we wouldn't repeat the same thing as easily again'. Or like this girl who estimates that no punishment means no interest: 'Yes, sometimes they should punish, because otherwise we think that they don't care'.

In sum, the majority of the children interviewed feel they are being controlled and disciplined by their parents and if some of them seem to accept and even appreciate the situation, a minority is critical. One may wonder whether the emotional support that most of them expect of their parents is given to them as well. If one third of the children feel they are unconditionally supported by their parents who understand them, console them, help them, offer them security and advice, the majority seem to lack support. Some think that what their parents are mainly interested in is that they do their homework and that they don't make trouble when at home: 'They are not really interested in my problems; just in my schoolwork'. Others specify that their parents' interest is conditional: 'They don't care about my problems with my friends, they say I have to resolve them by myself, they are more interested in my problems at school'. For some children their parents' interest misses the point and is seen as an intrusion:

> My mother, if I have some problems with my friends, she comes and says; 'oh, what's wrong, you must tell me, you mustn't have secrets from me', and I feel like telling her, these are my secrets and that's all! I have the feeling that I am a baby to them.

Finally for a few children parental interest is totally absent: 'We don't talk … they absolutely don't care. They don't take much interest in my life'.

The children's thoughts on their parents' child-rearing methods suggest that they expect affection and support as well as guidance and security. In everyday life, however, they feel more supervised than listened to, more controlled than supported. Further-more, when they give their opinion on what their parents should do in concrete problematic situations (their child's overeating, cheating, etc.), what they propose seems to correspond more to their everyday experience rather than to their expecta-tions. Children are quite marked by the control they concretely experience, even though they seem to know the limits of this control.

Emotional reactions to parental control

Powerful emotions are part of the children's experience of control. Anger is very frequently mentioned when their parents abuse their power: 'When I am punished for nothing, like yesterday, I get angry. Yes, I get irritated and then I stay in my room and I don't come out except to eat'. Injustice arouses anger:

> Sometimes my mother accuses me of having done some stupid thing, and in fact it's not even me, it's my sister! So they blame me because naturally I am the younger, so my mother thinks I'm being stupid. So, I don't agree and I get angry.

The absence of understanding or of attention from their parents makes some children furious. 'Sometimes I'm angry because as usual they haven't listened to me, and then I'm not happy and I get angry. I shout at them and then I go to my room. I've always been like this'.

Emotions often arise in expectation of parental control. Children mention fear when they anticipate the reaction of their parents when they bring home bad marks or bad remarks from the teacher in their notebook. Other emotions, such as shame or sadness, are mentioned following various situations when they break the rules or do something which they know their parents disapprove of. Children feel empathy when parental control is exercised over their siblings. More pleasant emotions, like joy or pride are also mentioned of course, but they are less associated with parental daily practices and more to particular family events and contexts, like birthday parties, family dinners, or holidays.

Some reactions to parental control

Children's reactions and strategies in relation to parental control and authority are manifold and vary according to the particular situations as well as according to their personality. Conformity is the most frequent reaction and corresponds to submitting to the parent without discussion. Children evaluate the pros and cons of deciding to conform. The following explanations are good examples. A girl whose parents forbade her to go out with her friends says: 'Well, I obey, because otherwise I would be punished if they see that I go out in secret'. A boy who is closely supervised says when his parents don't allow him to dress as he wants: 'I give up, because if I insist it's very likely that I'll be punished, so … With clothes I do what they say, I can't do otherwise'.

A frequent strategy consists in circumventing the parental injunctions. The children find a way to obtain what they want: 'If I really want to see a film that they don't want me to see, I keep changing channels and watch the film as long as possible'. Another strategy consists of wearing down the parental opposition. They repeat with insistence what they went until their parents give in: 'I ask them repeatedly, I wear them out, until they give in'. Some children adopt the strategy of the bad looser. They obey but not without showing their discontent and frustration: 'Well, I'm irritated, I slam the doors, then I go and have words with them'. Quieter strategies are also used. They use negotiation, for example, when children are ready to comply if their parents can show that their bans are grounded. They use arguments in order to persuade their parents that they deserve what they ask for. Some bargain; they agree, for example, to present no opposition to their parents in exchange for a promise to let them go out. A few mentioned the technique of the *fait accompli*: anticipating that their parents will forbid something they want to do, they do it anyway without asking for the permission, and wait and see. One boy said that he goes as far as terrorising his parents to obtain what they refuse.

Children are aware of their subordinate position in relation to adults and they adopt corresponding strategies when they are asked to do something for their parents. Most of them comply with parental requests most of the time. Obedience is often calculated. Even when it is a necessity, they do not obey blindly. Some obey because they don't want to be scolded or punished. Others acquiesce because they think that their parents do many things for them and that they have to do something in return. Still others allude to their status as children. One third of the children, however, resist parental authority. Some delay when they are asked to do something, knowing that if they wait long enough they will get what they want. Others find ways to avoid doing what parents demand, delegating to a younger sibling, or pretending that they are not well, or just ignoring the request.

These examples show that although children often feel obliged to obey their parents, they have many resources to subvert their authority. They do not always accept parental supremacy, they ask to be listened to and assert their rights. They are sometimes ready to admit their parents' demands as long as they can be justified. They claim a modern parental authority, open to discussion and negotiation.

The majority of the children interviewed wish to grow up soon. The main reason they give for this is that they look forward to being 'free at last', to have 'complete freedom' of movement and decision, to be able to do what they want, when they want, without having to ask their parents. For them being an adult means 'not having your parents on your back'. They also mention the desire to do things that are not allowed, such as driving a car, going to a disco, seeing all the films they want, coming home late at night, etc. Some mention the desire to have one's own space and things, not to have to share with their siblings, to be able to be alone. Other children stress the fact that they will be able to chose their own way of living, have a job they like, be more respected than they are now. The minority who do not wish to grow up express fears as regards the difficulties and constraints of adult life: heavy responsibilities, conflicts, financial difficulties, stress, illness and even old age. The children in the study realise that there are advantages to being a child: to be fed, sheltered, protected, having good time. Most of them, however, stress the fact that as children they are very dependant on adults as regards their freedom of action and decision-making as well as their material existence.

Experience of teacher authority and the desire for fairness

At school, children are immersed in a universe which is larger, more open, more particular than the small world of the family. Day after day they find themselves in an organisational and relational context which is imposed on them. Most often they are placed in a group they have not chosen, under the responsibility of a teacher, a key figure in their school life. The children are not passive spectators and have many things to say on their relations with their teachers (Cullingford, 1991).

Representations of teacher control

The analysis of what they consider a good teacher revealed three main qualities and shows that throughout the years spent at school children construe interesting representations of authority. The first dimension concerns the teachers' qualities as instructors. A good teacher is one who knows how to explain clearly and patiently what she or he wishes to transmit. Those who are imaginative, who know how to awake the interest of their students, how to motivate them through the originality and creativity of their methods, how to make schoolwork pleasurable are appreciated. A boy declares: 'When a teacher explains things well it is easier to work than when we have someone who tells us "do this do that" and then we understanding nothing and have bad marks'. The effort to innovate is underlined by a girl:

> With him we do many things that we have never done in other classes, research that we've never done before. I feel more like listening to him than I felt with other teachers. It's the way he conducts the class, and the timetable, we are told about what we'll do during the week.

A similar explanation is given for a woman teacher: 'We liked her because she explained well and she always wanted us to understand. She was still young, she wanted to try new things'.

The children also mention an ensemble of human qualities appreciated in a teacher, consisting of listening with interest, looking with a friendly eye, being accessible when there is a problem, showing empathy and understanding and having a good sense of humour: 'She understands us well, she knows when we have too much work, when we have problems; she helped me a lot when I had problems getting used to school again, she agreed to talk'. Gender identification is appreciated: 'Yes, perhaps I prefer a woman, because she is the same as me, and then sometimes we understand each other better, whereas men are different'. Humour is mentioned very often: 'Yeah, she was very nice, she made jokes, but not like some of the other teachers do. When we gave a wrong answer she made a joke out of the answer'.

Qualities which one can describe as pedagogical were also mentioned by the children. They appreciate the teachers who are demanding but fair, who require effort but in acceptable limits, who are strict but within limits, who are equitable, impartial, who do not abuse their power and encourage the pupil's autonomy. This requires a subtle equilibrium of demands and stimulation. 'She doesn't shout at us, she gives us some freedom in the class, but we mustn't go too far', says a boy of his favourite teacher. And a girl: 'I think that he was quite severe; but his severity was stimulating'.

The children seem to be looking for a fair authority. This appears more clearly when they talk about their representations of the teachers they don't like. What they dislike most is the excessive strictness of teachers who punish on any occasion, who leave no space for freedom, who tolerate no deviation in conduct, who overload them with work. In fact they are much more loquacious about their teachers' defects than about their qualities.

> There was a teacher I didn't like at all because she was too severe and she didn't understand us, she did as she wanted. We were little and when we did a small mistake she used to reprimand us very very hard.

says a girl. Sometimes the children try to understand this severity: 'She used to punish us a lot, she didn't ask herself what would her own child think if he were in our class. All of sudden, she would give us a test, and we had no time to revise, nothing'. Physical violence is given as an example of where extreme severity can lead:

> X used to hit us with wooden rulers, yes. But later he stopped, because a friend of mine used to go home with a red face, so his mother sent a message, that if he continued in this way she would denounce him, so he stopped.

Some children, knowledgeable of modern methods, don't like their teachers to give them activities that do not take account of their needs: 'He would impose too much work, we could never do something, for example write a text for ourselves. If we had to write a text, it had always to be a dissertation'.

The absence of humour, teachers who never smile, never laugh, who are very serious, arouses many comments: 'That one in third grade was pretentious, she would never smile, never. And she used to walk like this, straight, moving just her legs, and the only thing she thought about was work, never anything else'. The teachers who don't care about the climate in the classroom are less appreciated than the ones who show enthusiasm: 'He's somebody who has remained young, all the others are old mummys, strict, for whom school is just a place of work, to be serious, where you can't have fun'.

The children of course dislike teachers who have their favourites. Injustice is not tolerated, even by those who profit from the situation:

> The best (girls) were her favourites, and I was her favourite, one of my friends as well, but the boys since they are not as good as the girls, except two, well all the other boys it was as if they were not there.

Many examples of the teachers who show no signs of empathy or sympathy and who humiliate the children or indulge in verbal violence were given: 'I don't think she's nice, she says in front of the whole class, "X made 14 mistakes!", well I don't think this is nice, I don't like her at all'.

Teachers who don't teach well, who don't explain clearly, who have no imagination are also disliked. Some children try to understand them. One girl, after having reproached the injustice of her teacher, concluded: 'But it's normal that she's like that, because she's been a teacher for twelve years now. I understand she's tired. On the one hand I like her and on the other hand I don't like her too much'. A boy who criticised his teacher, added: 'We were making trouble all the time and so we were told off, in fact we searched for it, to be told off, but well, it was like military service'.

In sum, it is power abuse that the children disapprove of most frequently and the reasons they don't like some teachers have often to do with the problem of their asymmetrical relations.

Emotions and teacher control

A very rich palette of emotions accompanies their interactions with their teachers and the children give many examples of anger, fear, shyness, hate, shame and jealousy. Anger is aroused by injustice: 'Sometimes I find that the teacher scolds us for nothing. Generally I stop working and I stay like that, I wait until it is over because I can't work when I'm angry', says a boy. And another further explains: 'When the teacher shouts at us and we've done nothing, I am angry, I think of all the things I could do to annoy her, in order to make her pay for what she has done to me'.

Fear is often the result of the teachers' severity and is also present when the children anticipate their reaction. A girl says:

> I think that he should not exaggerate, because you should see how he is with us, eh, sometimes I'm really frightened with the way he tells us off, afterwards I'm afraid to raise my hand out of fear he will tell us off!

Shyness is sometimes encouraged by the teachers' methods: 'When he questions us I don't answer, because I'm shy in the class, so eh, I don't dare. And sometimes, my answer would have been correct'. Shame occurs in similar circumstances: 'When the teacher makes a remark to me I'm a little bit ashamed, because everybody looks at me, I'm embarrassed, I try to be noticed as little as possible, so that nobody sees me, nobody looks at me'. It also happens, as in the family context, that emotions are felt in relation to a schoolmate who is the victim of a teacher's remarks: 'Sometimes I feel pity for a friend who has been told off by the teacher, I find it's not fair'. Another example:

> There are always five or six boys who always have bad grades and Mr X does nothing to help them understand better. He says 'This is wrong', but he doesn't say where to look in our books, so I feel pity for them.

Jealousy among the children can be provoked by teachers who don't use the same criteria in their evaluations:

> When Y (a good student) has good marks, Mr X is always congratulating him. He should encourage us more, those who have done better. I am jealous of Y because he receives all the praise and when we try to work better well we get almost nothing.

More pleasant emotions, pride for example, are sometimes related to the situation when a student gives the right answer to the teacher. More often though it is related to receiving good marks without a direct interaction with the teacher. As for joy, it is principally associated with relationships with peers, recess time, and school outings. Unpleasant emotions are more frequently mentioned by the children than pleasant ones when they talk about their teachers and they seem to be mainly related to the demands and abuse of authority by the latter.

Some reactions to teacher control

How do the children act or react in the various situations in which they are involved with their teachers? What do they do when for example a teacher makes a negative statement as regards their conduct, reprimanding them for talking too much for example? The majority of the children say they accept the remark, they say that they recognise it is correct, they listen and comply. 'I stay quiet, but I don't put up my hand, because I don't like remarks; I listen but nothing more. I feel a little bit upset', says a girl. A boy has a similar attitude: 'I shut up and then I try to get on normally as if she had said nothing. Then I try to be less talkative. I think she's right'. Children take very seriously what may appear a simple comment: 'When the teacher makes remarks, I go to the toilets and then I talk to myself. I like this and sometimes I say: "you are stupid, why did you do that. Now you look stupid in front of the class"'.

Acquiescing to the teacher has a price, however, and all the children are not ready to pay it. Some children say that they pretend to accept the remark, they pretend they obey whilst they don't care, and even continue as before: 'I feel embarrassed when he makes remarks in front of the others. But afterwards we laugh at this, so as to show we are ... (we don't care), yeah, we laugh because what we did was funny'. Here is another example of this type of reaction: 'I shut up to start with. I'm upset at this, so I say "hm hm" like this, but not in front of him, he can't see. I say this to myself, inside'. Some other children react by answering back, sulking, or sometimes by refusing to participate. This child controls himself in front of the teacher but states quite explicitly what he thinks:

> Well, I stop talking but afterwards I say to the others 'yeah, he's a con', and things like that. Sometimes he's (the teacher) nice but sometimes he gets on my nerves and I feel like hitting him. I don't open my mouth the whole day when he asks questions, and then this bothers me, because sometimes there are things that I know and perhaps I am the only one to know and I never say.

A few children contest what the teacher reproaches: 'Well, I tell him it's not right, I want to say what I think, because I think that children have a right to express themselves, not only adults'.

Being defensive, expressing contempt or counterattacking occur less often than accepting the teachers' remarks. This is not surprising when one thinks of the relatively fragile position children occupy when they are pointed out by the teacher and risk losing face in front of their peers. Even the alliance with their peers is of little help in such situations.

Do children feel freer at home or at school? The majority of the children state that they feel freer at home than at school. As in Edward's study (this volume) of children's understandings of parental involvement in education, the home is described as a space of relaxation, leisure and freedom. It is the place where they feel comfortable, where they feel they can be themselves, where they can play, say what they want, shout, sing, relax, let off steam. They say that at home they can do the things they like with the people they like. Their discourse confirms Mayall's (1994) observation that life at school offers less scope for negotiation than in the family.

The company of peers and the construction of autonomy

The role of peers in the social development of children has been studied for a long time. In the sixteenth century, Comenius emphasised their importance:

> Parents and tutors are very useful for children but the company of other children is even more so. They tell each other stories and play together. Children who are equal in age, knowledge, politeness, mutually sharpen their minds … Nobody would doubt that a child contributes more than anybody to sharpening the mind of another child.
>
> (Prévot, 1981: 157)[4]

According to Piaget (1932) children's interactions with their peers contribute not only to their cognitive development but also to the development of their autonomy. In his analysis of children playing with marbles he showed that if interactions with adults are marked by constraint and heteronomy, interactions with peers are characterised by cooperation and autonomy (see also Sullivan, 1953 and Youniss, 1980). Psychologists and social psychologists have produced an impressive amount of studies on the role peers play in the development of children's social competencies (Shantz, 1987; Hartup, 1992) and socialisation (Harris, 1998). More recently, sociologists have started addressing the subject as well (Corsaro and Eder, 1990).

In our Genevan study the children spontaneously talked about their peers and friends, about the opportunities they share with each other to gain more autonomy and about the role they play in alleviating the weight of adult authority. Going downtown is a kind of adventure for children who up to recently were not allowed to. Once there, they go the movies, to the 'Mcdo' (Mcdonald's), to the skating-ring, and to the pool. These Saturday evening outings, without their parents, are opportunities to gain freedom of movement, to avoid parental control, occasions to exercise their autonomy.

Children learn many things in the company of friends: techniques in different sports, game rules, how to work for various school requirements, all kinds of information concerning the world of music, sports, shopping, etc. The exchange of knowledge that takes place amongst peers contributes to their autonomy as well: the information comes from different sources, they can compare what their parents or teachers say.

Children learn how to interact with others from their friends: how to respect one another, how to be tactful, how to share, how to dare communicate, how to make and keep friends, how to analyse feelings, including their own. They learn things about themselves. All this contributes to their autonomy:

> 'Since I've become one of them', says a girl, 'I have opened up. Before, I was in a little corner, never talked to the others. Now, when we enter a shop, I'm no longer afraid to go to somebody and ask where is this and that. Before, I didn't like to go up to other people, now it's much better. We opened up together, all of us'.

For many children peers are the only satisfaction they find in school life. They communicate curiosity, feelings; they contribute to modifying each other's ideas and tastes. If they often imitate each other, which can be considered as a sign of dependence or heteronomy, they also make efforts to be special, different, and contribute in the development of each other's identities.

The choice of friends is in itself an act of autonomy. Friends are quite often chosen for practical reasons, because they live close by, for example, but an autonomous choice is often involved as testified by the fact that the friends they choose are not always appreciated by their parents or teachers. Friends are chosen because they are attracted to each other, because of certain affinities and common tastes, because they get along well. They are chosen when there is a feeling of mutual trust. A friend is one to whom one can confide without fear, confide one's problems with parental authority, teacher injustice, or one's plans to avoid adult control.

Furthermore, the children have given many examples of the way they collectively appropriate the world around them. The rituals and games they create or carry out among peers, the language they use, are part of their micro-culture. In as much as they are not shared with the adult world they are manifestations of their autonomy.

CONCLUSION

Day after day children spend most of their time under the authority of their educators. When invited to talk about this experience, they make interesting observations on their parents' and teachers' practices. Even though they have some instrumental expectations from those involved in their socialisation – material support from their parents or professional competence from their teachers – they mostly expect from them affection, understanding and stimulation of autonomy. They observe, however, that their parents and teachers seem to be more preoccupied with everyday aspects of family and classroom life, supervising homework, getting ahead with the timetable, than with the affective dimensions in parenting and teaching. The research in Geneva shows that the children's experience is quite typical of a post-industrial society on the brink of the year 2000, valuing emancipation and autonomy but maintaining institutional dependencies and constraints.[5]

The experience children have of control and authority both at home and school consists not only of their representations; it comprises vivid emotions and imaginative behaviour as well. Both at school and in the family children show many ingenious strategies to curb their parents' and teachers' demands and control. They are conscious of the asymmetry of means between adults and children and many of them await with impatience being considered adult. Their rapport with authority is quite pragmatic. What else can they do in front of an adult who is not always sensitive enough to their situation and whom they understand, love and appreciate most of the time?

When one listens to the children's accounts, however, one sees quite clearly that they are not conditioned by the various socialisation agents and agencies. They are co-producers of the competencies and knowledge they develop in interaction with significant others, among which their peers occupy a special place.

NOTES

1 For a more complete presentation of the conceptual framework see Montandon (1997, 1998).

2 It is to be noted that the subject of the research was not authority, control or autonomy. These concepts were not explicitly defined in the research project. This chapter highlights elements in the data which have some connection with these issues.

3 It is very difficult to translate the children's language. I hope that I have not totally betrayed what they meant.

4 Prévot (1981) translated into French Comenius's *Opera didactica omnia* (Amsterdam 1657 – Prague 1957). The above citation, which I further translated into English, belongs to the chapter *Schola infantiae*.

5 The children's experience is often related to structural elements, to gender and social milieu. For example, anger and sadness in the family is more often mentioned by girls whereas pride and boredom by boys. Girls expect more empathy and imagination from their teachers; boys expect more fairness. In this chapter, however, emphasis was given to the asymmetrical relations children as a segment of society have with adults.

REFERENCES

Alanen, L. (1990) 'Rethinking Socialization, the Family and Childhood', *Sociological Studies of Child Development*, **3**, 13–28.

Buchner, P., du Bois-Reymond, M. and Kruger H.-H. (1995). 'Growing up in Three European Regions', in Chisolm, L., Buchner, P., Kruger, H.-H. and du Bois-Reymond, M. (eds), *Growing up in Europe. Contemporary Horizons in Childhood and Youth Studies*, Berlin: Walter de Gruyter, 43–60.

Corsaro, W.A. and Eder, D. (1990) 'Children's Peer Cultures'. *Annual Review of Sociology*, **16**, 197–220.

Corsaro, W.A. (1997) *The Sociology of Childhood*, London: A Pine Forge Press Publication.

Cullingford, C. (1991) *The Inner World of the School. Children's Ideas About Schools*, London: Cassell.

Harris, J.R. (1998) *The Nurture Assumption: Why Children Turn out the Way They Do*, New York: Free Press.

Hartup, W.W. (1992) 'Conflict and Friendship Relations', in Shantz, C.U. and Hartup, W.W. (eds), *Conflict in Child and Adolescent Development*, Cambridge: Cambridge University Press, 186–215.

James, A. and Prout, A. (eds) (1990) *Constructing and Reconstructing Childhood*, London: Falmer Press.

Jenks, C. (ed.) (1992) *The Sociology of Childhood. Essential Readings*, Brookfield, VT: Gregg Revivals.

Kellerhals, J. and Montandon, C. (1991) *Les stratégies éducatives des familles*, Paris: Delachaux et Niestlé.

Mayall, B. (ed.) (1994a) *Children's Childhoods: Observed and Experienced*, London: The Falmer Press.

Mayall, B. (1994b) 'Children in Action at Home and School', in Mayall, B. (ed.), *Children's Childhoods: Observed and Experienced*, London: The Falmer Press, 114–127.

Montandon, C. (1997) *L'éducation du point de vue des enfants*, Paris: L'Harmattan.

Montandon, C. (1998) 'Children's Perspectives on their Education', *Childhood*, **5**, 3, 247–263.

Piaget, J. (1932) *The Moral Judgment of the Child*, London: Routledge and Kegan Paul.

Pollard, A. (1985) *The Social World of the Primary School*, London: Holt, Rinehart and Winston.

Prévot, J. (1981) (ed.) Comenius. *L'utopie éducative*, Paris: Bélin.

Qvortrup, J., Bardy, M., Sgritta, G., Wintersberger, E. (eds) (1994) *Childhood Matters. Social Theory, Practice and Politics*, Hants, UK: Avebury.

Shantz, C.U. (1987) 'Conflicts between Children', *Child Development*, **58**, 283–305.

Sullivan, H.S. (1953) *The Interpersonal Theory of Psychiatry*, New York: Norton.

Waksler, F.C. (1991) 'Studying Children. Phenomenological Insights', in Waksler, F.C. (ed.) *Studying the Social Worlds of Children*, London: The Falmer Press.

Youniss, J. (1980) *Parents and Peers in Social Development*, Chicago: The University of Chicago Press.

7 Minding the gap

Children and young people negotiating relations between home and school

Pam Alldred, Miriam David and Rosalind Edwards

INTRODUCTION: PLACING HOME–SCHOOL RELATIONS POLITICALLY

In this chapter we explore how the children and young people in our study negotiated notions of 'family', 'home', 'education' and 'school' in relation to each other and their perspectives on parental involvement in their education. Do they see home and school as inter-related, or as separate spheres, with a clear boundary between them, and what would they prefer? Does the London Underground 'Mind the gap' warning[1] have resonance, such that any 'gap' between home and school represents risky dissonance between spheres? Or is it, instead, a separation with which they are comfortable; a boundary that can guard their personal privacy, where attempts to close the gap can threaten to intrude? Do they therefore *mind* a 'gap' between home and school in the sense of being bothered by it, or do they '*mind it*' in the sense of looking after and maintaining the separation between home and school?

Our study, *Children's Understandings of Parental Involvement in Education*[2], explored how children and young people with diverse backgrounds and identities – in terms of 'race', ethnicity, age, family and socio-economic circumstances, and at different schools – described their experiences of relations between home and school. We wanted to hear their *own* views, feelings and experiences, not as reported or mediated by their parents, teachers or schools. Although we set out to study accounts given in both home and school settings, because most participants chose to be interviewed at school, our study was, in the end, predominantly school-based. Elsewhere we discuss the particular ethical and methodological issues which are raised by the study of children or young people in school (see David *et al.* 2001).

The study was initiated during a period of Conservative rule in the UK (Edwards and David 1997), but conducted between 1997 and 1999 in a rapidly changing political and policy context, and during the height of the discourse of family-school partnerships. We were aware of this political context of powerful rhetoric about the importance of education, and, more specifically, as it was impacting within the particular schools in the study to produce a moment of self-consciousness (as well as compulsion) about their policy and practice regarding children's homes and families.

For children today, family and home do not necessarily coincide (David 1993; Haskey 1998; Silva and Smart 1999). Some public policy accounts of family in the UK are perhaps beginning to recognise diverse family forms and that changing within them are relationships between parents and children, and between men and women as adults, and as parents. Understandings of school and of education have also shifted as education policy and rhetoric have applied neo-liberal marketisation and indiv-idualist consumer rationalities to education. Changing discourses of education construct particular family and parental obligations. The discourse of parental choice in education which had become dominant by the end of the 1980s (Bowe *et al.* 1994) was part of a continuing shift from the language of state provision to private responsibility, such that families today are increasingly seen as the 'consumers' of public services such as education, yet also further drawn into provision.

These shifts in family–education relations gathered pace with the coming to power of New Labour in 1997. The consumerism of the parental choice discourse that dominated Conservative agendas in the UK in the 1980s and 1990s (David 1998; Gewirtz *et al.* 1995), was not rejected, but was further elaborated. There have been general initiatives on home–school relations, such as home–school agreements and the specification of homework policies for both primary and secondary school-aged children (David 1999; Edwards and Alldred 2000). The 1998 School Standards and Framework Act mandated written agreements for parents to sign, which set out parents' responsibilities for their children's school attendance and punctuality, home-work completion, discipline and good behaviour, as well as for informing the school of any problems affecting their children and generally supporting their schooling. In turn, schools agree to let parents know about their children's progress and any problems associated with their schooling. The central government Department of Education and Employment has also recently issued Parents' Guides to the National Curriculum, in an effort to encourage parents to get involved in their children's school project work, buy relevant books and CD-roms, and take their children to visit libraries and museums.

The government has additionally emphasised home–school relations for particular developments, such as parental involvement in children's education and social development, in identified areas of economic and social need. Education Action Zones (Department for Education and Employment 1998a) combine state provision with business enterprise to try to ensure parental involvement in children's education. Partnerships with parents are seen as the way to renew 'failing' schools (often those in poorer neighbourhoods). The focus on family or community agency in 'third way' political thinking encourages an individualist understanding of inequalities, and of responsibility for tackling them, downplaying wider social and economic forces and government responsibility for challenging them (Franklin 2000).

Family-school 'partnerships' have thus predominantly come to be seen as the means to raise educational standards and to develop opportunities for children. While posed as a 'partnership' between home and school, and/or parents and teachers, as pointed out in the introduction to this volume, from a more critical stance it can appear to be the incorporation and colonisation of the home by educational meanings (David *et al.* 1993; Edwards and Alldred 1999; Phoenix and Woollett 1991). Virtually everything that goes on in the home between parents (which in practice mostly means mothers) and their children potentially becomes defined as education, teaching and learning. For instance, the Government's rationale for strengthening home–school links stated that: 'Parents are a child's first and enduring teachers' (Department for Education and Employment 1998b: p. 3). As the introduction to this volume makes clear, a major thrust of current home–school relations policy is to break down divisions between home and school. The language of partnership masks the unequal nature of the relationship between home and school that reaches its height in the potentially intrusive and surveillant initiatives that have been piloted which involve teachers and community groups visiting the homes of parents who are unable or reluctant to come to school to discuss their children's education (e.g. the Alliance Schools Initiative, Foundation for Civil Society).

Thus 'family', and in particular 'parents', are heavily implicated in education policy, and parenting is increasingly constructed as an educational enterprise. Whether or not education policy is interpreted as having an ideological agenda regarding 'the family', it nevertheless impacts on families in normalising ways to validate certain domestic arrangements and family relationships and not others. Where children's family or home life does not conform to 'traditional' notions of the family, a (cultural) 'gap' between home and school or private and public spheres might be widened, but this might be preferred.

Having set out the political context for this study, we will now discuss how we saw the significance of place in our study – the regional and school settings. We will then describe the meanings children and young people gave to 'home' and 'school' as places and socially meaningful spaces, including how they position themselves in relation to home–school links. First, we isolate understandings of home and school artificially in order to discuss them, but secondly, we show how, in practice these understandings cannot be taken in isolation, how 'home' was understood in relation to, and sometimes in contrast with 'school' by children and young people.

PLACES AND SPACES: OUR STUDY

The post-war era has seen a 'polarisation' of urban space, reproducing social hierarchies in terms of residential segregation in cities and their suburbs (Byrne 1997) and concentrating deprivation and affluence spatially (Hudson and Williams 1995). In particular, there are interactions amongst 'race'/ethnicity and social class in urban space in relation to education. Particular minority ethnic populations are concentrated in deprived city areas – in London, Bangladeshi and African-Caribbean, as opposed to South Asian (Dorset 1998); and middle-class parents often move home to maximise their children's chances of attending a 'good school', while the working classes are more locally constrained (David *et al.* 1998; Gewirtz *et al.* 1995). So, education policies that encourage schools to look increasingly to the parents of the children attending them to meet shortfalls in resources further exacerbate the spatial polarisation of resources, including school facilities.

In order to include children and young people from a broad range of backgrounds in our study, we selected a primary and secondary school in each of three contrasting places: inner London, a London suburb and a town in the south east of England. We talked in-depth, in small groups, in pairs and individually, to just under 70 children overall in Year 6 and Year 9 classes in these schools, that is at 10 and 14 years respectively (for further discussion of the research process see Edwards and Alldred 1999; David *et al.* 2001). The discussions and interviews were concerned with understandings and experiences of parental involvement in their education and home–school relations more broadly.

We chose these locations, and certain schools within them, in order to produce a diverse population of potential participants. Schools whose 'catchment areas' had markedly different demographics were selected, since schools in different places might have different school cultures, and we used eligibility for free school meals to indicate levels of deprivation, as a proxy for social class. In terms of ethnicity, in London, the inner city primary and secondary schools each drew pupils from a range of ethnic groups – mainly African-Caribbean, South Asian and White. In these schools, over half the pupils received free school meals because their parents claimed state benefits. The London suburban primary and secondary schools also contained pupils from a range of ethnic groups – mainly Asian and White. However, in these schools only 10 per cent of the pupils had free school meals. The schools in the town in the south east of England had much less ethnic diversity, being overwhelmingly White, and had around 20 per cent of pupils claiming free school meals, which is close to the national average. The participants therefore lived in varied socio-economic circum-stances and family forms.

We were interested in place both in terms of the coalescence of particular pupils in relation to class and ethnicity in particular urban locations, and also with place in the sense of home and school as distinct social spaces that children and young people are located within and move between. Furthermore, we were interested in how these two might interact such that school and home are experienced within particular localised social contexts, for instance, as a young woman from a minority ethnic group in a school with a high or low minority ethnic intake situated in a corresponding locality.

Conceptualising school and home

School and home are everyday spaces in and through which children's identities and lives are shaped and remade, in ways which then feedback into and shape the meaning of those spaces. As settings, school and home map onto, and are part of, notions of public and private spheres of life, which have received much feminist analysis and critique (see Edwards 1993; Edwards and Ribbens 1998; Ribbens McCarthy and Edwards 2001). Public and private – and within them, school and home – can be identified by reference to physical location, but can involve contrasting principles of social organisation (Cheal 1991), or different modes of organisational consciousness (Smith 1987), comprising psychological space and ontological experience as well as social relations and activities. Nevertheless, public sphere policies, activities and trends, and private sphere processes, relations and practices, are overlapping and inter-dependent, as interactions between education reform and family life suggest, and 'partnership' policy interventions illustrate vividly through their challenge to divisions between school (as public) and home (as private).

The politics of everyday life is not protected from the politics 'out there' in the public sphere. Despite this, as we will see, in people's everyday understandings and experiences there may be a distinct 'gap' between the two spheres in terms of their cultures. In the children and young people's accounts, 'school' and 'home' obviously indicated distinct physical spaces, but furthermore, were often posed as contrasting social spaces and experiences involving different sets of values. When policy aims are to integrate school and home, two value systems may clash, and one of them has institutional power through the practices and rhetoric of schooling and of education.

Particular constructions of the constitution of, and relationship between, home and school are embedded in policy discourse, and particular understandings are embedded in the accounts given by young people. Elsewhere we have produced a typology of parental involvement in education centring on children and young people, highlighting the way that they may initiate, facilitate, go along with, discourage or resist aspects of their parents' involvement in their education in complex and strategic ways (Edwards and Alldred 2000). These various approaches to parental involvement, and the children and young people's positioning in relation to separating or connecting their school and home lives more generally, are underpinned by certain understandings of the nature of home and school, of education and of family. We will now set out these meanings separately, and overview the patterns across our sample as a whole. First we discuss the meanings of 'school', and then of 'home', but we would stress that each of these cannot be taken in isolation. Our empirical material does not easily provide two distinct descriptions because the children and young people we spoke to constructed and understood 'school' and 'home' *in relation to*, and often in contrast to, each other.

Meanings of school

School is a particular aspect of the public sphere – a formally organised and institutionalised (both internally and externally) educational setting, separating children off from, but equipping them for an (adult) future in other aspects of the public. It is a space in which children are sequentially segregated with their peers according to age, and linked to levels of educational attainment. In turn, progression into and through the school system by age defines the time of 'childhood' (as noted in the introductory chapter to this volume). This fixed age-sequential segregation and progression also means that children are viewed as a group and so essentially the same (Mayall 1994), and merely at different stages along a unitary developmental pathway (Burman 1994). School modes of social organisation are shaped around compliance to order, convention, regulation and hierarchy (or resistance to it), within both the everyday formal and informal curricula. Allison James and colleagues (1998) emphasize the formal division of the day into time-tabled segments in which different skills are taught, and the placing of children in classrooms to facilitate learning and discipline, and the informal re-inscription of gender and other social divisions. The segmented regime imposed by the school system also shapes children and young people's experiences of friendship (Amit-Talai 1995).

Indeed, in our research, the children and young people characterised school as involving formal rules and timetables, and general constraints upon feelings and behaviour. The inability to eat when you wanted, or to lose your temper or generally be 'loud', were often used as illustrations of the constraints involved. It was these regimented aspects of school life as part of the group 'pupils' that featured large in the children and young people's accounts rather than education and learning, although some did refer to schooling as preparation for, and important to, their future (adult) prospects of 'getting on' in life.

'Bad' teachers were described as those who took the regulation and control of children too far; who would not listen, shouted at them, and ordered them around peremptorily. They might also be too 'nosey' about children's lives outside the classroom, and be 'boring' as educators. Good teachers possessed a variety of characteristics, including being funny, listening and understanding, not being 'nosey', and were occasionally referred to as stimulating and lucid educators.

School was also spoken about as a place for mixing with friends and peers. The conduct of peer and friendship relations was often posed as being shaped and constrained by the institutional structuring of rules and timetables, for example in being unable to talk to your friend in class. However, experiencing the regime of the school mode of social organisation did not necessarily equate with feelings of safety: fears of threats and bullying and/or having been bullied by peers or picked on by teachers were also an aspect of some children and young people's accounts.

Meanings of home

The setting of home is informally (but nonetheless institutionally) organised around familial and intimate relationships, and bearing the history of the material and ideological association of women and children with the 'haven' of the private domestic sphere (again, as noted in the introductory chapter to this volume). Home modes of social organisation, for children, are shaped around particularity, (inter)dependency, care and surveillance. Work addressing this area of children's lives often points to issues of gendered and generational power within households and families, and makes clear that the home is not necessarily a haven for children, being a site of (adult) control and most sexual abuse (James *et al.* 1998), although some commentators address the way that it provides a more negotiable context (in comparison with school) for children as individuals (Mayall 1994).

The idea of the home as a regulated socialisation space for children did not feature much in our empirical data. In explicit contrast to their accounts of school life, the children and young people largely emphasised their freedom from restraint, and the intimacy available within the home. Home was portrayed as a place where they could relax and do what they wanted when they wanted. Freedoms in relation to watching television, eating, and getting angry and being 'noisy', were often mentioned.

Getting angry, of course, implies someone to be angry at. Home life was also about being an individual in familial relationship to others, as daughter/son, sister/brother, grandchild, cousin and so on. Other family members were often posed by the children and young people as providing them with support and someone they could talk to, just as much as argue with. Indeed, as we have pointed out elsewhere (Edwards and Alldred 2000), children and young people's activities in relation to parental involvement in their education – both facilitation and resistance – mostly occurs on the basis of the familial intimate connection between themselves and their parents, especially their mothers, rather than on educational grounds.

If the children and young people themselves could be loud and angry at home, then so could other family members. Mothers in particular were often described as sometimes shouting and 'getting stressed', as well as being caring and loving most of the time. In contrast to teachers though, such behaviour did not mean that they were regarded as 'bad' mothers.

The privacy of the domestic sphere was also a strong feature of the children and young people's accounts, resonating with their dislike of 'nosey' teachers. In particular, they felt that details of their home lives should only be made public to the school if it was seriously affecting their education or if child protection issues were involved. Even so, they wanted to decide whether and which teachers were approached about any problems. This was emphatically an area of home–school relations in which the children and young people 'minded' the gap: they 'minded' in that they cared about there being a privacy gap in relation to the school's knowledge of their family and home lives, and they 'minded' in that they 'policed' this gap as far as they could.

An overview of differences in home–school boundaries or connections

The meanings accorded the 'gap' between school and home in the children and young people's accounts form the basis on which they also negotiate and experience home–school relations. We have indicated how they attach quite different, contrasting, meanings to home and school as specific and concrete private and public modes of social organisation. It does not follow necessarily, however, that children and young people want or experience only a gap between these two aspects of their lives.

Taking an overview of our sample of children and young people's stances towards relations between home and school we can identify some patterns around the construction of boundaries between the two, or efforts towards connecting these places and spaces in their lives. Those from the inner city schools were far more likely to maintain a gap, or to experience a separation, between their home and school lives, as were children in working class circumstances (that is, from working class families and/or attending a school with a predominantly working class intake) across all ethnic groups, as well as those of South Asian origin generally. Age is also a factor, with young people in the secondary schools talking more about separation in home–school relations and parental involvement than their younger peers.

In addition, girls tended to talk more about being active in initiating or facilitating their parents' – especially their mothers' – involvement in a broad range of aspects of their schooling, while boys who involved their parents tended to focus more on doing this in relation to their formal schoolwork. Both boys and girls, however, most often did this in relation to parental involvement in the home setting than in school.

This sort of patterned overview by social characteristics of the construction or maintenance of gaps and boundaries between home and school lives, or the building or sustenance of links and connections, while it has some uses, does not allow for an appreciation of the complex interactions and negotiations that children and young people undertake. It gives little sense, in particular, of the concrete ways that gender, class and ethnicity interact to shape children and young people's understandings and experiences of home–school relations in a localised and personal context. In this respect, case studies can better illustrate the particular and the holistic. In the next section we present three case studies of individual children or young people who took part in the study.[3] These explore how the meanings of school and of home are intricately interwoven in the context of individual children's lives, and their different negotiations in relation to the two settings. We look at: 'Nisha',[4] who actively 'minded' the gap between her home and school lives; 'Sonia', who experienced a high degree of connection between her home and school lives; and 'Gibson' who steered a middle course between these two stances. In these three cases, we are not concerned with 'typicality' and representativeness (in relation to the stances in our overview above), but with demonstrating the everyday confluence and juxtaposition of modes of social organisation. Looking at these as manifested within specific contexts allows a deeper understanding of the processes underlying, and practice of, home–school relations for children and young people.

Home–school boundaries or connections: particular children, particular lives

Maintaining the gap: policing the boundaries between home and school

'Nisha' is a 13-year-old South Asian girl who goes to the suburban secondary school. She lives in a 'nice' owner-occupied area, with her mother, father and older brother. Her account is striking for being characterised by a strong sense of separation between her home and school life, which she consciously articulates, and a strong preference for a gap, which she defends robustly. At home she feels well understood: 'my mum just knows there's something up as soon as I come home', and she does not think it appropriate for teachers to ask about her home-life or for the school to have any knowledge about her family that she has not volunteered. 'It's my life!', she says indignantly, conveying her desire for privacy and autonomy.

She spontaneously and happily tells her mother, father and brother what she wants to about her school day and feels she can speak openly with her parents. She describes a range of issues concerning school and friends which she talks to them about and says how much she values this openness for the support it gives her, and in particular, for the intimacy that confiding in her mother engenders:

Sometimes I think of my mum as my best friend, …'cause I can talk to her about anything, all the things about school. Some of my friends can't talk to their mums about boyfriends or anything, but I can tell her even really personal things. I don't tell my dad those things, 'cause it's different, and he's just really protective of me.

She feels positive about her parents' responses and, for instance, is confident that in the (unlikely) event of a bad school report, they would be concerned and ask her about it in an understanding, not angry way. However, occasionally she gives only brief answers to their questions (especially her dad's) on matters that she does not wish to discuss. Nisha is therefore highly active in the maintenance of firm boundaries between home and school, and in decisions about what exactly to tell people on either side of them. She likes to be in control of the flow of information between her family and the school. She is highly conscious of privacy issues and her own personal boundaries around, but also *within* the family, and discusses these in detail by contrasting her own views on what is appropriate with anecdotes revealing those of her friends and year group. Nisha's account clearly illustrates that a strong preference to retain boundaries between the two spheres, and, in particular, to keep family life separate from school and outside the school's gaze, is not necessarily linked to little general communication between a child and their parent/s or a feeling of being unable to confide in parents. Indeed, her interview involved lots of discussion about communication within the family and between its members, which she appreciates as one of the things she likes best about her family and is keen to reflect upon.

She values home as a place to relax and unwind after school, but she also maintains a busy schedule of leisure activities. For instance, learning Indian dance is important to her as a cultural activity. However, domestic activities, which may be valued additionally for their cultural significance, can be compromised by education:'I cook rice, chicken, curries, all that sort of stuff, but I don't cook every day 'cause my mum thinks studies are more important than cooking. She's right!' Furthermore, Nisha can actively work to connect her education with her family at home as she sees fit. If she needs any help with homework she goes to her mum or brother, and specifically to her dad for any help with mathematics. She values being able to ask her brother things: 'Cause he's already been through everything', although she can sometimes reciprocate by helping him with homework that requires conversation or practice (e.g. languages or drama). At home, the involvement and support of her brother is important to her. Her strong sense of herself as active in making decisions about her life means that her parents are cast in merely supportive roles, whereas regarding decisions about her education, her brother's views are very significant. Such support from siblings is under-recognised in the education discourse of '*parental* involvement in education'.

Nevertheless, despite the fact that she says:'I think studies are the most important thing in my life because I want to be a doctor', Nisha actively discourages links between her family and the school. In terms of parental involvement in education, Nisha's parents are involved, but she allows their involvement strictly in the home only and not in (or with) school. For instance, she welcomes their support and encouragement for her education, but is certain that she does not want them to get involved at the school or in its running. Similarly, the idea of a teacher visiting her at home is a 'Nightmare!', even though she knows her family would be very hospitable. For her this would be a breach of privacy and she would rapidly find an excuse to leave the house politely.

As indicated earlier, home is a site of affirmation of Nisha's cultural identity and heritage. Although she describes her values and aspirations as 'Western', her identifications with home and family must also be seen in the context of her consciousness of racism in school and in society at large. As well as being generally articulate about racism, she has personal experience and describes the family's experience of discrimination from a traffic warden: 'he didn't put [a ticket] on their cars 'cause we're coloured. If we were White I'm sure he wouldn't, you know', and the, 'Go back to your own country, you pakki', abuse her father faced in the business her parents used to run.

Nisha describes herself as quite popular at school and as self-confident enough to gain respect for expressing her own views even where these clash with those of her peer group. Despite this, she perceives differences between how she behaves at school and at home: 'Basically I'm very shy and quiet at school, and I'm the loudest person alive at home!', and she has a sense of moderating her behaviour: 'I just can't find myself to be myself at school'. She identifies some contradictory elements though, such as the fact that she swears at school (where is it 'part and parcel of being young'), whereas she wouldn't at home because it would upset her dad. This hints at the complicated interrelation of the gendered, sexual, ethnic and 'classed' identities Nisha occupies, as well as her personal maturity and confidence. 'You have to play many roles', she says: 'When I'm with my friends I'm loud, but when I'm around boys, I'm quiet', partly because all the girls get loud and showy and she 'can't get a word in edgeways!', and partly because she rejects their self-conscious ('Is my hair alright?') behaviour. The two spheres of home and school for Nisha then are clearly characterised by different local value systems amongst the specific people around her (e.g. her dad's objection to swearing, the peer group culture among her friends). The cultural gap between home and school needs careful negotiation on Nisha's part.

It is therefore possible to work to maintain the gap between family and school and to discourage extensive parental involvement in one's education, whilst having a strong sense of family as being about 'togetherness', and supporting and talking to each other. In addition, for Nisha, despite her separation of school from home, home is a positive place for education, where she decides when and how her parents are involved.

Close connections between home and school

'Sonia' is the same age as Nisha and goes to the town secondary school. She is of dual heritage, having a White European mother and a father from South East Asia. She lives with her mother, father and older brother, Phil. She actively connects home and school spheres in some ways and in other ways experiences particular overlaps and connections between them which are beyond her control.

Sonia's mother is a teacher at the secondary school she attends and is therefore known to many of her peers. She describes having her mum teaching at her school as 'a bit irritating!' and the irritations she describes are all about how it positions her in the eyes of other pupils (as opposed to her own boundaries). She has contact with her mother during the day at school, both in her role as a teacher (to whom she goes for extra work), and as a mother, to whom she goes to get money. The particularities of Sonia's situation raise some fascinating issues of separation and connection. It sets up certain tensions for her such as that whilst she believes that teachers generally shouldn't know about pupils' home lives because it's 'none of their business', some teachers from school, because of their friendship with her mother, occasionally visit her home. Similarly, while she resents being known as 'Miss Long's daughter' or 'Phil Long's sister', she values the fact that her mother knows 'what's going on at school' both in terms of her educational progress and for the protective function this could have in case of trouble. 'Trouble' and 'safety' are significant themes in Sonia's account. The sense of danger at school or in town is notable and the threat to her, as to her brother, could come from the fact that their ethnicity means they 'look different' in the predominantly White environment of school and town. There is an overall theme of connection between home and school for Sonia, in spite of the sense she has of her peers as potentially threatening, and her desire for a degree of separation on certain issues.

Sonia has a strong sense of school as restrictive and enjoys 'being different' outside of school by wearing 'wilder clothes' and the sense of greater freedom of emotional expression. At school, she feels she has to 'act happy and not lose my temper, but, at home, they understand'. In each of these, and regarding food differences too, the version at home is preferable to that at school. Similarly, her mother is perceived as 'strict' at school, but 'nice' by friends who meet her at home as 'Sonia's mum'. Despite these differences between home and school for her sense of self, in terms of her home as a place, Sonia gives the strong impression that her home is suffused with educational meanings and pressures, in part at least because of the literal overlaps and connections between her family and her school. Home is not in contrast with the business of education, although Sonia does also describe it as a place to relax and play with her pets. She discusses at length her own academic successes and those of her family members, and clearly takes pride in these. Not only are both her mother and her father very clever, but so too is her brother and many members of her extended family. She argues for the importance of education, and of the need to be pushed to work hard and set targets to achieve, but that 'it's probably [down to] genetics', so there's no point telling people off for poor schoolwork because 'some people will be not particularly bright all their lives … You're just born with it'. She talks of her own educational motivation too, but does say that she thinks her family are 'too education orientated':

> It's like education, education, education. Can we talk about something *else* please?! It's a really big thing because my mum's a teacher, dad was offered a degree at Oxbridge, one of those you don't have to work for, you're just capable of, so they say 'have a degree', my brother's a complete genius, my uncle's a professor and we've got engineers in the family, a great artist, a vicar…

The ambivalence Sonia shows towards education is paralleled in her relationship to her brother: she finds Phil very irritating and sees him as different from herself, even as she admires his 'genius'. Both her mother and father are involved in her education at home: her mother gives critical feedback on her work and sets her extra work, and her father offers to ask teachers for more homework; but so too are other family friends, and she enjoys the fact that they take an interest and encourage her. This probably extends the sense of education yet further into Sonia's home life. However, alongside this pressure, she does feel she has some autonomy: 'They think you've got to get a good education or you'll not get anywhere, so it's really hard ... [but] they wouldn't make me do it if I didn't want to'. Many adults give her advice on education issues, but she feels clearly that such decisions are her own.

Sonia's positive view of education does not correspond to being totally pro-school, in spite of her academic success. The relative lack of the usual gap between home and school for Sonia is not of her choosing and places her preferences for connecting or separating home and school in a very particular context. Many of the ways in which she acts to maintain close links between home and school relate precisely to her mother's presence in the school. Some are about personal concerns (e.g. safety) and others are educational issues. However, not all the children and young people who share Sonia's sense of connection between their family and school lives are pro-education in the way that she is. Part of her preference for some forms of connection between home and school seems to relate to her ethnicity, or rather, her sense of her ethnic and other particularities. Many minority ethnic children prefer to keep their home and school lives separate, as the previous section outlined, but Sonia's circumstances mean that this option is not available to her: she cannot keep her home and school lives separate. Instead she accepts and sustains the links that exist for her. Not only does her ethnicity make her visible, her academic success and her being a teacher's daughter each mark her out at school. This illustrates how the protective function of a gap between home and school may be reversed for children or young people who feel they are, or are seen to be, different in yet other ways. It also begins to point to layers of individual, peer, family, school, local area and policy contexts which may be significant in understanding pupils' preferences regarding home–school relations.

Mixing connection and separation between home and school

'Gibson' is a 10-year-old African boy who goes to the inner London primary school. He lives with his mum, his aunty, two older brothers and his sister. He talks a lot about the meaning of family and describes many family moments, rituals, rules and understandings. The family are practising Christians and say prayers at the breakfast and supper table. Gibson usually welcomes his mother's questions about how his day has been, and reciprocates by asking her about her day at work. He is positive about education and says that he 'always' does his homework. His mum helps with it and, if she's not in, his aunty does, but it is striking how much 'education' goes on at home for him. In particular, domestic tasks and skills are posed as education and are highly valued:

I mostly have homework in the weekends, so my mum helps me then if I've got a lot. And she teaches me how to use the computer. She teaches me nearly everything. We have discipline lessons and we have to go to the library as well (PA: *What's 'discipline lessons'?*). Like sometimes we have to learn to cook something, and sometimes we have to learn how to set the table and stuff and how to do things – what we're going to be doing when we're older.

The 'we' is Gibson and his brothers, and the considerable value accorded household tasks might relate to the high value placed on family life. There is also a future orientation to this type of education: equipping him with skills 'because they'll be good for me during my future', as well as to his sense of the value for the future of education in the school sphere. Academic learning also extends across both home and school spheres, particularly around computing.

Whilst educational meanings pervade Gibson's home life, there are few connections to his family from school. Indeed, although there is one particular connection that is outside of his direct control, in areas that are within his control, he works to limit and block connections between home and school in the form of school-based events. The connection that he involuntarily experiences is a friendly relationship between his mother and his teacher, which means that his (female) teacher has occasionally come to his home for tea. The boundaries Gibson spontaneously describes as important are that his mother must respect that he may wish to keep some parts of his day or his experience of school private from her in their 'after school/work' discussions. Similarly, he wants some control over the information that his teacher might give to his mum at home, which means that although he wouldn't chose to have his teacher come to his home because 'it's private!', if she does, he wants to be present to hear what is said.

On issues where Gibson has more power to influence the degree of connection between home and school, he is very clear and eager to explain his reasons for limiting connections, which generally centre around a notion of privacy. On talking to his mum at home about school, he says:

> Sometimes I don't tell her every single thing, because sometimes it's private and I can't tell anyone [PA: *What sorts of things do you keep private?*]. Relationships, erm, if I was bad or not. I tell her if it's just a bit, but not if it's too bad.

About having his mum come into school or mix with his school friends, he says:

> I would not like her to come on a day trip, no, not even a monthly trip, but only on a trip like to the River Thames because that's boring. I'd like her to come on a trip like that. But when there's a trip to go somewhere, like stay with your friends only, I'd not like her to do that because I think that's a bit private. It's a bit like time spent away from home. It's time for you with your friends and not family time.

So Gibson has a strong sense of himself as separate from his family and wants some control over his relationships outside the family. In particular, he maintains a gap between his relationships with his school friends and with his mother and family, and whether it is regarding everyday involvement at school, school trips or visits to a friend's house, he wants and expects a degree of privacy.

At home, Gibson is happy to allow and to create connections between his education and his home life, but at school, there are firm limits on the links with his family. Some of the connections he does encourage, for example telling his mother about school, appear to relate to intimacy and 'getting it off your chest' far more than to educational concerns, as was the case for Nisha too. He also describes wanting to control the limits of this and therefore is not always straight-forwardly connecting the two spheres. Gibson combines preferences for connection and for separation between home and school that show how complicated a mixture there can be of involving a parent yet of guarding against their intrusion into school life or relationships with friends.

CONCLUSION: MINDING THE GAP BETWEEN HOME AND SCHOOL

Our three case studies show the relations between home, school, education and family in the lives of particular children and young people. They begin to show how separations or connections between the spheres of home and school can relate to each other in different ways. The separations or connections that children and young people experience as already existing, those that they try to create or maintain, and the values of the different cultural settings they occupy, inter-relate in complex ways.

Each of our case studies are of people who were generally positive about education, and in each case, fairly positive about school. They were also each positive about their relationship with their family. The studies illustrate how intimacy and family relationships can be a more significant motivation for some children and young people's involvement of their parents in their education than instrumental educational reasons. Nevertheless, as did many of the minority ethnic children in our research, they each preferred to keep their home and school lives largely separate. In Sonia's case, her particular circumstances meant that this option was not fully available to her: it was not possible for her to be unmarked at school or for her family/home life to be kept separate from the school context. A limited degree of choice about the gap between home and school might well alter or impinge on children and young people's preferences about separation and connection.

Examining our material through case studies allows recognition of the complexity of relations between the spheres. The valuing of one sphere is not necessarily at the expense of the other, as for Nisha and Gibson. The values of home can be contrasted with education or seen as compatible with it, or this relation may be much more complicated. For Gibson, the family sphere is highly valued relative to the school sphere, yet home and family are themselves imbued with highly educationalised meanings. However, education can also be defined differently at home, to encompass broader activities or aims and to include activities (such as home-making) that might not be recognised as educational or valued highly by schools. Education policy discourses can be narrower in other ways too: the discourse of parental involvement in education constructs parents as the important players in a pupil's family life, occluding the significance of others, where siblings in particular may well be significant (see also Edwards and Alldred 2000). The meanings of education that schools increasing export to the home sphere – making this space less 'private' and more associated with education (in its particular institutionalised sense) – are particular understandings of education, not necessarily the first or only educational meanings to pervade the space.

A gap or separation between home and school can be a boundary that provides a marker, and over which children and young people negotiate in order to secure the privacy and separation that they expect or prefer between family relationships and identities and school and peer relationships and identities (in either or both directions), as for Nisha and for Gibson. Alternatively, a gap can highlight the potential threat of clashing value systems, cultures or meanings. Something that seems threatening emerges within Sonia's account, although it is paradoxical. The different value systems of classmates and family that Nisha straddles regarding issues such as swearing and how loud she is, might have their echo in Sonia's account of the pro-education family, but 'trendy' (not 'boffin') friends, although the connections and continuities between her home and school lives leave less room for her to 'be' different. Yet Sonia is also able to make furthering the connections work for her, so that her mother's access to the school situation is protective.

The overall, and important, lesson emerging from our discussion of home–school relations and our case studies is that policies and interventions seeking to build links between parents and schools, are entering into particular and diverse – but also much broader structural – issues that are embedded in the relationship between home and school. Here we have particularly concentrated on the concrete ways that ethnicity and gender relations can interact to shape children and young people's understandings, experiences and negotiations of home and school, in localised and personal context. Existing approaches to home–school relations in policy and practice arenas seem to have hardly begun to engage with the diversity of meanings 'home–school relations' might have, the functions they might serve for children and young people, and the underlying broader structural issues involved.

NOTES

1 At many underground stations a warning is broadcast asking passengers to 'mind the gap' between train and platform.

2 Funded by the Economic and Social Research Council under grant no. L129251012, as part of the *Children 5–16: Growing into the Twenty-first Century* research programme.

3 Each of the children represented here as case studies chose to be interviewed on their own (rather than the 'pair interviews' that just over half of the participants chose to do with a close classmate): Nisha at her home, and Sonia and Gibson each at their own school.

4 The names used here are pseudonyms, which in most cases participants chose themselves. We have changed other names or other identifying features as we felt appropriate.

REFERENCES

Amit-Talai,V. (1995) 'The waltz of sociability: intimacy, dislocation and friendship in a Quebec high school', in V. Amit-Talai and H. Wulff (eds) *Youth Cultures: A Cross-Cultural Perspective*, London: Routledge.

Bowe, R., Gerwirtz, S. and Ball, S. (1994) 'Captured by the discourse? Issues and concerns in researching "parental choice"', *British Journal of Sociology of Education*, 15, 1: 63–78.

Burman, E. (1994) *Deconstructing Developmental Psychology*, London: Routledge.

Byrne, D.S. (1997) 'Chaotic cities or complex cities?', in S. Westwood and J. Williams (eds) *Imagining Cities*, London: Routledge.

Cheal, D. (1991) *Family and the State of Theory*, Hemel Hempstead: Harvester/Wheatsheaf.

David, M.E. (1993) *Parents, Gender and Education Reform*, Cambridge: Polity Press.

David, M.E. (1998) 'Education, education, education', in H. Jones and S. McGregor (eds) *Social Issues and Party Politics,* London: Routledge.

David, M.E. (1999) 'Home, work, families and children: New Labour, new directions and new dilemmas', *International Studies in the Sociology of Education*, 9, 3: 209–229.

David, M., Davies, J., Edwards, R., Reay, D. and Standing, K. (1998) 'Choice within constraints: mothers and schooling', *Gender and Education* 9, 4: 397–410.

David, M., Edwards, R. and Alldred, P. (2001) 'Children and school-based research: 'informed consent' or 'educated consent'?', *British Educational Research Journal*, 27, 3: 347–365 .

David, M., Edwards, R., Hughes, M. and Ribbens, J. (1993) *Mothers and Education: Inside Out? Exploring Family-Education Policy and Experience*, Basingstoke: Macmillan.

Department for Education and Employment (1998a) *Meet the Challenge: Education Action Zones*, London: DfEE.

Department for Education and Employment (1998b) *Home–School Agreements: Guidance for Schools*, London: DfEE.

Dorset, R. (1998) *Ethnic Minorities in the Inner City*, Bristol: Policy Press/Joseph Rowntree Foundation.

Edwards, R. (1993) *Mature Women Students: Separating or Connecting Family and Education*, London: Taylor and Francis.

Edwards, R. and Alldred, P. (1999) 'Children and young people's views of social research: the case of research on home–school relations', *Childhood: A Global Journal of Child Research* 6, 2: 261–81.

Edwards, R. and Alldred, P. (2000) 'A typology of parental involvement in education centring on children and young people: negotiating familialisation, institutionalisation and individualisation', *British Journal of Sociology of Education*, 21, 3: 435–455.

Edwards, R. and David, M. (1997) 'Where are the children in home–school relations?', *Children & Society*, 11: 183–193.

Edwards, R. and Ribbens, J. (1998) 'Living on the edges: public knowledge, private lives, personal experience', in J. Ribbens and R. Edwards (eds) *Feminist Dilemmas in Qualitative Research: Public Knowledge and Private Lives*, London: Sage.

Franklin, J. (2000) 'What's wrong with New Labour politics?' *Feminist Review* 66: 137–141.

Gerwitz, S., Ball, S.J. and Bowe, R. (1995) *Markets, Choice and Equity in Education*, Buckingham: Open University Press.

Haskey, J. (1998) 'Families: their historical context, and recent trends in the factors influencing their formation and dissolution', in David, M.E. (ed.) *The Fragmenting Family: Does It Matter?* London: IEA Choice in Welfare 44.

Hudson, R. and Williams, A. (1995, 2nd edn) *Divided Britain*, Chichester: Wiley.

James, A., Jenks, C. and Prout, A. (1998) *Theorising Childhood*, Cambridge: Polity Press.

Mayall, B. (1994) 'Children in action at home and school', in B. Mayall (ed.) *Children's Childhoods: Observed and Experienced*, London: Falmer.

Phoenix, A. and Woollett, A. (1991) 'Motherhood: social construction, politics and psychology', in A. Phoenix, A. Woollett and E. Lloyd (eds) *Motherhood: Meanings, Practices and Ideologies*, London: Sage.

Ribbens McCarthy, J. and Edwards, R. (2001) 'Individuality and connectedness in the lives of mothers and children: maintaining a perspective on public and private', in A. Carling, S. Duncan and R. Edwards (eds) *Analysing Families: Morality and Rationality in Policy and Practice*, London: Routledge.

Silva, E. and Smart, C. (eds) (1999) *The New Family?*, London: Sage.

Smith, D.E. (1987) *The Everyday World as Problematic: A Feminist Sociology*, Boston: Northeastern University.

8 Priming events, autonomy and agency in low-income African-American children's transition from home to school

William A. Corsaro and Katherine Brown Rosier

INTRODUCTION

In a series of papers over the last ten years we have developed an approach to children's socialization that we have referred to as interpretive reproduction (Corsaro 1992; 1997; Corsaro and Molinari 2000; Corsaro and Rosier 1992). This approach differs from traditional theories of human development and socialization in several important respects. First, we place special emphasis on language and children's participation in everyday cultural routines. As Elinor Ochs has argued, language is central for children's socialization both as a 'symbolic system that encodes local social and cultural structure' and as a 'tool for establishing (i.e. maintaining, creating) social and psychological realities' (1988: 210). These dual aspects of language as a symbolic system and as tool of cultural production are 'deeply embedded and instrumental in the accomplishment of concrete routines of social life' (Schieffelin 1990: 19). The habitual, taken-for-granted character of everyday routines provides actors with the security of belonging to a social group. At the same time, this very predictability empowers routines, providing actors with basic frameworks (Goffman 1974) within which they can produce, display, and interpret sociocultural knowledge.

Second, the interpretive approach extends traditional theories of socialization which view development as children's linear progression from immaturity to adult competence. From our interpretive perspective, the cultural-developmental process is not linear but reproductive. It is reproductive in that what children do with adults and other children involves the use, refinement, and transformation of cultural resources (see Corsaro 1992). In this process of interpretive reproduction, children become a part of adult culture – that is, contribute to its reproduction – through their active negotiations with adults and their creation, with other children, of a series of peer cultures (also see Prout and James 1997). Thus, socialization is not merely a matter of acquiring culture at the level of the individual child but also a collective process of innovative or interpretive reproduction.

Central to the interpretive perspective is the documentation of key transitions in children's lives. The most appropriate method for such documentation is comparative, longitudinal ethnography (Corsaro 1996). Such ethnographies allow us to capture ongoing productive-reproductive processes in children's lives as they move from the family to other social institutions, and examine how children negotiate these transitions in a number of embedded local cultures such as the family, school and peer group. In this chapter we draw from interview and observational materials collected in a three year ethnography of nine African-American families living in poverty to examine everyday occurrences which focus children and their parents on coming changes in the children's lives. We refer to these experiences as *priming events* because they involve activities in which children, by their very participation, attend prospectively to anticipated changes (Corsaro and Molinari 2000). In this chapter, we focus on the language and communicative styles that parents, teachers, and children employ in their participation in the priming events embedded in everyday cultural routines. We give special attention to the active involvement and autonomy of the children as they negotiate challenges in the transition process with parents, teachers, and peers.

ETHNOGRAPHIC CONTEXT AND DATA

This chapter is based on a project that began as one component of a larger, comparative study that examined preschool children's peer cultures in three settings: an Italian nursery school, a private American preschool learning centre, and an American Head Start centre (see Corsaro 1994; Corsaro and Rosier 1992; Rosier 2000). Unlike preschool systems in most European countries, US preschool education is primarily provided by private organizations, and available only at considerable expense to families. An exception to this is the Head Start programme. Head Start is a 35-year-old federal programme for low-income children and their families, with centres located in urban and rural communities throughout the United States. Intended to provide children with a 'head start' on schooling, the programme is conceptualised as compensatory for material and social deficiencies of low-income families (see Zigler and Muenchow 1992). In this chapter, we draw on data from our ethnography of peer culture in the Head Start centre only. The centre was located in a large Midwestern city, and in line with Head Start income eligibility requirements, participants were from low-income homes. In the classrooms we studied, all of the teachers and all but one of the children were African American.

Our research in the Head Start centre involved careful field entry and acceptance by the children and teachers, participant observation throughout the school year, and collection of field notes and audiovisual recordings of representative episodes of peer and teacher–student interaction. During participant observation, we were often fascinated by the children's incorporation of many issues and themes relevant to their families' economic status into their play and peer interaction. These and other observations convinced us that our understanding of the social worlds of the children would be greatly enhanced by completing interviews with their parents and observing in their homes and communities. We also felt that our research in the centre had provided us with a strong and unique foundation from which to begin a longitudinal study of family–school linkages and socialization processes. Over the last two decades, home–school relations have taken an increasingly prominent place in discussions of US educational policy and practice, with educators and policy-makers alike calling for ever greater levels of parental involvement in children's schooling (see, e.g. *Goals 2000* 1996; for more critical treatments, see Lareau and Shumar 1996; Rosier forthcoming; Van Galen 1987). Thus we initiated an intensive study of a small sample of families whose children attended the Head Start centre, to examine the strategies that parents and children employed in collectively making the transition from the home, to preschool, and on to elementary school.

We completed tape-recorded interviews in the homes of nine Head Start mothers during summer 1990. At that time, each mother had a five-year-old child expected to begin kindergarten in the autumn.[1] Our sample contained mothers who varied greatly in age, education, and employment history. Although all but one had some history of welfare receipt, only one mother was a young, single parent with no formal employment history, receiving AFDC since her oldest child's birth.[2] There were a variety of family types included in the sample: two nuclear family households, one step family, four households composed of a single or separated mother and her children, and two other homes in which unmarried mothers and their children live with other adults – both relatives and non-kin.

In addition to requesting demographic information, our open-ended interviews encouraged the mothers to talk extensively about their families' circumstances and their children's daily lives. The mothers were gracious and candid, and the first set of interviews provided us with a wealth of information about the families. Encouraged by the mothers' enthusiasm, we maintained regular contact with these families as the children moved into the early elementary grades. After observing the children throughout their Head Start year, we completed four sets of intensive, open-ended interviews with the mothers over a three year period. We also observed informally in their homes and communities, joining them for dinner or spending time with the children as they went about their daily activities. Finally, we interviewed the children's kindergarten teachers in the spring of 1991 and first grade teachers one year later. We also completed some limited observations in several of the children's first grade classrooms.

This rich and extensive data from both family and preschool settings informs the identification and analysis of priming events that we present in this chapter. We concern ourselves with routine events in which adults and children actively attend to and ready themselves for this important transition from the family to formal schooling. We first examine priming events in the family, then go on to consider such events in teacher-directed and peer activities in the Head Start classrooms.

PRIMING EVENTS IN THE FAMILY

The mothers involved in this study, like their children's teachers who we have interviewed, believe that educational success begins at home, and parents must prepare children for schooling in positive and inspiring ways. In our interviews, all the mothers stressed the importance of their children doing well in school and at least obtaining high school diplomas. They clearly viewed education as vital for children's attainment of satisfying and productive lives, and most expressed both regret over past choices regarding their own education and concern that their children might repeat these mis-steps. Their efforts to encourage the children's motivation and achievement appeared to emerge from both prospective and retrospective thinking as well as from assessments of present realities.

In this section, we discuss two general types of strategies the mothers employed in support of these views. First, we examine their efforts to prepare and motivate the children for challenges of formal schooling. These strategies included both instruction in basic skills and attempts to instil a high valuation of education in the children. Second, we look at mothers' efforts to prepare children for peer and neighbourhood influences that they feared might hinder their children's academic careers. In this case, mothers' efforts were focused primarily on encouraging attitudes and values that would help their children withstand such potential future pressures.

Drawing attention to and preparing for the challenge of formal schooling

We have elsewhere discussed the mothers' in-home educational activities prior to and during their children's transition into formal schooling (Rosier 2000; Rosier and Corsaro 1993). Throughout the summer between the Head Start and kindergarten years, for example, all the mothers reported regularly engaging their child in educational activities, and several insisted on time devoted daily to such activities as writing ABC's and numbers, doing simple calculations, drawing and colouring, and reading with parents and siblings. Educational toys, workbooks, and television programmes were also important parts of most children's routines during this transitional period, and one mother constructed and regularly made use of numerous home-made matching and number games.

In addition to emphasising such activities and encouraging the development of concrete skills and knowledge, the mothers' reports suggested that they often forecasted coming changes in their children's lives prior to their entry into kindergarten, and also prior to first grade, when they would begin attending school for a full day. One mother told a story about her son, who she had repeatedly reminded that he would attend kindergarten when he was five years old. It seems that the day after his fifth birthday in May, he awoke, dressed and announced to his mother: 'Well I'm ready to go to kinnygarten, Mamma, walk me to kinnygarten'. When she told him he had to wait until autumn, he reportedly said 'But I don't wanna go to Head Start no more, I'm five years old!'

The mothers also routinely stressed both the practical and moral value of academic pursuits. Children were encouraged to view present activities as foundations for the future. This forward-looking perspective is nicely illustrated by one mother's tactic of capitalizing on her son's admiration of sports personalities to encourage perseverance and diligence in repetitive tasks. In our first interview with Amy, she reported that when Jeremiah complained about having to write his ABC's everyday, she responded that 'Air Jordan practise basketball everyday, the same thing day in and day out'. In a later interview, Amy recounted a similar conversation, in which she stressed to Jeremiah that if he wanted to be like Michael Jordan, 'you have to work on your studies ..., you have to practise every day. You think Air just shoot a basketball once and said, well, I'm gonna be great? And never picked up a basketball again? No, he practise every day. Now you gonna have to practice ...'.

The experiences and words of another mother and family best illustrate how the mothers stressed not only practical rewards of schooling, but also took a more philosophical approach to the benefits of educational achievement. Rhonda was 23 years old and the single parent of three preschool children when we first met in the summer of 1990. She lived with her children, mother and brother in the same apartment in a public housing project that she had lived in since she was a preadolescent. In our first interview, Rhonda described how she used the analogy of steps on a ladder out of poverty in her talk about education and learning with her daughter Cymira. She stressed that in order 'to get to that second and third step, you're gonna have to learn ... If you ever want to be one of the Chargers [those who make purchases on credit], you gotta learn'. She also noted her grandmother's saying that 'ain't a day goes by you don't learn something', and advised Cymira to 'stand up there with your spine straight', while learning the lessons of both school and life. She summed up her beliefs about education as the foundation for a dignified life by again evoking her grandmother's words: 'Why get on your knees all your life, when you can stand tall and proud to make this walk?'

Rhonda and other mothers routinely drew on such metaphoric imagery when they talked with their children about education. The rich oral tradition the women apparently grew up with was an important resource that helped them to make sense of their often chaotic world, and also to instil values in their children. When Rhonda repeated her grandmother's words, it was clear such folk wisdom was a vital source of inspiration and pride for her. It was also clear that this colourful language helped her to pass on feelings of pride and dignity to her daughter, and inspire Cymira to achieve all she could.

Although the mothers mentioned a variety of specific advantages provided by schooling (e.g. more satisfying work, more money, better character, and the ability to help their families and communities), they all shared the valuation of education articulated by Marissa when her oldest child was in kindergarten:

> When they get to a certain age, and they think they know it all, and they're out of your control, you can't really do nothin' but tell 'em, you know, sit down and tell 'em that *school will help you get through life*. [our emphasis]

Despite their children's young age, references to expected upcoming rebelliousness and trials of adolescence were frequent, and the mothers' talk often betrayed considerable anxiety and feelings of impotence in the face of monumental obstacles they feared their children would face. We discuss these expected obstacles below, and the mothers' efforts to ready their children for them.

Preparing for future transitions: temptation, responsibility, and decency in challenging environments

All the mothers feared negative aspects of the neighbourhoods and peer cultures that their children might soon confront. In line with this anxiety, they often described priming events, or activities that drew their children's attention to these potential future influences. The mothers primarily focused on restricting children's activities, and/or encouraging attitudes and values that would help them to withstand future pressures.

Nearly all the mothers repeatedly voiced concerns about truancy, drugs, shootings and other violence, gangs, and early sexual activity and pregnancy. For example, only a few minutes into the first interview with Amy, she expressed her apprehensions about their neighbourhood, and the rules she enforced to protect her five-year-old son from exposure to its dangerous features. When asked what Jeremiah needed 'to learn and to know in order to get along well and be successful in his community', Amy replied:

> The first thing, especially in this community, you have to be very particular about who you play with. You need to protect your child like this, because there's gang problems over here bad. Now, I do not allow him to go up here [indicating stairs leading to a small public housing project], 'cause there's lots of trouble, and I do not allow him to play with anybody who lives up there … he don't interact with any in the community, because I just don't trust 'em … 'Cause there's so many problems here.

Other mothers echoed Amy's concerns in this earliest round of interviews, and described similar restrictions on activities. For example, Annette and her husband preferred that their six children (aged 1–7 in 1990) play only with one another. While she occasionally allowed other neighbourhood children to visit, at no time were the children permitted to leave the house or front porch unaccompanied by an adult. Another mother reported that she instructed her son to 'just get up on the front porch', when he saw a group of teenagers coming down the street, because 'you never know, kids have access to everything now, guns, and I don't want to be a statistic'.

Such concerns increasingly preoccupied the mothers as their children matured and made more bids for independence in their neighbourhoods. In most cases, mothers who initially placed severe limits on their children responded by loosening these restrictions somewhat. This was viewed as developmentally appropriate, but it added to the anxiety the mothers felt.

As behavioural restrictions were relaxed, mothers increasingly emphasised other strategies to help their children meet the challenges confronting them. The mothers concurred that the best defence against drugs, violence, and other peer pressures was a set of attitudes and values that included self-esteem, achievement motivation, and a strong sense of morality and 'decency' (see Anderson 1999). While priming activities began to focus less on behavioural rules and more on values as the children matured, this was primarily a matter of bringing the emphasis on values from background to foreground (see also Corsaro and Molinari 2000); the moral foundations had been steadily constructed throughout their children's young lives.

All the families lived in low-income neighbourhoods characterized by high rates of school dropout and unemployment, but the level of observable poverty and violence varied considerably. Only Rhonda's family lived in a public housing complex, and it was here that gang activity, drugs, and violence was most readily apparent. Concerns about the dangers of the housing complex were prominent in all interviews with Rhonda. For example, in our second interview, she noted how commonplace guns and violence had become in her neighbourhood:

> Gunshots are like wakin' up and lookin' outside the window ... Over here, a shot fired is like – hmmm, you count your kids, and you know – whew! – wipe the sweat off, and continue walkin'.

Perhaps ironically, Rhonda was among the least restrictive mothers, allowing her children to visit with friends and to play outside for extended periods with limited supervision. While she clearly recognised dangers and negative influences that her children were exposed to, she realistically concluded:

> Where I live at, the things that are happenin', the only way that I could not show her [daughter Cymira], I would have to blindfold her and walk her through everything. I would have to walk her through life with this blindfold not to show her.

Rhonda had explained in our first interview that while she encouraged non-judgmental attitudes in her children ('I want 'em to know that drug addicts and people like that are people, too'), at the same time she stressed that: 'Momma's not like that. I live in that environment, but we're not like that. We can beat this.'

Rhonda's words suggested a daily battle with her environment for her children. She and other mothers recognised the power of their adversary and at times expressed somewhat fatalistic views about their chances of success (see Corsaro and Rosier 1992; Rosier 2000). Yet they continually encouraged their children to aim high, and not allow anyone or anything to limit their aspirations. Rhonda believed Cymira could achieve whatever she set out to, but she worried a great deal about the anti-intellectual climate she recalled clearly from her own adolescence (see Adler and Adler 1998; Fordham and Ogbu 1986). Rhonda often used her own past as a guide for what not to do, warning her daughter about peers who would try to discourage her from taking education seriously, as she does in the following quote (from June 1990):

> There's nothing out here in this great earth that won't be here in four years or two years ... That person that's tellin' you, lets go to this party, wished she hadn't went to that party. I'm the person that went to the party. I tell her all the time,

'I'm the girl that cut, and went to McDonalds. See me. And, let me show you my friend who works at Dow, drivin' this '90 [laugh]. I could've been in that '90, I mean, I am the other side, I am the example.

Two years later, Rhonda's poignant comments during an informal visit elaborated on this theme. She told how she had been a very studious youngster, but friends had belittled her, saying 'all you know is books'. She reportedly swung '360' away from that at their urging. Now, she 'sometimes sit[s] up thinkin' about all these wonderful things I see in Cymira,' (college, being successful etc.), 'and then sometimes I just cry, because my mother saw all the same things in me'.

Rhonda very deliberately 'primed' Cymira for the peer pressure she expected her daughter to meet, and we saw evidence that Cymira took her mother's cautionary tales to heart. We visited Cymira's first grade classroom one afternoon and watched with some amusement as she went about her schoolwork in a very serious manner. During a lesson on measurements, the children estimated weights of a watermelon and a bunch of bananas. The teacher asked her class: 'Who eats bananas without peeling them?' When no one could produce the desired response, Ms Nelbert told the children to 'go home and ask Mom, or Dad, or Grandma, or Auntie, or your cousin: Who eats bananas without peeling them?', Cymira smiled, leaned over and whispered quietly to us: 'Gorillas. Gorillas and monkeys'. But she did not share her knowledge with her classmates.

Cymira seemed to monitor herself so as not to appear the 'know-it-all' of the class, and this restraint was apparent throughout the afternoon. We noticed that a couple of girls watched Cymira closely and occasionally attempted to get her attention, but Cymira attended to the tasks at hand and did not acknowledge their attempts. These classmates included a friend who often visited Cymira's home to watch television, play school, or play 'Barbies'. Rhonda had reported that Cymira was impatient with Felicia: 'Cymira thinks Felicia doesn't listen enough, she's too busy tryin' to see what the boys are doin'. Ms Nelbert also noted Cymira's seriousness, and commented that while Cymira was well-liked and respected by her classmates, she 'knows that she's supposed to do certain things, and she takes her school work pretty serious'. As Ms Nelbert perceived and as Rhonda stressed repeatedly, Cymira had a job to do at school, and she managed relationships with peers so as to minimize their interference with her 'on-the-job performance'.

Cymira was often present and participated in our interviews with Rhonda, and it was clear that she was granted near-adult status during these conversations. Rhonda reacted matter-of-factly to Cymira's interruptions, viewing them as relevant and informative contributions. Mother and daughter at times collaborated in telling of an event, with Rhonda occasionally altering her story to reflect Cymira's corrections or elaborations. Rhonda once pointed out with pride that 'If an adult is wrong, Cymira's gonna let you know – no, you're wrong, this is how it go'. She recounted a humorous event where Cymira had confronted a male friend of the family about behaviour the child knew her mother did not condone. Although Rhonda had ignored the behaviour and was embarrassed by Cymira's action, she allowed Cymira to speak her mind, and she concluded: 'if there's somethin' that you just have to say, say it'. From every indication, Cymira's intellect, competence, and right to participate in family affairs was fundamentally respected by her mother.

Other mothers employed similar tactics, with similar results. Samantha, for example, also coached her son on resisting peer pressure to under-achieve, and he was proud of his identification as a 'gifted' child, despite the harassment he often endured. He was encouraged, or 'primed', to be an autonomous individual so as not to waste his 'special talent', and his behaviour at home and school suggested he applied these lessons to his interactions with adults as well as peers. His mother often responded positively to his adept negotiations with her concerning, for example, television rules, bedtime, or where the family should go for dinner. And Samantha, like Rhonda, also permitted what some might consider disrespectful behaviour toward other adults. This was illustrated by an incident that occurred during Ramone's kindergarten year.

Ramone's uncle had agreed to collect him from school one afternoon, but arrived very late. Ramone did not panic, but rather waited outside the school until his uncle finally arrived. His displeasure was clear, however, and he refused to speak to his uncle throughout the long ride home. The uncle was angry with Ramone's lack of respect, and told Samantha he believed the child should be severely punished. Samantha scoffed at this idea, however, and said simply: 'Well, you should have picked him up on time'.

As these final examples demonstrate, the children were active interpreters of the priming events we have described. In their interactions with peers, teachers, and other adults, they made their mothers' lessons their own through innovative processes of appropriation, extension, and elaboration. Ramone and Cymira in particular repeatedly collaborated with and received the approval of their mothers in their enactments of precocious independence and autonomy, as did other children to a lesser but still significant extent. Only time will tell us if these children are able to avoid the negative outcomes that their mothers feared. It is not too soon to note, however, that while these mothers' focus on independence was well considered given all-too-common outcomes for youth in their communities, the children's autonomous behaviour was often not well suited for or viewed as appropriate within the structure of their early elementary classrooms (see Rosier 2000 for elaboration on this finding). Below we turn now to an examination of priming events in the Head Start centre, some of which were explicitly aimed at preparing children for structural features and constraints of the educational settings they would soon enter.

PRIMING EVENTS IN THE HEAD START CLASSROOM

In the Head Start classrooms, priming events were interwoven in the fabric of everyday activities in structured and unstructured teacher–child interactions in the school culture and in the activities of the children's peer culture. We have space to discuss briefly only a few examples from each.

Priming events in the head start curriculum

Most teacher-directed activities at Head Start involved cognitive and language drills that were carried out in strict accordance with written instructions in curriculum materials. These drills all involved variants of questions from teachers which were to be answered in complete sentences by the children. The underlying rationale for these drills was that economically disadvantaged children lacked competence in language skills and that the Black dialect spoken in lower class African-American communities is an underdeveloped language style.

Many anthropologists and linguists dispute such beliefs (see Heath 1983: Labov 1972). However, regardless of one's position on this issue, a major problem with such drills was that they normally involved teachers asking Wh-questions (e.g. 'Where is the bird?') in which a normally perfectly acceptable answer like 'In the tree' or 'On the branch' was deemed incorrect by the teachers without explanation *because they were not full sentences* (i.e. 'The bird is in the tree'). As a result, the children sometimes became confused, believing that there could only be one correct answer to such questions. This belief often led to children becoming quite anxious about volunteering responses even when they knew the right answer.

In addition to language drills, the curriculum also included perceptual tasks where again teachers were instructed only to note when an answer was correct or incorrect and not give reasons why some answers were not acceptable. These drills were structured like the language drills with the behaviouristic assumption that children lacked certain skills that they could learn through modelling and reinforcement. Like the language drills these procedures caused anxiety for the children, especially in tasks where children were not provided enough contextual information to make judgments. Consider the following example.

Example 1 Stand In Front of the Longest Line

The teacher had the children sit as a group facing her. Between the teacher and the group of children were three lines (strips of tape attached to the floor) of differing lengths. The researcher (Bill Corsaro) sat next to the children (see Figure 8.1). After consulting the lesson plan in a book, the teacher asked one of the children (Jerome) to: 'stand in front of the longest line'. The researcher immediately thought that there was some ambiguity to this question because (at least to him) standing at point 1 or 2 (given the point of reference) could be seen as correct. Jerome moved quickly to the longest line, straddled it for a second, and then stood at point 1. The teacher said that was incorrect and asked Jerome to sit back down. She then called on Alysha. Alysha quickly walked up and stood at point 2. To the researcher's surprise, the teacher said that Alysha's response was incorrect and that she must return to the group and sit down. At this point a general 'sigh' went up among the children. The researcher was also confused about what the teacher thought the right answer was. She then called on three more students. The first two tried points 1 and 2 respectively, and were again told that they were incorrect. The third student, Zena, stood in back of the shortest line which was, of course, also incorrect. The researcher had by this

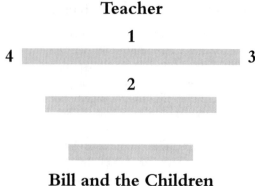

Teacher

1

4   **3**

2

Bill and the Children

Figure 8.1 Stand in front of the longest line

time decided that point 3 or 4 must be the right answer. However, given that there was no arrow or any point of reference, he was not sure which answer the teacher (or more importantly, the lesson plan) considered correct. The teacher asked all the children, and they all failed to get the right answer. Finally, she asked the researcher to come up and display the correct answer. He did so with some caution, selecting point 3 in the end. She said this was correct, and praised the researcher's choice. The teacher then moved on to a new task ('Stand in back of the shortest line'), and from this point most children produced the 'correct' response. However, they proceeded with a great deal of caution and anxiety in making their decisions.

Our point here is not to criticise the teacher. She faithfully followed the lesson plan laid out in the book. Later when we pointed out the ambiguity to her, she agreed that it could be confusing. However, she noted that it was important to stick with the lesson plan and to eventually elicit a correct response for the children to model.

Despite these negative features, the drills did prepare the children for the participant structure format that is so common in American kindergarten and first grade classrooms (see Mehan 1979). For this reason, the drills can be seen as priming events. However, while contributing to needed knowledge of the participant structure of future classroom lessons, these priming events appeared to foster an anxiety and a 'perfectionist' attitude in the classroom performance of some children in kindergarten and first grade (see Corsaro and Rosier 1992).

Other features of the curriculum that can be seen as priming events are projects and field trips that drew attention to the children's community – its history, organisations, activities, leaders, neighbourhoods, families and workers. In these projects children not only learn about their community, but also about themselves and their constantly changing place in the community as developing members. Such projects therefore encourage children to attend prospectively to coming changes in their lives.

For example, there were week-long projects on family, community helpers (including neighbourhood walks, and visits to a fire station, post office and a department store), and African American leaders like Dr Martin Luther King, Jr. During the week before the celebration commemorating King's birthday, a teacher read a story that recreated his life. The story was quite detailed, containing pictures and discussion of King's childhood, youth, encounters with segregation, activism against racism, and ultimately his assassination. The children listened very attentively and occasionally made comments like 'I know about him', and 'My Mommy told me about that' (these activities therefore nicely linked family and school practices and emphases). At the end of the story the children asked a number of interesting questions. Having experienced several recent field trips, Steven asked if we could go to see King's boyhood home. The teacher responded that maybe Steven could go sometime, but that it was in Atlanta and too far for the class to go. But Darren said: 'No, you shouldn't go because you'll get killed'. The teacher said that Steven would not be killed and that it all happened a long time ago. Another girl, Denise, then asked if we could go to Martin Luther King's funeral. The teacher smiled and said no. But before she could go on, Anne asked if Martin Luther King was going to have a birthday party. The teacher then said that Martin Luther King died a number of years ago so we could not attend his funeral, but we could celebrate his birthday with a party of our own during the holiday from school.

Although the children's comments and questions reveal temporal confusion about events, they also clearly show that the children were relating King's story to their own lives and attempting to tie it to the school projects and field trips. This type of retrospective–prospective thinking is a key outcome of priming events as children link information from the past to their current and future lives.

Other priming events were embedded in field trips to different parts of the community. One such trip involved a walk around the neighbourhood where the school was located. The teachers pointed out community helpers in line with the curricular theme of that week. At one point we waited at a bus stop and the teacher discussed the service bus and cab drivers perform for the community. After a few minutes a bus pulled up alongside us. When the driver opened the door, the teacher told him that the children were learning about community helpers and wanted to thank him for his work. All the children cheered and the bus driver smiled and honked his horn as he pulled away. Later as we continued our walk we saw some men collecting garbage and the scenario was repeated.

These experiences got the children talking about other community helpers (e.g. postmen, fire fighters etc.) as we headed back to the school. However, this trip into the community drew the children's attention to some of the negative elements of the neighbourhood as well. As we stopped to read the sign for a barbecue restaurant, a number of children pointed to the bars on the window and broken glass on the sidewalk. Further along our route we encountered several men standing outside a convenience store drinking from bottles in paper bags. The teacher hurried us along and did not respond to children's comments and questions about the men.

These examples demonstrate the complexity of priming activities at the Head Start centre. In both the structured classroom lessons and the projects and field trips, the preparatory or prospective power of the priming events was tempered by the challenging circumstances of these children's lives. The classroom drills provided children with needed practise for the discourse participant structure that would dominate in elementary school, but that is very different from typical discourse in the family and peer group (see Heath 1983). At the same time, however, the drills created an uncertainty and anxiety in the children regarding their ability to display their knowledge and skills. Similarly, the priming events embedded in field trips and related projects drew the children's attention to both positive and negative aspects of their community. The children prospected to their increasing participation and involvement in a community with positive role models (both revered leaders and everyday heros) and in the life of the streets with all its problems, dangers, and enticements. Much like priming events in the family, then, priming events embedded in the Head Start centre routines also focused children's attention on future consequential choices they would confront.

Priming events in peer culture

Of the many types of priming events that occurred in peer interaction, here we consider only those related to the children's production of dramatic family and occupational role play. In dramatic play, children reproduce the complex social relations of adults in their lives and, in turn, prospect about their eventual movement into and enactment of these adult social positions. In the Head Start centre we frequently observed the children engaged in such role play in which they pretended to be employees in fast-food establishments, harried single mothers frustrated by their children's constant demands and misbehaviour, parents taking sick baby dolls to the clinic, and police ordering suspected drug dealers against the wall to be searched.

We were struck by the high drama, exacting detail, and complexity of the Head Start children's role play compared to that of American upper middle class children (see Corsaro 1993). We have space here for examination of only one short sequence of family role play involving Debra and Zena pretending to be mothers having a phone conversation that we recorded on videotape. The sequence begins as Debra dials the toy telephone and initiates a conversation with Zena:

Example 2

78 D: What you been doin'?
79 Z: Hah. Cookin'. Now I need to go to the grocery store.
80 D: I got to take my kids to the party store, they told me. I said –
81 Z: My kids – my kids want me to take them to the park.
82 D: What?
83 Z: My kids told me to take them to the park, and then, and
84   then the bus had to come and get 'em. That's gonna be a
85   long walk for to here! And then the bus would have to
86   come and get us!
87 D: Well, we have to wait for transfers, then I have to buy
88   groceries, we have to buy some groceries. And um –

89 *Z*:   Guess where my kids told me to take them? To the
90   store. When the bus comes by (my kids waitin' for it). I
91   don't got time to do that.

In this segment the girls, through their use of what Goodwin (1990) terms 'format tying' (the systematic use of the surface structure of speech for orderly sequencing in informal talk), establish shared agreement regarding a general topic for their telephone talk. In response to Debra's question in line 78, Zena notes she is cooking but needs to go to the *grocery store*. Debra ties her turn at 80 to Zena's previous turn by noting that: 'I got to take *my kids to the party store*' (a smaller store for buying things like milk, bread and snacks). Zena then picks up on Debra's introduction of kids (81), using the same exact phrase *my kids* and noting that they want to be taken to the park. Zena expands her description at lines 83–86 by introducing the information that the kids will have to take the bus because it is too far to walk to the park. At line 87, Debra continues the orderly sequencing by semantically tying her turn to Zena's earlier mention of *the bus* by stressing the requirement of having to *wait for transfers*. Finally, in lines 89–91 Zena ties her turn to Debra's prior turn by noting that she does not have *time* to be waiting for the bus.

The girls' skilful building of coherent discourse through the repetition of syntactic features and the semantic linkage of developing ideas in the discourse is important because it enables the collaborative construction of a shared topic: Problems of parenting in poverty. Here several key aspects of the content of the sequence are important. It is not just that the mothers (here animated by the children) have to do everyday chores like shopping; their children expect them to provide a number of additional services. However, the children's discourse reveals that it is not easy to meet such expectations if you do not have a car and must deal with a limited and time-consuming bus service. As the episode continued beyond what is included here, the girls introduced several other routine demands that 'their kids' placed on their very limited resources.

We see then that dramatic role play of this type is an important priming activity in that its very production enables the children to practise their developing language, cognitive and social skills and to prospect and anticipate their movement into the adult world. In this sense, dramatic role play contributes to the children's development of a set of predispositions (Bourdieu and Passeron 1977) through which they confront the objective structures or circumstances of their present and future lives (see Corsaro 1993).

CONCLUSION

In this chapter we have examined priming events in the lives of several African American families living in poverty. We have looked at the nature and significance of priming events in the family as revealed in in-depth interviews with mothers and observations in the home. We have also discussed priming events that occurred regularly in teacher–child and peer interaction in the Head Start centre the children attended. We have tried to demonstrate how the children's participation in these priming events prepare them for present and future challenges of formal schooling. We have also argued, more generally, for the importance of such priming experiences for the children's anticipating, securing, and transforming their lives as they move from childhood toward preadolescence.

We have stressed that children do not merely and individualistically incorporate the intended lessons of adult-initiated priming events into their developing expectations and conceptualisations of self. Rather, they actively and collectively appropriate and apply these lessons in ways that reflect the objective circumstances of their lives and their own concerns about what the future has in store.

A key finding was the complex, multi-layered effects of the priming events in the lives of these children. Given the harsh and challenging demands of their political and economic circumstances, the priming experiences of these children drew their attention to: (1) a set of dichotomous value orientations including hard work and perseverance versus play and fun, personal responsibility versus dependence, community versus personal gain; and (2) the sober recognition of daunting challenges they face in embracing these values and realising their consequences. Priming experiences can certainly help individuals to confront, adapt to, and sometimes transform the objective structures or circumstances of their daily lives. However, the ultimate power of unequal and discriminate structures can not be matched by the mere espousal of positive values and morals. While the children's active agency is clear throughout this analysis, we must conclude by noting that the structural constraints and barriers that these children and their families confront are all too often insurmountable.

NOTES

1 Most US children begin their elementary schooling with one year of kindergarten prior to first grade, and virtually all public elementary schools include kindergarten classrooms. There is variation among the American states, however, on whether or not kindergarten is mandatory. In the state where we completed this research, it is not, yet over 90 per cent of children do attend kindergarten. Localities and even individual schools within the same school system also vary on whether kindergarten classes meet for half or full days; some of the kindergarten classrooms attended by the children involved in this study met for half-day sessions, while others met for the entire day. Less than 50 per cent of school districts in the US have full day sessions, and the overwhelming majority of the school districts in the state where the kindergartens we studied were located offered only half day sessions.

2 There are many social welfare programs in the US (e.g. school lunch programs, unemployment insurance, food stamps, and various forms of subsidised housing), but the term 'welfare' is commonly used only in reference to AFDC (i.e. Aid to Families with Dependent Children) and its recent successors. The 1996 Federal Welfare Reform Legislation changed the nature and the availability of welfare programs for poor children and their families quite dramatically; prior to this legislation, AFDC was the main federal-state income support for poor families. Even before 1996, there was always much state-by-state variation in the amount of AFDC grants; in 1990 (when this research began), the median state's maximum benefit for a family of three was $367 per month, while in the state where we did our research, the maximum grant for a family of three was $288. AFDC was distributed in the form of a monthly grant check, which recipients used to meet housing, clothing, and personal needs. Any transportation or childcare costs were also paid out of the grant, although modest allowances for these items were added if the recipient was completing training or working.

Most families who received AFDC were also eligible for and received Food Stamps (which spend like cash for groceries) and Medicaid (which provides health coverage for low-income families with children). Good sources for further information on AFDC are Sidel (1992) and Edin and Lein (1997).

REFERENCES

Adler, Patricia A. and Peter Adler. 1998. *Peer Power: Preadolescent Culture and Identity*. New Brunswick, NJ: Rutgers University Press.

Anderson, Elijah. 1999. *The Code of the Streets: Decency, Violence, and the Moral Life of the Inner City*. New York: W. W. Norton & Company.

Bourdieu, Pierre and J. Passeron. 1977. *Reproduction in Education, Society, and Culture*. Beverly Hills, CA: Sage.

Corsaro, William A. 1992. 'Interpretive Reproduction in Children's Peer Cultures'. *Social Psychology Quarterly* 55: 160–177.

Corsaro, William A. 1993. 'Interpretive Reproduction in Children's Role Play'. *Childhood: A Global Journal of Child Research* 1: 64–73.

Corsaro, William A. 1994. 'Discussion, Debate and Friendship: Peer Discourse in Nursery Schools in the United States and Italy'. *Sociology of Education* 67: 1–26.

Corsaro, William A. 1996. 'Transitions in Early Childhood: The Promise of Comparative, Longitudinal Ethnography. 419–457 in Richard Jessor, Ann Colby and Richard A. Shweder (eds), *Ethnography and Human Development: Context and Meaning in Social Inquiry*. Chicago: University of Chicago Press.

Corsaro, William A. 1997. *The Sociology of Childhood*. Thousand Oaks, CA: Pine Forge Press.

Corsaro, William A. and Luisa Molinari. 2000. 'Priming Events and Italian Children's Transition from Preschool to Elementary School: Representations and Action'. *Social Psychology Quarterly* 63: 16–33.

Corsaro, William A. and Katherine Brown Rosier. 1992. 'Documenting Productive-Reproductive Processes in Children's Lives: Transition Narratives of a Black Family Living in Poverty'. 5–23 in William A. Corsaro and Peggy Miller (eds), *Interpretive Approaches to Children's Socialization*. San Francisco: Jossey-Bass.

Edin, Kathryn and Laura Lein. 1997. *Making Ends Meet: How Single Mothers Survive Welfare and Low-Wage Work*. New York: Russell Sage.

Fordham, Signithia and John U. Ogbu. 1986. 'Black Students' School Success: Coping with the Burden of "Acting White"'. *The Urban Review* 18: 176–206.

Goals 2000: Increasing Student Achievement through State and Local Initiatives. July 1996. Report to Congress, United States Government Printing Office.

Goffman, Erving. 1974. *Frame Analysis*. New York: Harper & Row.

Goodwin, Marjorie Harness. 1990. *He-Said-She-Said: Talk as Social Organization among Black Children*. Bloomington, IN: Indiana University Press.

Heath, Shirley Brice. 1983. *Ways with Words: Language, Life and Work in Communities and Classrooms*. New York: Cambridge University Press.

Heath, Shirley Brice. 1989. 'Oral and Literate Traditions among Black Americans Living in Poverty'. *American Psychologist* 44: 367–73.

Labov, William A. 1972. *Language in the Inner City: Studies in the Black English Vernacular*. Philadelphia: University of Pennsylvania Press.

Lareau, Annette and Wesley Shumar. 1996. 'The Problem of Individualism in Family–School Policies'. *Sociology of Education* 69 ('extra issue'): 24–39.

Mehan, Hugh. 1979. *Learning Lessons*. Cambridge: Harvard University Press.

Ochs, Elinor. 1988. *Culture and Language Development: Language Acquisition and Language Socialization in a Samoan Village*. New York: Cambridge University Press.

Prout, Alan and Allison James. 1997. *Constructing and Reconstructing Childhood*. London: Falmer Press.

Rosier, Katherine Brown. 2000. *Mothering Inner-city Children: The Early School Years*. New Brunswick, NJ: Rutgers University Press.

Rosier, Katherine Brown. Forthcoming. '"Without the Parent You Lose the Child": Teachers' Expectations and Parents' (Non-) Involvement'. In David A. Kinney (ed.) *Sociological Studies of Children and Youth*. Stamford, CT: JAI Press Inc./Ablex Publishing Corp.

Rosier, Katherine Brown and William A. Corsaro. 1993. 'Competent Parents, Complex Lives: Managing Parenthood in Poverty'. *Journal of Contemporary Ethnography* 22: 171–204.

Schieffelin, Bambi. 1990. *The Give and Take of Everyday Life: Language Socialization of Kaluli Children*. New York: Cambridge University Press.

Sidel, Ruth. 1992. *Women and Children Last: The Plight of Poor Women in Affluent America*. New York: Penguin Books.

Van Galen, Jane. 1987. 'Maintaining Control: The Structuring of Parent Involvement'. 78–92 in G.W. Noblit and W. T. Pink (eds) *Schooling in Social Context: Qualitative Studies*. Norwood, NJ: Ablex.

Zigler, Edward and Susan Muenchow. 1992. *Head Start: The Inside Story of America's Most Successful Educational Experiment*. New York: Basic Books.

9 Negotiating boundaries

Tensions within home and school life for refugee children

Mano Candappa and Itohan Egharevba

INTRODUCTION

This chapter focuses on children who have come to live in the UK in the context of forced migration from their home countries. It is concerned with tensions the children face in their daily lives in the home and in the school, and the issues involved in their negotiation. Two sets of relationships are focused on: parent–child relationships within the home, and peer relationships in the school, reflecting key relationships in children's lives. The chapter explores these and considers whether and how they influence each other.

We take as our starting point the notion that the home is the locus of family care; that care involves labour as well as love (Finch and Groves, 1983), and that care encompasses caring for as well as caring about (Graham, 1983). Caring relationships can be both symmetrical and asymmetrical (Waerness, 1984). In family relationships, parents are normally seen as the providers and supporters of children's needs, material, social, and emotional, with children as their dependants. Parents are the carers, children the cared-for. Within families, relationships between the generations have been described as governed by generational contracts (Alanen and Bardy, 1991). These contracts are informal, initiated by adults, and based on adults' understanding of the division of labour in society, and what is allowed and required of children within that framework. Care relations within the family are central to the generational contract. Mayall (1994) argues that within this (inter-)generational contract, children's interactions, *inter-alia*, vary according to social context. Thus ill-health could be one factor that reverses the terms of the inter-generational contract, when a disabling illness could make children the carers of their parents.

Moving to the second setting – the school – which, as an institution, fosters standardised modes of behaviour (Radcliffe-Brown, 1940), children must negotiate school environments, including its hierarchical structure, and in particular, peer relations. Relationships between peers can be conceptualised as intra-generational contracts. These contracts, again, are informal, and within them the rules of engagement are dynamic and have to be negotiated. This process therefore raises issues of value and identification. As Mayall (1994) points out, people may have different degrees of identification in relation to different social settings and arenas.

Describing relationships between generations and between peers as contract, does not, however, imply equality or symmetry. As with the formal labour contract, in inter- and intra-generational contracts, relationships are based on equivalence, which imply underlying difference. Thus, age and gender factors could operate within the inter-generational contract, and class, 'race', and gender factors could operate within the intra-generational contract, and influence power relations within them. This chapter will explore these and other issues raised above in relation to refugee children. In particular, the chapter will explore care relationships between the generations in a context where social norms have been put to the test through war, flight from home country, and re-location in the UK. Within the school, a focus on children who have recently migrated to the UK, and who, as a group, have a low social status within the country, enables us to explore the children's emerging self-identities in relation to the competing norms of home culture and peer culture. These issues are discussed against the background of the children's refugee experiences: experiences of war, of flight, and of relocation in a new country. Firstly, however, a brief description of the research on which it is based.

THE RESEARCH STUDY

The basis for this chapter is recent research into the lives of refugee children, called *Extraordinary Childhoods*. The study was conducted at the Thomas Coram Research Unit at the Institute of Education, University of London, and implemented in collaboration with the British Refugee Council. The project was supported by an Advisory Committee, which included representatives of refugee community organisations and professionals working with refugee children. As social actors in their own right, children were active subjects in the research. Children participated in the research process by assisting in the development of research instruments, and in editing their stories for inclusion in a reader for schools on refugee issues (Rutter and Candappa, 1998). The term 'refugee' was used in the study to include asylum-seekers and those granted exceptional leave to remain in the country (ELR status), as well as those granted refugee status (i.e. it was self- rather than the legal definition).

The study was called *Extraordinary Childhoods* because of the upheavals and trauma many refugee children have experienced, and the changes they have had to come to terms with and to cope with. The overall aims of the research were:

- to contribute to knowledge of the lives of refugee children; and
- to provide information that will be useful to policy makers and others concerned with the welfare of refugees.

Research questions focused on refugee children's experiences in their *families*, e.g. the different roles, responsibilities, and relationships they have in their households; their *social relationships,* and activities such as their experiences of clubs and sports, friendships, religious activities; the children's experiences of *services*, such as schools and health care; and the children's expectations of the *future*. The study began in December 1996 and covered a period of 16 months. It utilised a range of research methods, and centred on children aged 11–14, the first years of secondary schooling, a time of significant transition in children's lives. Work was conducted in two complementary stages.

Stage 1 consisted of a series of case studies. Its main focus was a group of 35 refugee children who arrived in Britain around 1994, drawn from the main groups of asylum seekers to arrive in the country at that time: namely, Bosnians, Somalis, Sri Lankan Tamils, and Turkish Kurds. In order to gain insights into the children's lives, the research issues were explored in-depth with these children, in semi-structured interviews, conducted in English. So as to gain a better understanding of the children's lives and the changes they had had to undergo, children were asked about their experiences of war, flight and relocation. For similar reasons they were also invited to reflect on and compare their present experiences of home, school and social life with previous experiences in their home countries.

Children, roughly equal numbers of girls and boys, were accessed through schools, refugee community organisations, and other welfare agencies; and interviews were conducted in a variety of locations, ranging from schools to family homes. In order to compare the refugee children's present social lives with those of indigenous children, the research issues were explored at this stage with a similar number of girls and boys who were born in Britain. The comparison group was ethnically mixed, and included children who attended the same schools as many of the refugee children.

Stage 2 complemented the interview data, by providing quantifiable data on the lives of refugee and non-refugee children. It consisted of a survey involving 312 children from Years 8, 9, and 10 (the first three years of secondary education) in two London schools. Stage 2 employed a self-completion questionnaire, which was structured around issues arising from stage 1, so as to test stage 1 findings with a larger population. The questionnaire was administered by the researchers in whole classes, in school time. The objective of the survey was to find out how children and young people felt about their lives, particularly their families, their schools and their friends; how they spent their time, and what things were important to them. The questionnaire was confidential, and children were not required to write their names on it.

Out of the 312 children who participated in the survey, 228 (73 per cent) indicated that they were born in the UK. Of those children born outside the UK, 22 children indicated that they had come to the UK because of war or fighting in their home countries, and were identified as refugees for the purposes of analysis and comparison, with other non-UK born children defined as non-refugee migrant children. Because of the small numbers of participating children who could be identified as refugees, tests of statistical significance were not applied. Comparative data presented below should therefore be treated as indicative only. However, it should be noted that case study data was found to be broadly in line with survey data on the issues discussed.

LIVES OF REFUGEE CHILDREN

Refugee children often have experienced intense disruption and upheaval in their lives. They are a diverse group, coming from a wide range of countries, and from different cultural and social backgrounds. A common feature among children who participated in the study was that they all had led fairly comfortable lives in their home countries, since it is usually wealthier people who are able to flee to foreign countries. The children were aged around 8–12 when they arrived in the UK. But because flight to a safe country could sometimes be long and involved, many of them had been 3–6 years younger when they fled their home countries. These children represented the range of experiences associated with war and political conflict, witnessing atrocities, flight to safety (often routed through three or four other countries), family separation, severe hardship, periods of living in camps, and being at the mercy of unscrupulous intermediaries. Some of these experiences are captured in the story of Sheikh, who speaks of what a child might be caught up in in times of war, and those of Bazi and Radhika, who tell of what flight to safety might involve.[1]

The chaos of war: Sheikh's story

Sheikh is a Somali Brava boy, 10 years old at this time.

> I was playing outside when somebody [thugs] came and tell me, 'Go and knock at your neighbours' door and speak Bravanese. Tell them to open the door or I am going to shoot you'. And then I went to knock. (They told me, 'Go and knock at that door' because they can't speak my language.) I said, 'Don't open it, there are some robbers here'. And they [thugs] thought that I said, 'Open the door'. They didn't open the door. And I say [to the thugs], 'They don't want to open it.'
>
> The robbers say, 'Tell those people to open it'. And I say to my neighbours, 'Don't open the door because they are still here. They kill people'. They [thugs] say to me, 'You lie to us'. They hit me with a gun! The gun never had any bullets, they just use it to hit my legs. Now I've a problem with my legs. They give me pain. When I came to this country I had to go to hospital to get an operation. (…) I have to take tablets now.

Death at sea: Bazi's story

Bazi is a Somali Brava boy, who was 11 years old at the time of these events.

> One day we leave by boat … but the boat broken in the middle of Somalia and Kenya and some of our family fell in the water and drowned – our cousin. And we just prayed to God, and God pushed us through the sea to the land … It was very deep in the middle of the sea … It was night and everybody was praying. The boat was slowly going down to the sand, until it got to the sand. In the sand there was nobody and one day we slept on the sand. And another day, we were scared, some people came … Some people came by small boats and they came to collect us and they took us to their island. We was very hungry that day. They gave us food … And then we stayed for week … After two weeks, some people

say that our family sent small ship from Mombasa to that small island … and they took us and then we got to Kenya. We got to Kenya.

We stayed in place for refugees [a refugee camp]… There was bad disease in there. My Grandma, she died from malaria… My Dad … he said that this is no good country. There is much disease …

Radhika's journey

Radhika is a 14-year-old Tamil girl from Sri Lanka, who fled her home in Jaffna when she was seven.

> They asked my brother to join with them, Tigers [guerillas]. My mum didn't let him (…). we had to leave. (…) We had to pay money I think, we had to pay money to army but she said, 'I didn't pay because I talk to them, "Look my children, I don't have any money, (…) I have many girls and I haven't got any money"…'
>
> We stayed in Colombo about five years … We buyed a small house, only one room with a kitchen … [and] one bathroom … We was learning, we was studying there … Best friends are there … And then the fighting started … the fighting was round the corner …
>
> We left Colombo, and we went to Moscow, and we stayed there two days, and then we went to Nigeria. We stayed there one week, two weeks … Agency was helping us … So many countries we stayed … In Moscow it was all snow … in Nigeria, really hot there … There was a man. He was taking us to there. A Tamil man. He take us for the flat to live in, to stay for one week. There isn't really good food down there, we just ate bread … Then another place … I don't know what the place called – there was all Tamil, Muslim peoples living – one room for one family – and we was cooking all together in the kitchen. And they cooked food, like rice and curry … Lots of Tamil people …
>
> When we come to London we don't know whether we are going to live here, if we are going to stay or we might go back …

The war situations in their home countries meant that some of them, especially among the Somali children, had had very little formal schooling. Others, like some Kurdish children from Turkey (where it was forbidden to speak Kurdish until 1991), had had little opportunity to learn their mother tongue. Still others, like some Sri Lankan children, attended school to the sound of guns and bombs (see Rutter and Candappa, 1998). There were also examples of courage and bravery such as in Sheikh's story, above, that could test conceptualisations of childhood where children are seen primarily as vulnerable beings in need of adult protection, and where children's own activity in developing their own social positioning, among other things, is not recognised.

With the exception of the Bosnian children who came to the UK through the agency of the Red Cross, all the children had come at their families' personal expense. For some children this had meant taking a flight from their home country to London, for others, like Bazi and Radhika, the experience was more traumatic. Some children arrived in the country as unaccompanied minors.

For many refugee children their arrival in the UK was a mixed experience: relief at being in a safe country, tempered sometimes with guilt and sadness at having fled their homes leaving friends and family behind. Some children were uncertain whether they were safe from the persecution in their home countries or whether they could still be pursued. Many children had little knowledge of the UK when they arrived, and many experienced culture-shock and trauma on arrival. Most children spoke of the hardships they and their families experienced in those early days, living in cramped accommodation, numerous moves before they were given permanent housing, how they felt isolated, how difficult starting school was for them. Below, Fatma and Serap, two 14-year-old Kurdish girls from Turkey, tell of their early days in the UK.

Fatma's story

> We didn't have a house for about six months or something, so we had to move on to my cousins', my uncles', my aunties'. We had one week in each house. ... I wanted to have my own house, live with my own family, be together, because you have this – have the idea that because, my auntie and uncle have a row, I always thought that it's about us, because of us, innit, they can't be happy? ... They've got three children, [and] we three children and family – it was a bit crowded, and I felt really uncomfortable. I always used to tell my mum, 'Can't we have our own house?' But always we had to wait for the Council to make a decision. And then they gave us a small flat ...

Serap's story

> When we came to the house, there was nothing in there. We had to buy everything ... We stayed at my uncle's house for about two weeks, because we had to do everything, carpet, beds and stuff like that. ... You know we get Income Support? – they help us, but afterwards they cut it from the Income Support. ... We got carpet just for our rooms. Last year [i.e. two years later] ... we got carpet for the stairs and middle and corridor.
>
> It was very dirty, ... our wallpaper was ripped, some of it was coming off. That is why we had to clean it, it was dirty. You know, pigeon poo was every-where. Bathroom was like this – all the pigeon poo. My Mum had to clean it all.

The children's accounts speak vividly for themselves. After their arrival in the UK, they and their families would have also soon become aware of the hostility with which refugees and asylum seekers are often viewed. They would become aware of politically charged and emotive debates in the media about 'bogus' asylum seekers flooding the country and abusing the benefits system, taking housing and school places from locals, and somehow threatening jobs, which fan resentment against them.

It is against this background of painful experiences of war, flight, and relocation in a new country that we site our discussion of relations within the home and school for refugee children.

THE HOME AND FAMILY

Extreme social conditions have been known to challenge established social relations in any given society. War situations, for example, have often led to a change in gender relations, with women taking on traditional male roles as needs dictate (see Lammers, 1999). We are concerned here with how the terms of the inter-generational contract can change following displacement through war and relocation in a foreign country. More particularly, we are interested in children's roles within the inter-generational contract, and the shifting boundaries of the labour of care within the family that might ensue in these circumstances.

As a guide to the children's present lives, we will use the survey to provide an indication of caring tasks undertaken by refugee children for their families, in comparison with those undertaken by non-refugee children, which provide the norm. These are demonstrated in Figure 9.1.

The most striking differences between refugee and non-refugee children were in relation to taking care of siblings, taking care of elderly relatives, cooking, and translating, within and outside the home. These differences in responsibilities were also seen when comparing refugee children with non-refugee migrant children. These data, while indicating differences, at the same time reflect some of the changes that have taken place in refugee children's lives, and that have led to their more enhanced roles in the labour of care within their families. In discussing these changes we will draw on case study data.

With respect to the care of younger siblings and the care of elderly relatives, children's responsibilities here can be linked to loss of extended kin networks enjoyed in the home country, though affecting them in different ways. In relation to the care of siblings, very few, if any, kin were available locally to help with childcare if parents were working or otherwise busy; but the corollary of that was that there were therefore few elderly relatives who required assistance of the children. Cooking the evening meal also devolved upon older children, especially girls, if mothers were employed. The latter most usually undertook low-paid employment, often working unsociable hours, since refugees are among the most disadvantaged in the employment market (see Refugee Council, 1998), and which left older children playing a major caring role within the family. It might be argued, in this context, that in other societies older siblings play a greater part in caring for younger children than is usual in western societies today. However, it must be pointed out that in those societies, care of children by older siblings usually takes place under the watchful eyes, albeit at a distance, of adult members of the community; whereas the children in the study assumed sole responsibility for their siblings' care in the absence of their parent/s. In the changed circumstances, it would seem, the terms of the inter-generational contract are varied, giving children greater responsibility within the family.

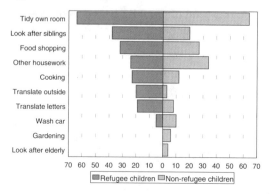

Figure 9.1 Responsibilities towards home and family: refugee and non-refugee children

The greatest change in relations between the generations, however, lay in children acting as translators, language brokers and advocates for parents less competent in English than themselves. Vasquez *et al.* (1994: 96) have pointed out that translating 'involves recourse to multiple sources of linguistic and cultural knowledge in order to create meaning, negotiate a task, or solve a problem'. As other authors have noted, such activities might be critical to the functioning of a family that speaks little English within an English-speaking society (Shannon, 1990; Kaur and Mills, 1993). Indeed, these activities were most acute for refugee families in their early months in the UK, when parents became crucially dependent on their children. At that time children, through schooling, had a better understanding of English compared with their parents, and had to translate for them at local authority offices, the DSS, GP practices, hospitals, and so on. This was at a time when the children themselves were not very fluent in English, and were adjusting to a new way of life and school. Many of these tasks lessened once permanent housing and benefits had been sorted out, but accompanying parents to doctors and hospitals, as interpreters, tended to be recurrent tasks over the years.

In situations such as these, a child could be described as being in an 'intercalary position' (Gluckman, 1973), facing their parents as child and as a carer at the same time, when relaying and interpreting information from the outside world to their parents, and transmitting the concerns of their (hierarchically senior) parents to the outside world. Having to rely on their children in this way results in a role reversal within the inter-generational contract, where parents are in a position of (asymmetrical) dependance on their children. It could, for example, involve parents having to reveal intimate details about themselves to their child for transmission to a doctor, in a way that previously might have been seen as culturally unacceptable. This made children's negotiation of different contexts and hierarchies a highly complex task. However, while children in general lovingly accepted their new roles within their families, and were proud to be able to help their parents in this way, the complexity of their position was not without its tensions. Some of these tensions are illustrated in Fatma's story.

Fatma's story

Fatma is 14 years old. Her parents go out to work, and her older sister is at college, so she has to bring her little brother home from school, take care of him, do the housework, and cook the evening meal for the family, before she can do her home-work. She seeks to justify this workload by saying, 'They [her parents] think I've got more time at home'. But she sometimes rebels and 'can't be bothered to cook', and gets in trouble for it. She has the best command of English in the family, so to her falls most of the translation and advocacy tasks as well. Here she talks, with justifiable pride, about a time when her skills were crucially important to the family:

> My Dad was gonna be deported – I was really sad about that. We had a court [hearing] last month … [Just before that] they send us a letter thing that he was to go back to Turkey. My Dad was really shocked, 'This can't be, we got court in a few days time, what's wrong with them!' It was me that sorted that. I phoned them up, I argued with them, 'How could you do this', and everything. Mr 'X' [a teacher] was helping us quite a lot.

However, although she performs these adult roles, she continues to be treated and disciplined as a child by her parents. While she accepts her status as a child within the family, she also seems to resent being treated in this way. She particularly seems to resent this attitude in her father, and demands to be treated differently. Her story continues:

> I *hate* it when they shout at me, I hate it. I don't mind my Mum shouting at me, but when my Dad shouts at me, he really – he really upsets me. I really get pissed off. I hate when my Dad shouts at me. When my Mum – I don't care … One minute I'm all sadness, the next minute I go next to her and kiss her and everything … When my Dad shouts? I – I tell him, like, what are you shouting for? … what was the reason for shouting, was there any need to shout? You could have said it properly. He goes to me, 'Yeah, I know I could have said it properly …'

The intercalary positioning of Fatma within her family is thus a source of tension. On the one hand, the parents are reliant on Fatma providing a major part of the care normally to be expected of parents. They are also dependant on her for language brokering in a variety of situations. However, in consequence, the hierarchical struc-ture of the family is eroded, and the parents seek to re-assert their authority over her. Fatma, on the other hand, seeks to negotiate her status as child within the family on different terms, and will not submit to traditional disciplining. It would seem that here the terms of the inter-generational contract are in the process of revision.

It was noted above that an aspect of care often provided by parents lies in supporting children's social needs. This includes providing children with norms and values to guide them in their social interactions. These often involve cultural, religious, and moral values, that could be reinforced or challenged by the society in which they live. As Dahlberg (1996) and Andenaes (1996) have pointed out, as children move between different contexts and boundaries they encounter different norms and values. Migrant children often find that some of the norms and values transmitted by their parents derive from their home countries, and are at variance with those of the countries in which they have come to live. They thus need to negotiate their way through the competing mores.

Negotiating their way through competing social norms and contrasting boundaries is the situation that most refugee children found themselves in. There were cultural and religious norms relating to how girls dressed, and how they behaved. For example, wearing shorts was considered inappropriate for most Muslim and Hindu girls in the study; non-Muslim Kurdish girls talked of short skirts being seen as inappropriate. Cultural and family norms also often governed whether refugee children were allowed to have their friends visit them at home; in most cases parents needed to feel reassured that the friend would respect their culture and traditions. These rules also applied to visiting the homes of their friends. There were also norms governing relations with the opposite sex, and in general even the older children in the study were considered by their parents as too young to have boy/girlfriends. These norms seemed to impact more strongly on girls than boys in the study, and are issues that will be taken up further in discussing boundaries encountered by refugee children in their school life.

THE SCHOOL AND PEER RELATIONS

For many young people, schools provide an environment in which values and rules are explicit, and behaviour such as racism, bullying, and sexism can be made accountable (see Holland and Thomson, 1999). While this means that a framework that upholds acceptable behaviour exists in schools, it does not imply that unacceptable behaviour does not occur there, or that perpetrators are always held accountable. In reality racism, bullying and sexism imbue (though are not confined to) peer interactions in school, and reflect power relations among different individuals and groups. For example, as in the wider society, visible differences such as skin colour, hair, and dress (see Rex and Mason, 1986) can cause certain children to be targeted for racist discrimination or bullying, these behaviours often reflecting children's own social hierarchies and prejudices. These in turn can affect the way children present themselves and how they behave. As stated above, we are concerned here with the intra-generational contract and peer relations at school, and the competing pressures of peer culture and home culture in the formation of refugee children's self-identities.

In recent research, Brannen *et al.* (2000) have noted that as new entrants to secondary school the children in their study were 'weakly positioned and occupied low statuses within the hierarchial structure of the school, with its formal hierarchies … and its informal cliques and peer groups' (p. 202). Refugee and other migrant children, whether starting at a primary or secondary school, are in a similarly weak, or weaker position upon joining, starting from outside of the intra-generational contract. They are the Other, and have to negotiate their way through existing hierarchies and groupings from a position of very little power. Refugee children are often in the weakest position of all, given the hostility with which they are viewed in society at large, and tell-tale signs such as cheap and unfashionable clothing, take-up of free school meals, and so on, which add up to negatively valued differences. Additionally, many refugee children may be particularly vulnerable, having been through major upheavals consequent on forced migration and, as outlined above, for some, formal schooling may be a completely new experience. As such, the social distance they need to cover, and the negotiations they have to make to be accepted among their peers will be greater than for most other children in British society.

Attending school can provide some sense of return to normality for refugee children. But the difficult process of negotiating the intra-generational contract, trying to make friends and become part of the school is largely left up to them. Whilst teachers can be significant others who can help in this process, our study suggests that refugee children receive little help in negotiating the social distances involved in starting school in a foreign country, in circumstances that they might find bewildering. Many refugee children reported feeling themselves vulnerable because of the low status of non-English speakers within the school culture. The experience of Serpil, a Kurdish girl from Turkey, on starting school, illustrates this point:

> Everybody kept staring at me. I was embarrassed, shy. ... Most of the people in this country doesn't like refugees as well. So, even in dinnertime, I was scared to have my dinner. ... They were talking about me. I know they were talking about me because they were calling my name in'it? So even though I didn't understand what they were saying, I understand that they were using my name. So they were kept staring at me, talking about me, saying bad things about me, keep laughing at me so I was really upset then.
>
> I told my Mum, my Dad and they told me that when I get to learn English, they wouldn't say anything to you. I kept crying and said to my Dad, 'I don't want to go to school, I don't want to see them laughing at me, see them talking about me'.
>
> I had two Turkish friends, but not that close. Sometimes they helped me but most of the time they didn't. ... When they translated anything, I think they were, like, embarrassed. They didn't want to talk to me. They were embarrassed that other kids will say, 'Oh, don't talk to that girl, she doesn't speak English' ...

It is particularly significant that Serpil is rejected by children from her own culture, children who she might expect to help her. But they had already negotiated the distance between English speakers and non-English speakers, and, seemingly, did not want to align themselves now with the latter group. This was not an isolated example. Another Turkish girl, from a different school, described how her compatriots would walk away from her in the playground. Two Sri Lankan sisters told of how the British-born South Asian 'befriender' allocated by the teacher kicked their feet when out of the teacher's sight, saying, 'You can't talk English', whilst ostensibly showing them where the coat pegs were.

Children soon realised that achieving competence in English was key to gaining entry to peer groups. However, there seemed to be a gender dimension to this behaviour: it was only reported by girls in the study. Boys reported speaking their home language with, and being helped by, other boys in their school, and one girl reported being helped by a boy from her home country. This suggests that competence in English as a status symbol that must be negotiated by children from ethnic minorities may be more important among girls' peer groups, rather than among boys', and also points to the importance of communication as the basis to many girls' friendships.

There are other social boundaries and hierarchies that refugee children faced, but which were less easy to negotiate. In particular, there are boundaries of 'race' and those relating to their status as asylum seekers/refugees. Negative images of refugees endorsed in the press have echoes in taunts thrown at refugees, for example, 'dirty Bosnians', 'go back to your country', and that refugees 'take too much money', mentioned by children in the study. Similarly, visible ethnic and cultural differences, noted above, made children targets for racist bullying. Children were aware (in common with children from ethnic minorities in the comparison group) that their minority status made them vulnerable to racism, but many of them felt that school authorities did not take effective action against bullies. In the absence of such support, children had to negotiate these situations as best they could. The more confident among them responded by 'cussing back'; one mentioned punching a perpetrator, but in the words of one child, many of them simply 'get used to it'.

'Race' and ethnicity can be important factors in children's friendships and social groupings. As noted, refugee children are often positioned as the Other when starting school in the UK, and must be 'let in' to friendship groups. Being excluded from the friendship of their compatriots left many refugee girls, in particular, feeling rejected and unhappy. However, all children reported an initial period of isolation, when they had no-one with whom to talk or to play. There seemed to be a 'sizing up' period before refugee children felt they were allowed in to peer groups. This typically lasted a day or two, but its effect on the children's morale was profound, as was apparent in the passion with which they spoke of that time. After this initial period, all refugee children in the study reported making some friends. However, the survey suggests that refugee children were less likely to have *many* friends at school, compared with their migrant non-refugee and non-migrant peers (Figure 9.2).

Two routes to forming friendships were mentioned by children: through work and through play. Hierarchies and power relations among children within school meant that a refugee child might ask for help with school-work, and hope that this might lead to more general conversation; but invitations to join in play had to come from the other children. In the former situation, refugee children reported being more likely to approach someone perceived to be of his/her own cultural group for help. Girls were more expansive on the subject of friendship than most of the boys. Many girls spoke of 'being friendly' with most of their classmates, as distinct from 'being real friends', with religious or ethnic factors being mentioned as a key to developing close friendships. Survey findings suggest that whilst characteristics such as being trustworthy, being someone you can talk to, being fun, and being kind were

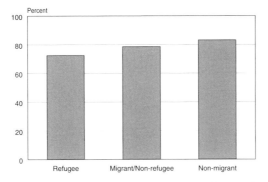

Figure 9.2 Many friends from school: refugee, migrant non-refugee and non-migrant children

highly valued in a friend by all children, similar religious and cultural backgrounds were more important for refugee children than for migrant non-refugee or non-migrant children in peer relations (Figure 9.3).

The value placed on religion and culture in close friendships among refugee children could be indicative of a sense of ease among familiar norms and values. On the other hand, it could also be the result of subtle pressures of social exclusion where low social status was an additional factor that militated against cross-cultural friendships. It should be noted, however, that this does not imply that all friends of the refugee children come from the same or similar ethnic or religious backgrounds as themselves.

In the previous section we noted cultural and family norms and boundaries that could impact on refugee children's social relations, and that they might find some of these at variance with those of their peers. Many of these affected girls more than boys; in particular, with respect to dress codes, visiting friends at each others' houses, and interactions with members of the opposite sex. Concerning tensions between home and peer norms and values, and how refugee children negotiate their way through these, the study found that in interactions outside the home, for the most part, children adhered to family rather than to peer norms and values. For example, girls seemed to identify with cultural norms that influenced their dress, especially in multi-cultural areas. Indeed, tension between home and peer norms was less prevalent here than might be expected in more monocultural areas: refugee girls could observe non-migrant children from different religious/cultural traditions observing similar norms. However, a Bosnian Muslim girl living in a monocultural area had to negotiate her way through both home and school norms. The school norm was for children to wear shorts when playing sports, the home-cultural norm was that girls should not be seen in shorts. Her solution was to wear shorts under a skirt when playing sports, thus seeming to satisfy both norms.

In interacting with friends, the children seemed to find their parents' rules regarding respect for each other's culture and values as a pre-requisite for visiting friends at each other's houses, reasonable. Here again, tension between peer and home norms was not very marked in the multicultural areas where most of the children lived. The

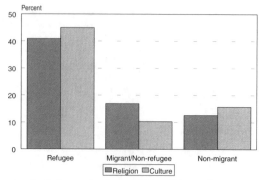

Figure 9.3 Importance of religion and culture in friendships: refugee, migrant non-refugee and non-migrant children

children could find similar rules among some non-migrant minority ethnic groups as well. For example, some British-born South Asian girls talked of their homes as places for interacting with family and other relatives only. Boys were less affected by this rule than girls, because, for the majority of them, playing football in the local park was the main source of social interaction after school, whereas girls were more likely to want to visit friends at home. This pattern of interaction is perhaps to be understood also in the context of refugee children having little money to spend on leisure activities.

Rules relating to interactions with the opposite sex seemed again to affect girls more than boys in the study, because most of the boys were at an age where they seemed to prefer playing football to going out with girls, while girls were showing a definite interest in boys. Refugee girls could therefore be facing peer pressure to have boyfriends, while their parents considered them too young for this. However, most girls in the study accepted their parents' reasoning, and focused on their education for the present. Overall, it would seem that cultural factors, with their gender implications, play a large part in the seeming ease with which the refugee children negotiate contrasting contexts and boundaries.

DISCUSSION AND CONCLUSIONS

In this chapter, we have considered parent-child and peer relations of children who have come to live in the UK in the context of forced migration, as a result of war or political conflict. We have been concerned with the effects of the social context on these two key sets of social relationships. Within the home and in terms of the inter-generational contract, we have found that as a consequence of displacement, and the unfamiliarity and difficulties of adjusting to life in the new country, parents may come to place greater reliance on children. Children may have to take on many of the caring tasks they would normally expect of their parents and community elders, thus upsetting the traditional balance of the labour of care in the family. We have also seen that whilst having greater responsibilities can enhance the child's status within the family, these changes in role can also give rise to tensions that have implications for the terms of the inter-generational contract, particularly governing parent–child relations within the home.

The refugee child's enhanced status within the home brought on through forced migration sharply contrasts with his/her status of powerlessness and vulnerability within the new school environment. In relation to the intra-generational contract, starting from outside of its boundaries, and as one of a group that is often negatively viewed in the wider society, the child's status is low, and the social distances to be negotiated in order to be allowed into peer groups can be great. Moreover, such negotiation cannot take place on the child's terms; because of the refugee child's low status in the pecking order, it must submit to established hierarchies in peer relations. The study suggests that home cultures and values play an important part in the children's negotiation of boundaries and pressures encountered at school.

In seeking to explain the dominance of home values for refugee children, we suggest that the connection between family and culture, and self-identity may be key in understanding decisions a child makes in the situations and contexts described. In a recent study of children aged 9–10 and 12–13 in a different context, Mayall (2000) concluded that children's identities are bound up with their family: 'family matters most to them' (p. 1). We would argue that refugee families' poignant experiences through war, flight, relocation, coping with straitened circumstances, and so on, serves to strengthen their family bonds and appreciation of one another. Similarly, experiencing as they do a foreign culture in their new country, could make them look with new eyes and appreciation at their own. This is borne out by the nostalgia and longing with which most children spoke of their home countries. Their past experiences, and the fact that their early experiences in this country, including school, were often less than happy, could have made them confront cultural issues in a way that children who experience more ordinary childhoods do not.

In discussing self-identity with the children, we found it to be strongly rooted in cultural identity for most of the refugee children who expanded on the subject. That such soul-searching does go on comes out most strongly in Fatma's account, at the end of which she said: 'I'm someone else, not the person I used to be. I feel really confident now, 'cos I know who I am. Not under pressure no more'. While this self-confidence would serve to strenghten her position in terms of the intra-generational contract, this is not to say that peer norms and values have no influence on refugee children. On the contrary, when Fatma sought to re-negotiate the inter-generational contract, described above, for example, she could have been influenced by other models of family relations she has encountered, at school perhaps. We would argue that, in general, a strong cultural identity developed in many refugee children helps them steer with seeming ease between conflicting boundaries and values of home and school.

NOTES

1 The children's accounts of their experiences have been edited, with their consent, to remove identifying features, and, where possible, children were consulted in the selection of their own pseudonyms.

ACKNOWLEDGEMENTS

The authors would like to thank the ESRC for funding the study (award nos. L129251009 and R000222952), and very particularly the children who shared their experiences and thoughts with us. We wish to acknowledge the contributions of the other project team members, Professor Peter Moss, Adviser, from the Thomas Coram Research Unit, and Matthew Grenier, Consultant, from the Refugee Council, in implementing the study. We are also grateful to Charlie Owen for his help and guidance, and members of the Project Advisory Committee for their valued advice and support.

REFERENCES

Alanen, L. and Bardy, M. (1991) *Childhood as a Social Phenomenon: National Report for Finland, Eurosocial Report*, 367, Vienna: European Centre.

Andenaes, A. (1996) 'Violation of canonical norms for family life – challenges and solutions for children with two homes', in J. Brannen and R. Edwards (eds) *Looking Backwards and Moving Forwards: Parenting and Childhood*, London: South Bank University/Institute of Education/ESRC.

Brannen, J., Heptinstall, E. and Bhopal, K. (2000) *Connecting Children: Care and Family Life in Later Childhood*, London: RoutledgeFalmer.

Dahlberg, G. (1996) 'Modern childrearing and family life – a complex process of negotiation', in J. Brannen and R. Edwards (eds) *Looking Backwards and Moving Forwards: Parenting and Childhood*, London: South Bank University/Institute of Education/ESRC.

Finch, J. and Groves, D. (eds) (1983) *A Labour of Love: Women, Work and Caring*, London: RKP.

Gluckman, M. (1973) *Custom and Conflict in Africa*, Oxford: Blackwell.

Graham, H. (1983) 'Caring: a labour of love', in J. Finch and D. Groves (eds) *A Labour of Love: Women, Work and Caring*, London: RKP.

Holland, J. and Thomson, R. (1999) 'Respect – Youth Values: identity, diversity and social change', *Children 5–16 Research Briefing*, No.3.

Kaur, S. and Mills, R. (1993) 'Children as interpreters', in E. Mills and J. Mills (eds) *Bilingualism in the Primary School: A Handbook for Teachers*, London: Routledge.

Lammers, E. (1999) *Refugees, Gender and Human Security*, Utrecht: International Books.

Mayall, B. (2000) 'Negotiating Childhoods', *Children 5–16 Research Briefing*, No. 13.

Mayall, B. (ed.) (1994) *Children's Childhoods: Observed and Experienced*, London: Falmer.

Radcliffe-Brown, A.R. (1940) 'On social structure', *Journal of the Royal Anthropological Institute*, 70.

Refugee Council (1998) *The Pan-London Refugee Training and Employment Network*, London: The Refugee Council (mimeo).

Rex, J. and Mason, D. (1986) *Theories of Race and Ethnic Relations*, Cambridge: Cambridge University Press.

Rutter, J. and Candappa, M. (1998) *'Why do They Have to Fight?' Refugee Children's Stories from Bosnia, Kurdistan, Somalia and Sri Lanka*, London: The Refugee Council.

Shannon, S. (1990) 'English in the barrio: the quality of contact among immigrant children', *Hispanic Journal of Behavioural Sciences*, 12 (3), 256–276.

Vasquez, O., Pease-Alvarez, L. and Shannon, S. (1994) *Pushing Boundaries: Language and Culture in a Mexicano Community*, Cambridge: Cambridge University Press.

Waerness, K. (1984) 'The rationality of caring', *Economic and Industrial Democracy*, 5, 185–211.

ung people between home
d school

Elisabeth Backe-Hansen

One perspective on adolescence is to understand young people as actors in a social landscape. This landscape can be divided into different arenas or contexts that represent both possibilities and constraints for the individual. Arenas are social meeting-places where activities take place, experiences are exchanged and skills developed through interaction with others (Øia 1994). The arenas of the family and the school are important for the development of young people in differing ways, in a period of their lives that is crucial for learning about cultural expectations in a wide sense.

Besides the emotional closeness and nurturing that is associated with family relationships, the family is an arena of informal education using everyday life contexts and episodes to guide children towards good and fulfilling adult lives (Valsiner 2000). At one level the school has the same goal, as cultural knowledge is transmitted here as well. However, the type of knowledge transmitted at school is outsiders' knowledge, oriented towards the establishment of values, loyalties, and ways of thinking and feeling that are in accordance with social units that are larger than the family or local community. This distinction between informal and formal education is marked by the setting up of clear geographical boundaries between the school territory and the outside world (Valsiner 2000).

Young people in modern, Western societies divide much of their time between the home and school arenas, and it is important to analyse how they understand and relate to the interrelationship between them in a psychological sense. In this chapter I use the concepts or dimensions of autonomy, connectedness and regulation as the point of departure for an analysis of this relationship. Autonomy, in the sense of a process of becoming an independent individual, is both a goal and a challenge of modern adolescence, while connectedness among other things is about enduring relationships between children and their parents that have to be renegotiated and reconstructed while children develop. In this analysis, regulation means the informal constraints imposed on young people by their parents as well as the formal ones imposed by the school, and both embody society's efforts to shape new generations.

These three dimensions will be used analytically in the discussion of some results from a primarily quantitative study of social competence among young people.[1] Data were collected from the young people themselves, their parents and teachers at two points in time, when the former were 13 to 14 and 15 to 16 years old respectively.

The original sample consisted of 806 young people from 10 strategically selected Norwegian municipalities, including small, rural communities. No particular emphasis was put on including schools with a high proportion of children from ethnic minorities, as they are fairly concentrated in the large cities. Besides, two recent studies have focused particularly on this issue (Bakken 1998; Sørlie and Nordahl 1998).

The multi-informant approach was seen as particularly important for this study, as one key research issue was the analysis of cross-informant similarity and variation. The teachers were asked to fill in questionnaires about their own pupils, and the parents were asked to answer many of the same questions about their children. All the teachers participated, while 86 per cent (693) of the parents returned their questionnaire. The overall participation rate was 65 per cent of the young people and thus fairly low, but comparisons with results from recent studies using the same instruments (Ogden 1995; Sørlie and Nordahl 1998) indicate that the attrition was regional and not limited to specific groups among the sample. Between municipalities the participation rate varied from 54 per cent to 85 per cent, with even more variation between the 32 schools included (Backe-Hansen 1998a). After two years about 15 per cent had moved or changed schools, and of the remaining sample the participation rate was 77 per cent (528). Teachers of 97 per cent (517) of the young people answered their questionnaires, as did 85 per cent (451) of the parents (for a more detailed discussion of the sample and procedures, see Backe-Hansen 1999).

The starting point of the analysis is that there will be a complex interrelationship between the enactment of autonomy, connectedness and regulation when home and school are seen in conjunction, and from the point of view of the three sets of actors involved. This is discussed in the next section of the chapter. The perspective of the young people is then discussed through the presentation of results about their views on good parenting and their school motivation. The perspectives of the parents and teachers are discussed through the presentation of results about collaboration between home and school.

A COMPLEX INTERRELATIONSHIP BETWEEN AUTONOMY, CONNECTEDNESS AND REGULATION

Before discussing the interrelationship between the three dimensions of autonomy, connectedness and regulation in more detail, some information about the Norwegian school system needs to be presented in order to contextualise what the school arena means to the young people participating in the study.

In Norway, secondary school comprises the three final years of compulsory schooling. Leaving primary school and entering secondary school, which takes place when young people are 12 to 13 years old, is a structural transition that poses several challenges for them as well as their parents.[2] The pattern of the Norwegian school system is to have local and often small primary schools with one or two small[3] classes at each age level, but central and often large secondary schools with three or four slightly larger classes at each age level and a catchment area of several primary schools.

The policy is to mix the pupils and not put more than five or six former classmates together in the new classes. This creates opportunities for forming new friendships that at the same time are more difficult to monitor for the parents, as the young people live much further away from each other than one is used to from primary school. As a consequence of this parents will know their children's friends, and particularly their parents, to a much lesser extent than formerly (Backe-Hansen 1998a, b). At least while parents get used to this transition, they can feel that they are less able to regulate their children at a time in their children's lives when they start worrying more about possible risks like alcohol, drugs, or other antisocial behaviour.

Children in primary school have one or two teachers who cover most of the subjects, while young people in secondary school have several teachers who cover one or two subjects each. While the primary school teaching model is fairly generalist, the secondary school model is thus subject-organised. One or two teachers will be 'class teachers' as well, which includes the responsibility for maintaining regular contact with the parents, but they will not necessarily be those who know the young people best. When meeting with parents to discuss a pupil's academic progress and behaviour, the class teachers will thus have to depend on reports from the other teachers as well as their own judgement. Although collaboration between home and school is seen as just as important – or even more important – in secondary school than in primary school, the basis for this collaboration is more formal and less personal.

In Norway, no grades are given until children start secondary school. In primary school quasi-gradings like 'smiling faces' or written comments are used to give the children and their parents an impression of the children's achievement level, but this is not formalised or standardised like the grading done later. Once grading starts, teachers, parents and young people alike will judge the latter's academic achievement by the grades they receive. This was obvious in the results from the first data collection. While the match between the children's own assessment of their academic achievement and that of the parents was low on the part of the 10-year-olds, it was high on the part of the 13-year-olds. The match between the children's and the teachers' assessments was higher for both age groups, but again highest where the 13-year-olds were concerned (Backe-Hansen 1999).[4]

The transition to secondary school is not necessarily negative. As part of the first data collection, the parents were asked if they could give examples of positive transitions in their children's lives. Not more than a sixth of the 658 parents then participating answered this question, but of these, one-third (36) mentioned the transition to secondary school. The reasons given were the aspects discussed above; that their child had profited by the change of friends and teachers, and that getting grades was a welcome academic challenge.

Interaction from different positions and perspectives

Within the analytical framework of autonomy, connectedness and regulation, young people, their parents and teachers interact with each other from similar but also different positions (see Figure 10.1), which will be discussed more in detail below. There will be connectedness between young people and their parents, but from a

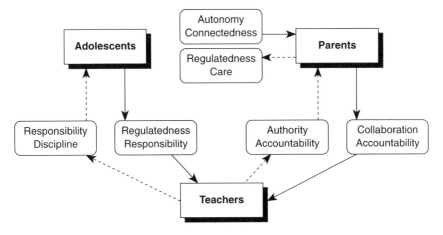

Figure 10.1 Model of the interrelationship between actors

position of increasing autonomy on the part of the former and decreasing regulation on the part of the latter. Young people and their teachers will interact with each other on the basis of reciprocal responsibility, but from a position of expected compliance on the part of the former and the right to effect regulation on the part of the latter. Finally, the common ground between parents and teachers will be one of accountability, but from a position of expected authority on the part of the teachers and of expected collaboration on the part of the parents. Thus, young people have the least influential position within this triad, but with most scope for change in the relationship between them and their parents. Parents occupy a more ambiguous position. They are still in a position of authority over their children, particularly on the home arena, but at the same time are expected to collaborate with their child's teacher in ways defined by the school (Nordahl 2000b). According to this way of thinking teachers will occupy the most influential position, as their role is attributed most authority in relation to pupils as well as parents. In today's society this system is not stable, however, and there will be room for fluctuation as well as change as a result of changing expectations relating to all actors in the triad.

When young people relate to their parents, they negotiate or take for granted a complex dialectic between connectedness and autonomy. As the results to be presented later show, this dialectic is not between opposites – connectness *or* autonomy – but rather a question of an increased demand for autonomy based on a connectedness that is taken for granted. On their part, parents have to accept that the ways they can regulate their children change over time, as well as the ways they can show connectedness with their children through expressions of care and love. This dialectic becomes even more complex because of two characteristics of modern adolescence. The first of these characteristics is that of adolescence being a period of social delay, or a mismatch between young people's competence and their actual independence (to be discussed further below). The second characteristic is that grown-ups tend to construct adolescence as a risky phase necessitating extra regulation through control.

The transition from primary school coincides with a time when the accordance of legal rights to young people has begun and will be increased step by step until they reach their majority at 18. From the age of 12 children are legally entitled to be heard (although not always listened to) when decisions are to be made that concern them, for instance in cases of custody disputes. From the age of 15 young people have the right to decide how they use money they have earned themselves, they sign the application to high school themselves, and they have reached the age of criminal responsibility. If they are involved in a child protection case they have the right to legal representation of their own. By 16, sexual acts are no longer criminal if they are voluntary.

A hundred years ago the great majority of these young people would already have left school and started working to help with the upkeep of their families. Many of them would have been learning a trade, whereas just a small minority would have gone on to higher education and later university studies.[5] At the same time, they did not reach their majority until the age of 25, which was the age set when the common vote was introduced in 1913 (Blom 1985). Today, all pupils leaving secondary school have the right to a further three years of education, and all but a small minority make use of this right.[6] Most expect to continue their education even further, through learning a trade, attending college or going to a university. Today's 16-year-olds know that it will be years before they are able to earn their own way and not depend on their parents for financial or practical support. Thus, young people are in a position where they are accorded increased autonomy through legislation, but at the same time remain dependent on parents who, conversely, are progressively losing their legal rights to make decisions on their children's behalf. The same seems to be the case in Great Britain (Brannen 1995). It may be argued that this double-edged position of both young people and their parents in itself creates a need for negotiations about regulation as well as autonomy.

The secondary school years coincide with the onset of puberty of most of the pupils, which may in turn be used to explain their moody and oppositional behaviour by teachers as well as parents. It is part of the common teacher lore that particularly during the middle of the three secondary school years classes can be difficult to control because so many pupils go through puberty just then, while things seem to calm down the year after. When the parents participating in the study were asked to describe their 13-year-olds in their own words, the relatively few descriptions that could be construed as negative were usually accompanied by reference to their puberty development, like: 'She has become more temperamental lately and does not accept our rules as easily any more, but I suppose this is due to her age'.

Historically, the notion of adolescence being a period of 'storm and stress' with puberty as the basis of a psychological crisis was brought into psychology by Hall (1904), with roots in the common sense of a society that needed the fostering of discipline and obedience of young workers in factories. The main concern at the time was young boys, as girls' socialisation was much more successfully controlled (Stafseng 1996). This legacy of adolescence as a transitional period creating an extra need for adult control has remained and been extended to girls as well, along with their changing status in modern Western societies, particularly where their sexuality is concerned (Ericsson 1997). Today the perceived need for regulation through control is fuelled by the persistent construction of adolescence as a period of risky and irresponsible behaviour by the media as well as various professionals, despite the equally persistent research results showing that the majority of Norwegian young people do well and end up conforming to dominant values and norms in our society. It can be argued that in modern (and postmodern) societies the issue of 'how to be a good parent' is likely to accentuate the issue of 'crisis of adolescence', since this crisis actually concerns parents' fear of loss of control over the development of their child (Valsiner 2000).

There is a paradox between this need for control and the co-existing idea that a successful development of the individual's identity and space in the society at large presupposes some kind of liberation from the social and emotional dependency on his or her parents (for instance Evenshaug and Hallen 1992). This liberation of course takes many forms, of which some are definitely unacceptable to adults, and some are destructive for the young people that engage in them as well. The point here is that there will be a tension between the need for control on the part of the parents, which again may lead to increased efforts to regulate their children's behaviour, and the parallel need to foster independence and self-sufficiency.

The balance between the need for control and the aim of increasing independence will be negotiated in different ways in the informal setting of the family and the formal setting of the school. Particularly after the major school reform of 1997, the public school system aims to foster self-esteem, social competence, and personal initiative and responsibility on the part of the pupils (Nasjonalt læremiddelsenter 1996). Indeed, such issues were prominent in the debate prior to this school reform (for instance Skaalvik and Skaalvik 1988). Thus, teachers have to integrate these aims with the aim of cultural knowledge transmission, which presupposes a more traditional pupil role. This tension is by no means resolved in the ongoing public debate about how Norwegian schooling is organised.

When young people relate to their teachers, they do so within a context where they are targets for collective-cultural interventions of various kinds. Formal schooling is a kind of role guidance, its content decided on by the social institutions wanting specific kinds of role enactment (Valsiner 2000). Young people are expected to act as responsible pupils, which means doing their best, being cooperative, and setting their own immediate interests aside for the common good. It is expected that pupils in secondary school conform to the regulation inherent in the way school is organised, for instance through sitting still during lessons and not talking out of turn, not being late, or not playing truant. Although the above-mentioned school reform in 1997 has led to a softening up of the formerly fixed schedules and somewhat changed role expectations, pupils are still expected to conform.

Young people are in a position where they have to comply with authority, since secondary school is compulsory. As most studies show (for instance Ogden 1995; Sørlie and Nordahl 1998; Nordahl 2000a), only a minority of pupils sabotage openly by playing truant. However, 60 per cent of the young people participating in a large-scale study in two Norwegian towns reported that they often found school dull and thought about other things during lessons (Sørlie and Nordahl 1998). School motivation decreased significantly from the first to the third year in secondary school in another study from a large suburban municipality (Ogden 1995). Within a context where there is a high degree of regulation, 'passive protest' is easiest.

On their part, the teachers are mandated to monitor the role guidance taking place through formal schooling. In principle they do this from a position of authority, which was self-evident some decades ago. Now, a teacher's authority over a class has to be earned. At the same time they are expected by parents and school authorities alike to succeed in this venture, and lack of success may be attributed to poor teaching and thus be the fault of the individual teacher. Particularly when a pupil has severe learning or behaviour problems, or there is conflict between the teacher and the parents about the right way to understand a particular boy or girl, an option for the teachers is to choose individual explanations ascribing the problem to the young person or the parents. When the problem is thus individualised the obvious solution is more resources in the classroom or extra tuition for the young person outside the class (Nordahl 1998). In this context, teachers need the power of definition, which can easily create conflicts between them and parents who want to have a say about the way their child is understood.

To sum up: The model used here to understand relationships between home and school for young people visualises a triad where the relative amount of influence will differ. The young people will have least influence over their own situation on both arenas, whereas the adults will have most influence on the home and school arenas respectively. When the adults interact through collaboration between home and school, the teachers will be more influential than the parents, however, adding some imbalance to the system. In the next sections, the perspectives and dimensions identified within the model will be discussed further, starting with an aspect of the relationship between young people and their parents.

CONNECTEDNESS AND AUTONOMY: VIEWS OF GOOD PARENTING

As part of the second data collection stage of my study, the then 15- to 16-year-olds were asked to write a few lines about their views on good parenting. The vast majority of the participants answered this question. A few did not take the question very seriously and gave responses like: 'Good parenting means giving me all the money and things I want and enforcing no rules at all', or just said 'I don't know', or 'Good parents are important'. Some were very literal and answered that good parents are either different from or similar to their own. Most took the question seriously, however, and responded in thoughtful and nuanced ways. Recurring themes in these responses were the perceived need for parents to show connectedness through caring in many different ways, and being accorded sufficient autonomy while at the same time expecting regulation.

The young people qualified these main themes in many different ways. Some focused only on the regulation part, writing things like: 'Good parenting means enforcing rules that discipline a child, to avoid spoiling or neglecting it'. These types of responses could be qualified even more, such as: 'Good parents have rules, but not too strict. They care, and become angry when the children do stupid things. They let their children take over some of the responsibilities of the household, so they can learn as they grow older'.

Some focused only on connectedness, writing things like: 'Good parenting means talking a lot with their children. It means showing that they love their kids enormously, and supporting them when they have difficulties'. Again, such responses could be further qualified, as in:

> You can tell your parents everything and they understand you. You can talk about everything with them and you feel safe when you are with them. They see to it that you are well and help you when you have problems, but they must not be over-protective. We must be allowed to have some fun even when something may go wrong.

These and other responses from the young people paint a picture of parental love as something that should be presupposed, with the parents representing a 'secure base' for their children.

When the young people reflected on both connectedness and regulation, they combined them or discussed them. Examples of combination were: 'Good parenting means taking good care of the children, care about them. Combine discipline and love, and give much praise. Keep the children away from unhealthy influences (television, bullies, gangs etc.). Support the children's interests', and 'Set limits to what children are allowed to do, show love. Strict and understanding. Easy to talk to'. Examples of discussion were: 'Good parents must set rules, so one learns to behave properly. They must still have a good relationship with their children and care about them (if this usually functions well). They must not give their children too much freedom, however', and:

> Good parenting means caring about what children do, setting limits. If the children do anything wrong, they must be punished just a little bit, as they need to learn the difference between right and wrong. Parents must care, but not be too kind. They must scold, but not be too strict.

In other words, the young people discussed two kinds of balance in their responses. The first was the balance between connectedness and discipline, or regulation, where both were seen as necessary. The second was the balance between too much and too little, where the young people discussing this underlined the need to find a suitable middle ground. This middle ground presupposed an understanding on the part of the parents about their need for autonomy.

While connectedness was presupposed, autonomy was a matter for negotiation. The young people wrote comments like: 'Good parents should set rules but not exaggerate. They should try to understand what it is like to be young today', or 'Good parents care, talk to you and ask about different things. They set rules, but not too strict, that are established through cooperation between the children and them.

Good parents show that they care'. One young person summed up modern thinking about the 'negotiation family' in a succinct way by saying that 'Child-raising is a cooperative venture between children and parents'.

While comments about connectedness in the guise of parental love and care took the form of general expectations, comments about the balance between regu-latedness and room for autonomy were much more specific. Regulating behaviour could mean knowing the young person's friends, keeping an open house for their friends, following up organised leisure activities, and knowing about what the young persons did and where they were during their spare time. Many wanted their parents to do these things but only as much as necessary. The need for autonomy was primarily discussed through comments about rules and money, about the option to stay out late at night, about the need for and right to be trusted by parents, and about being listened to as an equal by parents.

Some of the young people included homework and school in their specifications of what good parents should regulate, but the number who did so was surprisingly small. This does not signify that the parents did not follow up their children's school-work. On the contrary, most of the 15- to 16-year-olds thought that their parents were supportive in this area. The point here is that they did not automatically associate this with good parenting, as parents themselves may well do. A majority of the parents answering this same question included the school in their comments. This was either done indirectly, through statements like: 'Show an interest in the young person's activities', or 'Participate actively in whatever he does', or directly, through statements like: 'Being interested in what the children do at school and in their leisure hours'. Rather fewer included helping with homework, which is a reflection of the result that by the end of secondary school, only four out of 10 parents stated that they did so. Two years earlier, six out of 10 parents said the same. However, eight out of 10 parents responded that they usually asked their 16-year-olds about their homework.

This may be explained in the way Kjersti Ericsson (see Chapter 5) does when she discusses how a wish for parents to enter the school arena can be seen as a strategic choice on the part of children and young people. Another example may be sought in theoretical thinking about home and school as important arenas in young persons' lives. Although both are attributed a high degree of importance, they are at the same time qualitatively different. This difference is discussed by James, Jenks and Prout (1998), but even more specifically by Valsiner (2000). The basis for his argument is the difference between formal and informal education. While informal education takes place in everyday contexts, formal education is institutionalised. This creates a physical and symbolic distance between the two arenas. In informal settings the learners aim to master the socially shared know-how and skills, while the formal education framework introduces an institutionally promoted kind of knowledge which is not immediately available in the local community. Here I wish to point out that young people may well sense these inherent differences, and judge good and bad parenting in relation to the informal and not the formal setting. That teachers in general do not play a very important emotional role in the lives of the adolescents is underlined by their answers to a question about who they would go to if they had problems of some kind. While more than four out of five of the 15- to 16-year-olds would go to their friends or their mother sometimes or often, not more than one out of five would approach their teacher.

AUTONOMY IN A REGULATED SETTING

Most of the adolescents participating in recent Norwegian studies seem to accept that they have to attend secondary school, and few sabotage openly through playing truant or showing aggressive or destructive behaviour in the school setting (Bakken 1998; Ogden 1995, 1998; Sørlie and Nordahl 1998). Low and decreasing school motivation on the part of the adolescents can be interpreted as a more passive kind of protest, however.

Stability and change in school motivation was measured by administering the same questionnaire to the young people at the two points in time. The answers show a high degree of stability over that time.[7] Nevertheless, their average school motivation decreased significantly from the first to the third year in secondary school. In the first year, almost seven out of 10 responded that they liked going to school well or very well. Two years later six out of 10 gave this answer, while a third (as opposed to a quarter) said they liked going to school sometimes. More specifically, of the quarter who, at 13, were most motivated, not more than half were as motivated two years later. Of the quarter who were least motivated, two-thirds were as unmotivated two years later.[8]

At the time of the first data collection, a majority (92 per cent) of the parents thought that their children liked going to school well or very well (Backe-Hansen 1998a). Two years later the proportion of parents with the same judgement had decreased (to 81 per cent). On their part, the teachers gave similar answers, saying that most children (77 per cent) liked school well or very well, but that nearly a quarter did not like going to school at all. Thus, the overall decrease in school motivation on the part of the young people themselves was reflected in the overall judgments of both parents and teachers, even though the adults seemed to overestimate the overall level of the young people's school motivation.

The results presented in this and the previous section show, as might be expected, that the young people probably experienced their relationship with their parents as more dynamic and reciprocal than that with their teachers, or with the informal rather than the formal, cultural setting they were in to use Valsiner's (2000) terms. They probably expected regulation on both arenas, but had more to say, and probably expected to have more of a say, where their home arena was concerned.

The next section addresses changes in the perspectives of the two adult positions in the model of home–school relationships: that of parents and teachers.

COLLABORATION BETWEEN HOME AND SCHOOL

Collaboration between home and school is an important, official goal of Norwegian school politics, as Kjersti Ericsson describes in Chapter 5. The same is the case in the other Scandinavian countries, and has been a common trend particularly since the 1970s (Lindbom 1996). This collaboration takes place in two ways. The first of these can be called formal collaboration, and means parental representation and participation on school boards and other decision-making bodies in the school, or being parent representative in the class. This type of collaboration was not addressed in my study.

The second type is the contact and collaboration taking place between individual teachers and pupils' parents. This is formalised to some extent as well, as one class meeting with teachers and parents present will be organised by the school just after the start of the school year in the autumn. In addition there will be one or two individual consultations between the class teacher and the parents during the school year to inform them about their offspring's progress or problems at school. The young person will usually be present, unless he or she doesn't want to attend. If special problems should arise either the parents or the teacher may initiate extra meetings. No more than a fifth of the parents responded that such extra contact had taken place, however. In other words, when the parents and teachers in the study were asked how they viewed each other their responses were mainly based on the ordinary and rather limited amount of contact that is normal during a school year. Additionally, information will be exchanged and impressions will of course be formed through conversations between parents and young people about different aspects of school and schoolwork.

The parents' views of the teachers

At the second data collection, parents were asked how well they knew the class teachers. While the majority thought that knowing the teacher well was important, only just over half of the parents said they actually did know him or her well or very well. This mismatch reflects the earlier mention of a greater distance between secondary school and the home than between primary school and the home.

At both points in time, the parents were also asked whether they were in agreement with the teacher's approach to teaching and child raising. The response alternatives were 'agreement', 'neither agreement nor disagreement', and 'disagreement'. At both points in time, very few of the parents disagreed openly, and the majority were in agreement with the teachers on both counts. However, there was a decrease in agreement both concerning teaching strategies (from 76 per cent to 65 per cent) and child raising strategies (from 86 per cent to 80 per cent).[9] This may reflect the decreased level of school motivation on the part of the young people.

The parents were asked if they had any comments, which not many did. Some commented on disagreement about child raising strategies (14 per cent), and others on disagreement about teaching strategies (21 per cent). More than anything else, such comments reflect the great variation in expectations parents have of teachers in Norway's inclusive school system. Some commented on the way the lessons were organised, for instance: 'Too incompetent teachers, too much illness, too many temporary teachers', 'There is too much unrest in class during lessons, which the teacher does too little to stop. The rules should be stricter', and 'The work the pupils do should be followed up better, for instance through corrections of written homework'. Such comments clearly indicate a wish for more regulation and less autonomy on the part of the parents. The same pertains to the next comments, as some parents obviously thought that the recent school reform had gone too far in the direction of individual freedom for pupils, and made comments like: 'They are given too much freedom', or 'There is too little homework, too many exceptions from the curricula, for instance trips, theme weeks, etc.'.

On the other hand, others had the opposite opinion and commented that: 'The school should give the pupils more options concerning how they organise their time and their work in school', and 'Too little weight is given to creativity and variation. The evaluation of the pupils is too based on tests and reproductions of theory'. These parents obviously thought that more autonomy for the young people would be preferable.

Finally, some parents commented on the lack of respect accorded to themselves as parents by the teachers, as well as to the pupils, such as: 'The teacher has too little confidence in us as partners'. or 'Parents should be included when their child receives special tuition in the school setting', and 'The pupils are not sufficiently respected where their opinions and needs are concerned. They are often met with rigid and authoritarian attitudes'. One might say that parents who want more respect and room for individual activities conform to the modern thinking about school reflected in the school reform of 1997, while the others reflect more traditional views. It goes without saying that although most parents seemed sufficiently content, the diversity among those who were not as content posed many challenges to the teachers.

As mentioned above, many parents and teachers felt that they did not know each other well, although the proportion who did increased over time. At the same time, nine out of 10 parents thought that they and the teachers were sufficiently or very much in agreement about important norms and values, and almost all thought such agreement important. Thus, the parents did not need to know the teachers particularly well to feel in agreement with them, which probably means that most parents did not particularly feel the need for more collaboration or exchanges than the formal minimum.

The teachers' views of the parents

At the time of the first data collection, the teachers thought they knew just over a third of the parents well or very well (Backe-Hansen 1998a). Two years later this proportion had increased to above half. However, the teachers thought that there was a high degree of agreement between them and most of the parents about important norms and values at both points in time. When the response alternatives 'very high', 'high', and 'sufficient' degree of agreement were combined, they included a high proportion of the parents at the time of the first data collection (85 per cent), which rose even higher at the time of the second (95 per cent). When only the first two of the response alternatives were combined the rise was very large (37 per cent for the first data collection and 64 per cent for the second). Thus, knowing the parents over time seemed to lead to an impression of a higher degree of agreement even though the teachers did not meet with the parents very often.

At the time of the first data collection, a majority of the teachers thought that parental support for their children where school work was concerned was good or very good (81 per cent) (Backe-Hansen 1998a). Overall this had increased slightly after two years (to 87 per cent).

The survey questions about collaboration between home and school were general. Despite this, it seems fair to say that there appeared to be a generally positive attitude to the relationship between home and school on the part of both parents and teachers. The picture becomes less positive, however, when the answers to these questions are seen in relation to the school motivation of the young people at the time of the second data collection. Taking the quarter of the adolescents who were least and most motivated respectively, it becomes apparent that the teachers judged the parents' support as significantly poorer when the young people judged themselves as unmotivated. On their part, the young people judged parental support as poorer when they were unmotivated as well.

These results indicate that collaboration between home and school is a many-sided phenomenon, also depending on how the young people themselves construct their relationship with the school over time. As long as the young people do all right, and no big problems arise, a distanced but positive relationship between the teacher and the parents is probably sufficient. When problems or disagreements arise, however, other types of relationships probably need to be negotiated. Here, the existing power inequalities between parents and teachers, teachers and young people, and young people and their parents may make the development of functional practices more difficult. In the final section of the chapter, these complementary relationships will be further discussed with special emphasis on the possibilities of change from the young persons' perspective.

AUTONOMY, CONNECTEDNESS AND REGULATION IN CONTEXT

The model depicted in Figure 10.1 can be used as a starting point in the understanding of home–school collaboration from the perspectives of the three sets of actors concerned. Starting with the young people's point of view, what becomes evident is the difference in relationships between the young people and the informal setting of the family as opposed to the formal setting of the school.

The comments from the young people about good parenting underline ·that autonomy and connectedness need not be opposites. Whether their comments reflect cultural norms about parenthood or the young people's own situation, it was obvious that connectedness in the guise of making demands about parental care and concern was presupposed. This was the case even when parents showed too much care and concern, as some of the comments indicate. Autonomy was not related to increased legal rights, but to decreased constraints on the part of parents. From parents' point of view this is important to recognise because parents will often justify their use of regulation by calling it an expression of love. It is important as well to see this dialectic between autonomy and connectedness on the part of the young people and regulation and care on the part of the parents as a dynamic process. The relationship between the young people and the formal setting of the school, however, seems more static. The dialectic of responsibility and discipline on the part of the young people and regulation and responsibility on the part of the teachers is more pre-defined by the school setting, and less open for negotiations and development. Indeed, the decrease in school motivation that was found over time may reflect the way that this setting becomes less appropriate over time.

Another interesting finding was that most of the young people obviously separated the home and school arenas, in the sense that their ideas of good parenting did not include following up school work. On their part, parents as well as teachers may well think that such linking of arenas is an important aspect of good parenthoood, a point of view that is underlined by the state policy of collaboration between home and school, and probably even more paramount with today's emphasis on education. This may make parents feel an added obligation to discuss school at home, even though the young people themselves do not see the same need. It may be added that one of the factors that make young people school-motivated might well be proximity to friends and other social activities, not necessarily what they learn during and after school hours (Nordahl 2000a).

The relationship between parents and teachers can be construed as fairly static as well, with the power imbalance present throughout the school years regardless of how individual teachers and parents may communicate over time. In general both parents and teachers seemed reasonably satisfied with the degree of collaboration that took place, and most of them obviously expected that a basis for understanding existed through agreement about common norms and values. This is probably sufficient for most of the pupils, particularly since the school motivation reported by the young people was about average although it decreased over time. Unless it is possible to effect more fundamental changes in the way school is organised, which are based on knowledge elicited from young people about how secondary school can be a more motivating 'work-place' for them, it is probably better to 'let sleeping dogs lie' where this majority is concerned.

However, the picture changed when those who were least motivated were looked at more closely. Here, the collaboration between all three parties seemed more problematic. The nature of the data presented here preclude analyses of causation, but it points to the necessity for both teachers and parents to give particular consideration to the minority of pupils who are really unmotivated. Seen in relation to the model for understanding home–school relations set out and explored in this chapter, this means that it is necessary to develop a less static and more flexible view of collaboration between home and school. The evidence presented in this chapter is that, in addition to the formalised collaboration policies and practices pertaining to everyone involved, there is a need for more individual interventions, shaped around the situation for particular young people.

NOTES

1 The results derive from a study called 'Children's development and living conditions in a resource-oriented and holistic perspective' (1996–2001), financed by the Norwegian Research Council. The study includes two age groups, who were 10–11 years old and 13–14 years old at the outset. The discussion in this chapter is mainly limited to results about the latter age group.
2 The age cohorts follow the calendar year.
3 A quarter of Norwegian pupils of primary and secondary school age attend classes with up to 15 pupils, a quarter attend classes of 16–20 pupils, a quarter attend classes of 21–25 pupils, and the last quarter attend classes with over 25 pupils (Ogden 1998). However, class sizes in the secondary schools are generally slightly larger.
4 The actual intercorrelations were .22 and .52 on the part of the 10-year-olds, and .41 and .64 on the part of the 13-year-olds.
5 1 per cent finished high school in 1900, 3 per cent by 1933.
6 This right was established through a major school reform in 1994.
7 The correlation between the total scores was high, 57.
8 There were no significant gender differences at either point in time.
9 Again, there were no significant gender differences.

REFERENCES

Backe-Hansen, E. (1998a). *Mellom hjem, skole og fritid.* [Between home, school, and leisure time]. Interim report. Oslo: Prosjekt utvikling og levekår.

Backe-Hansen, E. (1998b). *10-åringer mellom hjem, skole og fritid.* [10-year-olds between home, school, and leisure time]. Interim report. Oslo: Prosjekt utvikling og levekår.

Backe-Hansen, E. (1999). Barn og unge sett med egne og voksnes øyne. [Children and young people seen through their own and grown-ups' eyes]. In Jensen, A.-M., E. Backe-Hansen, H. Bache-Wiig and K. Heggen (eds). *Oppvekst i barnets århundre. Historier om tvetydighet.* Oslo: Ad Notam Gyldendal.

Bakken, A. (1998). *Ungdomstid i storbyen.* [Being young in a large city]. Oslo: NOVA-report no. 7/98.

Blom, I. (1985). Kvinneliv i vårt århundre. [Women's lives in our century]. In Vogt, K., S. Lie, K. Gundersen and J. Bjørgum (eds). *Kvinnenes kulturhistorie.* Bind II. Oslo: Universitetsforlaget.

Brannen, J. (1995). Discourses of adolescence: Young people's independence and autonomy within families. In Brannen, J. and M. O'Brien (eds). *Children in families. Research and policy.* London: Falmer Press.

Ericsson, K. (1997). *Drift og dyd.* [Sexual drive and chastity]. Oslo: PAX forlag.

Evenshaug, O. and Hallen, D. (1992). *Barne- og ungdomspsykologi.* [The psychology of children and youth]. Oslo: Gyldendal forlag.

Hall, G.S. (1904). *Adolescence.* New York: Appleton-Century-Crofts.

James, A., Jenks, C. and Prout, A. (1998). *Theorizing childhood.* Cambridge: Polity Press.

Lindbom, A. (1996). Föräldrainnflytendes utveckling i skandinavisk grundskola. [The evolvement of parental influence in the Scandinavian compulsory school]. In Arneberg, P. and B. Ravn (eds). *Mellom foreldre og skole. Er et demokratisk fellesskap mulig?.* Oslo/København: Ad Notam Gyldendal/Unge Pædagoger.

Nasjonalt læremiddelsenter (1996). *Læreplanverket for den 10-åringe grunnskolen.* [Teaching plans for the 10-year compulsory school]. Oslo: The Ministry of Church, Education, and Research.

Nordahl, T. (1998). *Er det bare eleven?* [Is it just the pupil?]. Oslo: NOVA, report no. 12d/1998.

Nordahl, T. (2000a). *En skole – to verdener* [One school – two worlds]. Oslo: NOVA, report no. 11/2000.

Nordahl, T. (2000b). *Samarbeid mellom hjem og skole – en kartleggingsundersøkelse.* [Collaboration between home and school – an exploratory study]. Oslo: NOVA, report no. 8/2000.

Ogden, T. (1995). *Kompetanse i kontekst.* [Competence in context]. Oslo: Barnevernets Utviklingssenter, report no 3/1995.

Ogden, T. (1998). *Elevatferd og læringsmiljø.* [Pupil behaviour and learning environment]. Oslo: The Ministry of Church, Education, and Research.

Skaalvik, E. and Skaalvik, S. (1988). *Barns selvoppfatnin – skolens ansvar.* [Children's self-perception – the responsibility of the school]. Oslo: TANO.

Stafseng, O. (1996). *Den historiske konstruksjonen av moderne ungdom.* [The historical construction of modern youth]. Oslo: Cappelen Akademisk forlag/Ungforsk.

Sørlie, M.-A. and Nordahl, T. (1998). *Problematferd i skolen.* [Problem behaviour in school]. Oslo: NOVA, report no. 12a/1998.

Valsiner, J. (2000). *Culture and human development.* London, Thousand Oaks, New Delhi: Sage Publications.

Øia, T. (1994). *Norske ungdomskulturer.* [Norwegian youth cultures]. Vallset: Oplandske bokforlag.

Afterword

Similarities and differences

Rosalind Edwards

The chapter contributions to this edited collection have shown the myriad ways that children are active in and negotiate home–school relations, and have highlighted that this needs to be taken into account in policy initiatives and research studies addressing the topic. As noted in the introduction to this volume, the predominant concern in both policies and research has been with parents and/or teachers as social actors. The collection thus provides an important counterbalance.

Lack of attention to children's views and activities in home–school relations is further evident in their lack of a participatory voice in the education policies and practices that shape their lives. This is demonstrated in the first few contributions to this book especially. Priscilla Alderson discussed the lack of civil rights accorded to children in British schools, while Fiona Smith and John Barker were concerned with the ways that educational agendas rather than children's own perspectives were steering the development of British out of school services. Lise Bird showed the ways that recent reform in New Zealand similarly contained no space for children to express their views about education provision. These examples concern Britain and New Zealand, both of which are broadly liberal welfare regimes with a muted sense of children's citizenship. It is not evident from Kjersti Ericsson and Guri Larsen's and Elisabeth Backe-Hansen's discussions, though, that home–school relations policies in the social democratic regime represented here, Norway, have been open to children's participation in shaping home–school relations policies to any great extent (see also Flekkoy 1988).

Nevertheless, some interesting national differences do emerge around children's sense of autonomy. For example, there is some contrast between Cleopatra Montandon's findings that Swiss children emphasise connection and regulation as part of parent–child relations, and Elisabeth Backe-Hansen's that Norwegian young people focus on connection and negotiated autonomy. In part, this may be a reflection of the differing conceptions and positioning of family in the two welfare regimes and concomitant generational contracts. In the Swiss conservative regime, family is regarded as crucial to children's socialisation into norms of personal regulation and parents are held responsible and accountable. In the Norwegian social democratic regime, responsibility for children is shared between parents and state, and there is a greater citizenship and social emphasis on children's independence and competence. The tension between regulation and autonomy identified by Kjersti Ericsson and

Guri Larsen and by Pam Alldred and colleagues as a feature of contemporary childhood, then, may well be played out and experienced quite differently in different national and cultural contexts.

Indeed, it is evident from the contributions to this collection that social divisions and issues beyond the specific arena of home–school relations play an important part in those relations. Mairian Corker and John Davis showed how conceptions of disability impacted on and were engaged with a disabled boy. William Corsaro and Katherine Brown Rosier's discussion of pre-school African-American children's experiences, and Mano Candappa and Ito Egharevba's research on refugee children in particular revealed the ways that positions and practices of gender, race/ethnicity and social class, as well as poverty, and challenging environments and circumstances, shaped children's negotiation of the relationship between school and home. It may also be that age is an issue, for example as another feature of the Swiss-Norwegian contrast in conceptions of parent–child relations noted above.

In relation to the settings of school and home, and other educationally liked spaces, however, there appear also to be some important similarities in children's views and experiences. Many of the contributions addressed how each setting embodies quite distinct sets of institutional and familial values, modes of organisation and relationships, with different implications for children's regulation, autonomy and connection. Moreover, Kjersti Ericsson and Guri Laresen's research in Norway, Cleopatra Montandon's in Switzerland, Pam Alldred and collegues' in Britain, and William Corsaro and Katherine Brown Rosier's in the US, provide examples of the ways that children in these diverse national contexts appear, in the main, to value moving between different settings, and competently cope with the 'dissonance' that home–school links policies and practices can seek to reduce. Indeed, Fiona Smith and John Barker's work further showed that they seem to want out of school clubs to provide yet another mode of organisation beyond school and home.

The differences and similarities identified here, then, point to the importance of context in conceptualising and understanding school and home, and relations between them, for children. Taking account of this poses challenges for home–school links policies and initiatives.

REFERENCE

Flekkoy, M. (1988) 'Child advocacy in Norway', *Children and Society*, 4, 307–318.

Index